C000181264

MERCHANT SEAFARING
THROUGH WORLD WAR 1
1914 – 1918

MERCHANT SEAFARING THROUGH WORLD WAR 1

1914 –1918

PETER LYON

The Book Guild Ltd

First published in Great Britain in 2016 by
The Book Guild Ltd
9 Priory Business Park
Wistow Road, Kibworth
Leicestershire, LE8 0RX
Freephone: 0800 999 2982
www.bookguild.co.uk
Email: info@bookguild.co.uk
Twitter: @bookguild

Copyright © 2016 Peter Lyon

The right of Peter Lyon to be identified as the author of this
work has been asserted by him in accordance with the
Copyright, Design and Patents Act 1988.

All rights reserved. No part of this publication may be
reproduced, transmitted, or stored in a retrieval system, in any form or by any means,
without permission in writing from the publisher, nor be otherwise circulated in
any form of binding or cover other than that in which it is published and without
a similar condition being imposed on the subsequent purchaser.

Typeset in Bembo

Printed and bound in the UK by TJ International, Padstow, Cornwall

ISBN 978 1 910878 41 5

British Library Cataloguing in Publication Data.
A catalogue record for this book is available from the British Library.

CONTENTS

U-boat crews – 'Gentlemen Pirates' – Treatment of captured U-boat crews – Accounts of captured merchant seafarers on U-boats – War criminals – Condition of survivors – U-boat crew account of their own sinking

AUTHOR'S NOTE

The motivation in writing this book stems from my research into the career and experiences during the First World War of my maternal grandfather, Captain Harry Griffiths, to whose memory this book is dedicated. While I have learned much about the history of my family, I have learned much more about the history of my own profession which was seemingly accorded such little public regard. The limited information that I have been able to locate provides a vivid history of incredible hardship and endurance, against a background of little concern for the safety and protection of the British merchant seafarer. As civilians, the merchant seafarers had to face an enemy of such brutality as had never been witnessed before, apart perhaps from that displayed by the pirates of the 17th and 18th centuries. I believe their story deserves to be told and re-told and that it should never be forgotten that it was this disparate group of individuals who, against incredible odds, and despite great loss of life, maintained the supplies of food, troops and armaments that enabled Britain to survive to fight.

In carrying out my research I acknowledge, with gratitude, those who have preceded me in gathering and collating the scattered remnants of records and papers. I trust that I have shown proper recognition of their work and apologise if I have been remiss in this task. I am also grateful to those who have sympathetically guided me in my days at the various libraries and archives and to those who have patiently listened to my thinking aloud as the research progressed. I must give special acknowledgement and thanks to my wife, Margaret, for her most valuable support and advice, without which this book might never have been published.

Peter Lyon
West Sussex

PROLOGUE

Prior to the outbreak of World War 1 steam ships had emerged from the shipyards and slipways to replace their sail-driven forbears. The increasing demands of trade, fuelled by the expanding British Empire, had resulted in a huge growth in shipping, yet the reputation of British merchant ships and their seafarers was such that merchants sought other than British ships to transport their goods. So great was the concern in government circles that the Foreign Office, at the request of the Admiralty, sought opinions from British Consulates around the world regarding the standing and reputation of British ships and their crews. In 1843, having been given the task to collate and summarise the responses from the Consulates, a Mr Murray (later Sir James Murray), of the Foreign Office reported:

> '*It is stated from various parts of the world that persons placed in command of British ships are so habitually addicted to drunkenness as to be unfitted for their position, and it will be seen that Her Majesty's Consuls allude specifically to the notorious and gross intemperance, and to the ignorance and brutality of British ship masters, many of whom are totally void of education where bad conduct and ignorance is the rule, and intelligence and ability the exception.*'[1]

The shipowners were also given a poor report, this time from Mr W.S. Lindsay, a Member of Parliament, a prolific author of a four-volume treatise entitled *"Merchant Shipping and Ancient Commerce"* and a shipowner himself. In an address to the US Chamber of Commerce in October 1860, on the subject of Maritime Laws, he drew attention to the Shipowners' Society of London claiming they consisted of '*small political factions, got together ostensibly for the purpose of promoting the interests of particular branches of trade, but too prone*

---

[1] Hurd, *The Merchant Navy*, Vol.1, p.77

to ride hobbies of their own political dogma.' He further said that he was not very popular with these factions, claiming that to be partly due to him being a self-taught and self-made man, but most certainly because of his mission to improve the lot of the seafarer and the laws relating to the Mercantile Marine. In relating the views of some shipowners regarding the competence of their shipmasters, he was quoted as saying; '*In my own time I remember a shipowner saying to me that he would never have a "scholar" in command of any of his ships, because education taught him how to make up false accounts and the art of cheating'*. He concluded that ...*a large proportion of their* [British] *ships were commanded by and navigated in a manner reflecting discredit on our national intelligence, and injurious to the interests of Great Britain'.*[2]

As a consequence of the report of Mr Murray and of the efforts of those such as Mr. Lindsay, many changes were brought about, including the examination and certification of seamen and regulations relating to shipbuilding. Merchant shipping had become a highly profitable undertaking for some shipowners in that even ship losses were not regarded as a financial disaster. In 1884 Joseph Chamberlain, the then President of the Board of Trade responsible for shipping in Gladstone's Second Government, declared somewhat wryly that with the law and marine insurance protocols then applicable, the advice to aspiring shipowners and insurers could be understood as;

Buy your ship as cheaply as you can, equip her as poorly as you can, load her as fully as you can, and send her off to sea. If she gets to her voyage you will make a very good thing of it; if she goes to the bottom you will have made a very much better thing of it.[3]

These condemnations of the merchant seafarer and the shipowners gave an unhappy account of the state of Britain's Mercantile Marine in the years leading to the outbreak of war. It was a sad indictment of the country's ability to maintain the supply routes necessary for Britain to survive the forthcoming siege. At the end of the war however, after all the vicissitudes, horrors and dangers suffered by the seafarers, a Resolution of Parliament of August 6th 1919 placed on record;

---

[2] Woodman, *Masters Under God*, p.61
[3] Hurd, *The Merchant Navy.* Vol. 1. p.79

That the thanks of this House be accorded to the officers and men of the Mercantile Marine for the fine and fearless seamanship by which our people have been preserved from want and our cause from disaster.

The social historian Asa Briggs, recognising that the Mercantile Marine had succeeded in maintaining supplies to Britain described it as ...*the indispensible instrument of the country's wealth*.[4]

At the conclusion of hostilities, H.R.H. The Prince of Wales stated:

It is the glory of our Merchant Navy, and will be so acclaimed by generations to come, that they faced without hesitation the tremendous odds and the frequent hazard of death, undaunted in spirit to the better end. Let us not forget, also, that had it been otherwise this country of ours must have perished.[5]

The threat of war had been growing throughout 1913 and the spring of 1914. The 'Great War' began on 28 July with the Austria-Hungary declaration of war on Serbia and Germany's declaration of war with Russia, Belgium and France in the first week of August. The German invasion of France began on 2 August and Britain, with the nations of its Empire, declared war on Germany on 4 August. On 23 August, Japan declared war on Germany.

★ ★ ★

So what had happened to the Mercantile Marine between the times of the views put forward by Mr Murray and Joseph Chamberlain and the later statements of Parliament, Briggs and The Prince of Wales? This book attempts, initially, to provide some description of the period leading up to the war in terms of the regulations, practices and living conditions of the seafarers. It is followed by examples of the experiences of individual merchant seafarers and their passengers caught up in the war, with some personal experiences at the hands of their German adversaries and some views and experiences of their tormentors. It does not attempt to provide a history of the Mercantile Marine through the First World War; rather it is an attempt to sift from such

[4] Briggs, *A Social History of Britain*. p.251
[5] Hurd, *The Merchant Navy*. Vol. 3. Foreword.

histories some flavour of the war from the merchant seafarer's viewpoint and experiences. It includes a selection of stories and reports which provide colourful, if somewhat biased, accounts of individual events and indeed propaganda aimed at encouraging support to continue the fight against the enemy. It also provides accounts of hardship and brutality endured in the bitter struggle for survival.

Many records of merchant seafarers, ships' logs and crew agreements have been discarded or destroyed over the years. Crew Agreements, crew lists and records of births, deaths, desertions and disciplinary offences had been compiled and held by the Registrar General of Shipping and Seamen in Cardiff. In 1966 it was decided to cease the storage of these documents and to offer them to other archives, although many records have been lost in the exchanges. Surviving copies of Crew Agreements, ship's logs and ship losses are now held primarily at the National Archives at Kew, the Southampton Central Library and the National Maritime Museum at Greenwich. Additionally, maritime archives are retained at many regional centres, such as the Maritime Museum at Liverpool and at overseas archives, such as those held at the Memorial University of Newfoundland, which holds 75 per cent of surviving Crew Agreements and ships' logs for the period of the First World War. National and regional newspapers also retain records of significant ship losses.

Remaining sources often show discrepancies in dates and times and in spellings of names, even within the same document. Numbers of casualties for a given event also show quite wide variances. For example, some accounts of casualties include numbers of passenger losses, while others purport to show only crew losses. In arriving at the casualty figures, it must be allowed that those now shown must be regarded as a lower figure than actual losses, as some, if not many, will have been unrecorded. Nevertheless, every reasonable effort has been made to ensure the presentation of accurate dates, names and figures, with great reliance on the sources quoted.

Records and personal papers of merchant seafarers describing their experiences in the First World War are therefore limited to a diminishing collection at archives such that the ordeals, bravery and horrors experienced by the men and women of the British and Allied merchant fleets are seemingly given little currency. What is clear is that the merchant seafarers were generally regarded by British society as being of a low social status, often with little or no family ties or fixed address in the UK and living in the most basic conditions. They were, most certainly, often unruly, coarse, violent and difficult to discipline, many with backgrounds in the era of sailing ships and following a profession that was already fraught with danger without the added risks of war.

It should however be emphasised that the merchant seafarers were civilians, engaged in the commerce of their time, but drawn into military conflict. Some were too young to be called for military service and some too old. Ever since the origins of seafaring a bond had existed between seafarers of all generations and nationalities in the mutual understanding and sharing of the many deprivations and dangers inherent in taking ships to sea. These bonds can be seen to have existed between the belligerents in the early days of the war, where chivalrous and gentlemanly conduct was strictly adhered to by all sides and civilian status protected. Neither the warships nor the merchant ships were initially sure what was required of them, but it was not long before the humanitarian considerations disintegrated in the heat and desperation of the conflict and the age old bonds between seafarers were severed.

This book is aimed at identifying and preserving personal experiences of those who survived enemy action at sea from limited remaining official records and publications, supplemented by individual library collections and press reports. It cannot be comprehensive or complete but it is hoped that from these sources a powerful story emerges of the character and resilience of the merchant seafarer, both male and female, often in what must have appeared as the most hopeless and desperate of situations. Essentially this book is offered as a personal tribute to those who did survive and, even more so, to those who did not.

CHAPTER 1

THE PRE-WAR MERCANTILE MARINE

What might have inspired a young man, or indeed a young woman, to seek a career at sea in the Mercantile Marine (it was not referred to as the Merchant Navy until King George V so named it after the war) – and what legacies and traditions would be inherited? The majority of Britain's population lived in or around the sea ports – at that time some of the largest in the world and the home ports of many famous shipping companies. The boys and young men in those areas would have been exposed to ships and seafarers with many feeling attracted by the possibility of discovery and adventure. So, what was the background of the merchant seafarer at the outbreak of World War 1?

Most would have started a career at sea between the ages of twelve and fifteen, indentured to shipowners as 'sailor boys'. The reputation of seamen was poor and, judging by the view reported by Joseph Chamberlain, while he was a great advocate for the improvement of seamen's conditions, their lives were seemingly given little value. Many seamen of skill and diligence had found berths in the expanding American merchant fleets where conditions were better, the ships safer to work on and payment for their services guaranteed.

In 1835 the Board of Trade had introduced a system of central registration for all British merchant seamen in view of the high loss rate of ships and their crews. In 1836 the Select Committee on Shipwrecks suggested the way forward to reduce these losses was through education and certification which would also, it was claimed, lead to an improvement in moral character. It was hoped that such a path would bring British masters and crews to the perceived higher standards of the American, French and Scandinavian ships.

A move to improve recruitment was "An Act to amend and consolidate the Laws relating to Merchant Seamen; and for keeping a Register of Seamen of 5 September 1844". This Act deemed it lawful for Overseers of the poor to indenture boys as junior seamen from the age of eleven or twelve to any British shipowner for a period of seven years, or up to the age of twenty one, whichever was sooner. This was seen as a means also of offloading the parish poor – or killing two birds with one stone. The boys' parents, if alive, would need to be among the poor who were maintained by, or chargeable to, the parish, *'or who shall beg for Alms therein'*. As may be imagined, the fate of these young boys would not always have been a happy one and, with voyages often lasting more than a year, they were not able readily to settle on their return to life ashore. It is not surprising that many of these young men remained at sea, devoid of any family life and acceptable social skills. Shipowners preferred recruiting their seafarers at as young an age as possible to better accept the conditions and disciplines imposed upon them. A commonly held view, expressed by an experienced master of that time, Captain John Mason, was,

> *Young boys, as a rule, have not the sense to get scared, and they become so inured to hardships and dangers aloft and on deck that they take them as they come and think nothing of it all through life.*[1]

Boys from large families could be sent to sea to make room for younger siblings or as a punishment, as may be seen in the case of poor Alfred Dorling. Alfred was the thirteen year old half brother of Mrs Beeton, of later fame for her housekeeping books. He, according to the cautionary tale was;

> *so embarrassed by his parents' fecundity that he sent his father a condom in the post. Between them the parents brought four children each to their respective second marriages, and then added a further thirteen. Condoms were then regarded as prophylactic devices, used by men who frequented brothels, rather than instruments of birth control, and Alfred's act was therefore not merely impertinent but judgemental. As a punishment he was sent to join the Merchant Navy where presumably he learned all about condoms and a great deal more…Alfred drowned in Sydney Harbour three years later, an unfortunate end to a promising young fellow.*[2]

---

[1]   Woodman, *More Days, More Dollars*. p.55.

[2]   Ibid. p.56

Concern about the shipping industry nevertheless provoked considerable debate, where many believed that the high mortality rates and ship losses were the result of incompetent masters and crews, all of whom appeared to be subject to drunkenness and poor discipline. This was combined with an unfair insurance system whereby a shipowner could, in some cases, receive more in compensation for the loss of his ship than its value. Masters were often appointed on the basis of their being friends or relatives of the owner, or the owner himself, with little if any competence in navigation, seamanship or the ability to control a crew.

Certification of masters was introduced on a voluntary basis in 1845 following an Order in Council in 1844. There were however few takers, with little incentive offered in terms of improved remuneration for successful candidates and some companies offered their own examinations. The 1850 Merchant Shipping Act established a Mercantile Marine Office, the predecessor of the Marine Department, to *undertake the superintendence of matters relating to the British Mercantile Marine*; essentially to improve the safety standards of ships and the training and qualification of seafarers. Its activities, as a government department, were however not universally welcomed by elements of the seafaring fraternity and the distinguished commentator and historian of the time, Captain David W. Bone, wrote disparagingly of the new systems supplanting the traditional role of the Corporation of Trinity House;

> *For over three hundred years, our Alma Mater [Trinity House] flourished as the spring of our seafaring – a noble and venerable Corporation, concerned solely and alone with the sea and the ships and the seamen. The [Trinity House] Brethren saw only one aim for their endeavours – the supremacy of the sea trade, the business by which the nation stood or fell... While Trinity House was concerned alone with the conduct of shipping and sea-affairs, our new controllers of the Board of Trade have interests in charge as widely apart as the feeding of draught-horses and the examination of a bankrupt cheesemonger...Sullenly, we resent her dictation as that of a usurper – a lay impropriator of our professional heritage.[3]*

---

3 Bone, *Merchantmen-at-arms: the British merchants' service in the war*, pp.48–51.

The description of the general business of Trinity House, which was granted a Royal Charter by Henry VIII in 1514, had been given in 1746 by the Corporation's clerk, John Whormby, as

> *...to improve the art and science of mariners; to examine into the qualifications, and regulate the conduct of those who take upon them the charge of conducting ships; to preserve good order and (when desired) to compose differences in marine affairs, and, in general, to consult the conservation, good estate, wholesome government, maintenance and increase of navigation and seafaring men; and to relieve decayed seamen and their relatives.*

While Trinity House had undoubtedly been active in the direct promotion of measures of good seafaring practice for ship masters, adoption of such measures were generally localised and voluntary in acceptance. The Board of Trade believed that a more formal and national approach needed to be taken on shipping matters, including the examination, certification and registration of all seafarers.

Compulsory certification was introduced in 1851 for Masters and Mates of foreign-going ships following a series of examinations approved by the Board of Trade. Those on the coastal trades only (any port between the River Elbe and Brest) also had to be certificated as part of the 1854 Merchant Shipping Act. The certification of ships' engineers was introduced in 1862 and ships' cooks in 1906.

Examinations were based on the same curriculum throughout the country, but the markings of the papers by the new Board of Trade examiners were not standardised. Such was the variation in pass rates achieved in different parts of the country that a Commission set up to explain this apparent phenomenon came to the initial conclusion that '*those in the north of the country were less intelligent than in other parts*'. No doubt this conclusion gave rise to many a heated debate until standardised marking was implemented.

Despite those who complained so vociferously about the new powers invested in the Board of Trade's Mercantile Marine Office, it was recognised that new skills and standards were required, including those of navigation, ship construction and ship stability for the new generation of ships. A great advantage of the steam ship over sail was of course that steam ships could move against the wind and were thus able to maintain more or less a constant course and speed. This, coupled with the opening of the Suez Canal in 1869 meant that voyage times to and from the main trading ports to the east could be reduced significantly. The recently widespread availability of chronometers allowed navigation calculations using the sun and star observations to be made much more rapidly and with greater accuracy than the earlier laborious and lengthy lunar observations, with stellar navigation being introduced in examinations in 1898. These advances led to voyage scheduling and the birth of the scheduled liner trades; a side-effect of which was that a seafarer could look forward to the possibility of a relatively settled home life and thus domesticity and marriage became more common.

Various training establishments run on military lines had been set up to prepare boys for the Mercantile Marine and a training ship named the *WARSPITE* was acquired in 1876 by the Marine Society which was, and still is, a philanthropic body to give orphaned and other disadvantaged boys training to equip them with basic skills for a seafaring occupation. In 1883 sea training schools were set up for deck boys and apprentices throughout the country. (The year 1883 was particularly notable in bringing to the end the highly contentious practice of the Royal Navy commandeering merchant seamen for their own ships. This however was due mainly to the declining need of the Royal Navy for sail handling skills.) Additionally, the training establishments *CONWAY* and *WORCESTER* were set up for officer apprentices.

There were also reformatory ships, such as the *AKBAR* on the Mersey and the *CORNWALL* on the Thames, primarily for training particularly disadvantaged boys and under-aged criminals, which provided an inexpensive pool of labour for the shipowner. Although doubts were expressed about the recruitment and employment of some of these boys, this was seen as a convenient way of disposing of a potential source of nuisance and criminality. Lord Thomas Brassey, an eminent industrialist, adopted a more altruistic approach with,

Desirable as it is to make an effort to reclaim the unfortunate children of the pauper or criminal classes, it must be admitted that, in introducing boys of this class in large numbers into the merchant service, we incur a serious risk. The calling of the seaman must inevitably be lowered in the estimation of

5

the honest and independent working population, if we allow it to become a general and recognised refuge of the destitute … it is a grave error to suppose that the dregs of society can be educated for a sea life.[4]

By the 1880s many ambitious young officers, having served in sailing ships, were only too happy to transfer to the higher wages and improved conditions offered by steam ships on the liner trades. The contrast between those who served in the steam ships of the better shipping companies and the sailing ships was considerable, with the steam ship officers wearing the uniform livery of the owners and enjoying considerably improved working conditions and accommodation. Those who had been brought up in the sailing ships often had a difficult time adjusting to the new skills required for the steam ships and it was not uncommon for a sailing ship master to have to accept a position as a second mate when transferring to the new steam ships. Captain Sir Edgar Britten, a master in a prestigious Cunard liner, recalled a fifth officer of advanced years joining his ship who turned out to have been the master of the sailing vessel in which Britten had begun his apprenticeship.[5] Unsurprisingly there were certain resentments as steam replaced sail.

Not all steam ships however guaranteed easier working conditions and better accommodation with the 'watch on watch off' system common to sailing ships being continued on many tramp ships with only a chief officer and a second officer. These officers could often be found working with the seamen on menial maintenance duties while on watch at sea; the helmsman being provided with a whistle to blow to summon the officer to the bridge if another ship was sighted.[6] When in port, both would be fully engaged with the cargo work, supervising the loading and discharge of cargo and the associated paperwork. These officers could expect to work a minimum 12 hour day throughout the voyage, regardless of whether at sea or in port. On the passenger liners there were sufficient qualified officers to work the four hours on eight hours off watch system at sea, although they would also have other duties to perform on their 'off watch' periods. Rates of pay for equivalent ranks were highest on the passenger ships, although promotion

---

[4]   Woodman, *Masters Under God*, p.355.

[5]   Woodman, *More Days, More Dollars*, p.130.

[6]   Hope, *Poor Jack*, p.309.

and command generally came sooner on the tramps. Officers on scheduled cargo liners would have comparable pay and conditions to those on the passenger ships, although promotion and command would again usually be a little sooner. Certainly on the passenger and scheduled cargo liners, officers' accommodation would normally consist of separate cabins with stewards to ease the daily burdens of life. Chief engineers were paid more than the chief officers, although less than the master, and often a second engineer would earn more than a chief officer, fuelling the resentment felt by some who considered the engineers to be on a lower social and professional level.

There were masters on the large and luxurious passenger liners who mixed with the international society of the day, enjoying a high social status and running their ships against the background of company regulations with the assistance of a defined and supportive hierarchical structure. There were those on tramp ships who relied on their own and often highly individual judgement on matters of seamanship and crew management, although the qualification required for both was the same – a Master's Foreign Going Certificate of Competency.

While life on a steam ship was significantly safer than that on a sailing ship, seafaring still had a much higher mortality rate than any other occupation. Immediately prior to the outbreak of war, the disease and mortality rate of seamen was about 50 per cent greater than for occupational groups ashore and death from violence a shocking rate of over 400 per cent greater. The high loss of life at sea, notwithstanding the 'safer' steam ships, was often attributed to overloading the ship, with many coal-carrying ships foundering off the British coast, giving rise to highly charged debates in Parliament and elsewhere about such overloading, led mainly by Samuel Plimsoll. It was not until the Merchant Shipping Act of 1876 that it became mandatory for British ships to be marked to show the safe level of loading, but such was the opposition from shipowners that it was not until 1894 that the load markings were finally agreed and implemented.

It was perhaps a consequence of the harsh environment and working conditions of the seamen of that period that they were notoriously brutal in their treatment of local populations as they travelled around the world, often regarding the native populations as lesser breeds of humankind, although quite content to frequent the many local brothels and bars which sought to entertain them. Drunkenness, whoring and brawling were the norm, with consequential injury, robbery, imprisonment, desertion and venereal disease – indeed a life of adventure. Seamen failing to return to their ships after a run ashore were not uncommon, providing an additional problem for the ship's officers, not all of whom were themselves always immune from such activities. Such behaviour by crews of the better paying passenger and cargo liners would however preclude their further employment on ships with better pay and on-board conditions.

Other activities were gradually being made available to the seamen when ashore. The concerns of the Consulates and moral reformers of the day and of some shipowners, most notably the founder of the Blue Funnel Line, Alfred Holt, led to the provision ashore of places for reading, entertainment and socialising, along with facilities provided by various Missionary Societies. These were aimed more specifically at the younger seamen in the hope that the more unsavoury activities ashore could be avoided. No doubt it was felt that the older men were past redemption.

Discipline had always been problematical on British ships and was often imposed by violence and deprivation of rations. New legislation and the development of trade union activity tended towards the imposition of disciplinary measures beginning to swing away from the master who, in reality, had little authority over the behaviour of his crew other than the docking of pay and privileges. Should a master wish to make a complaint or punish a seaman, he could well find himself answering to a magistrate for his actions once the ship returned to a British port. Not surprisingly, masters had their own views of the quality of the men who presented themselves as crew and of the extent of legal disciplinary actions available to them, as well as the degree of support they may expect from the shipowner. For example, Captain Crutchley, who commanded in both the Union Line and the New Zealand Shipping Company fleets noted,

> *the democratic element was very strong, and Jack got to assume he was quite as good as his master ... The power of the master of a merchant ship ... is a very uncertain quantity, inasmuch as it is limited only by the necessity of the case that is being dealt with. In other words, you can act as you consider the occasion rightly demands you should do so, but you stand to be called upon to defend your actions when you get on shore.*

Captain Henry Moffat declared in 1911: '... *I certainly bear no goodwill to the drunken, good-for-nothing men who form a large percentage of the crews on board our ships and steamers*'.[7]

Many masters despaired at the lack of support given to them by the shipowners since some, if not many, considered the matter of a dispute between master and crew to be of little concern to them, unless of course the profits of a voyage might be compromised. Captain Crutchley regretted that the discipline clauses of the Merchant Shipping Act gave great discretion to the magistrates who, in his opinion, could be unduly lenient. Much concerned about this matter and the lack of support from shipowners he stated: '*Again, I am well aware of the gravity of the words I am using, it is not the Board of Trade that has whittled down the master's authority voluntarily, but it is the deliberate action of ship-owners, who, curiously enough, have done more than any other agency to destroy authority on board ship*'.

The Regulations for Maintaining Discipline, sanctioned by the Board of Trade in pursuance of Section 114 (2) of the Merchant Shipping Act 1884, were set out in the Crew Agreement, which listed the various offences punishable by fines which could be levied by the master. In essence these offences were of violence, including the taking or keeping of any weapons, drunkenness and insolence, each of which would incur a fine of five shillings for a first or subsequent offence. (At the outbreak of war in 1914 an able bodied seaman was earning about £7 a month.) On completion of each voyage, the Agreement would record the conduct of each crew member and any wages due, to be signed by the master.

The Crew Agreement issued by the Board of Trade had to be signed by every person, including the master, and recorded the names, home addresses and wages to be paid (other than the earnings of the master), prior to the commencement of every foreign-going voyage. On the first page of the Agreement it was stated,

And the crew agree to conduct themselves in an orderly, faithful, honest, and sober manner, and at all times to be diligent in their respective Duties, and to be obedient to the lawful commands of the Master, or of any Person who shall lawfully succeed him, and of their Superior Officers, in everything relating to

---

[7]   Woodman, *More Days More Dollars*, p.19.

*the said ship and the Stores and Cargo thereof, whether on board, in boats,
or on shore.*

The Agreement also showed, in a tabular format, the Scale of Provisions, or
food allocations, by day of the week as drawn up by the Mercantile Marine
Committee 1902 and incorporated in the Merchant Shipping Act of 1906.

The move from sail to steam had brought additional problems of discipline
with the necessary employment of engine room firemen and stokers who
worked in particularly difficult and dangerous conditions, and whose standards
of disobedience and indiscipline matched if not exceeded their shipmates
working on deck, much to the despair of the engineer officers. These engine
room worthies seemed almost a race apart. Their gear on joining a ship
was said to be little more than a pack of cards and a sweat rag, which later
became a serious impediment to survival when having to abandon ship in an
emergency. They had the unenviable reputation of considerable belligerence
when ashore, often resulting in injuries and/or the inability to return to their
ship. While predominantly engaged in work requiring considerable physical
strength, stamina and an ability to withstand long periods of extreme heat, a
measure of skill was necessary to optimise the throw of coal into the furnace.
It was said that a stoker could not be considered to be truly competent until
he could show he could shovel coal through a suspended barrel with both
ends removed, without any of the coal touching its sides. Following a watch
in the stokehold it was not uncommon for these men to suffer from the
extremely painful condition known as 'fireman's cramp', caused by excessive
consumption of cold fluids after having been exposed to the prolonged and
intense heat of the stokehold, with muscles in the *hands and feet so contracted
that they look like claws.*[8]

Relationships between master and chief engineer could be fractious; a
particularly common complaint of the master being that the chief engineer
could rarely provide an accurate figure of coal consumption or of the quantity
of coal remaining on board to enable an accurate calculation to be made of
the steaming range. The very act of coaling covered the ship with coal dust,
with its ability to penetrate accommodation, clothing and food; a further
aspect which those working on deck considered to be a penalty for having

---

[8]   Hope, *Poor Jack*, pp.304–305.

steam-driven ships. Often the ship would depart from its bunker mooring with coal still piled on deck, which had then to be laboriously shifted into its bunkers as space became available.

However, the various Merchant Shipping Acts heralded a number of reforms to improve the lot of the merchant seafarer, albeit at a slow rate. Shorter voyages and more frequent returns to home ports brought about by the realisation of schedules gave greater facility for the imposition of formal disciplinary regimes, as well as more access to family life and society ashore.

The requirements laid out in the Merchant Shipping Acts of 1854 and 1906 for crew accommodation and food were of particular importance. In terms of crew accommodation, the requirement was made for the first time on merchant ships that a seaman should have his own designated space for sleeping and for keeping his kit, whereas previously he would often have to sleep in whatever space he could find amongst the stores or cargo. The 1906 Act increased the living space to be allowed to 120 cubic feet.

Despite the Board of Trade recommended food provision, poor food on board ship had often been a major and regular source of discontent and in some cases mutiny. It may be noted that the improvements in feeding applied only to ships of 1,000 tons gross and upwards, whereas the great majority of the coastal fleets and some on foreign-going voyages would be of a lesser tonnage. The position of ship's cook could become extremely hazardous should he be suspected of sharp practice – murders of ships' cooks were not unusual. To combat scurvy the 1854 Act required the provision of lime juice, presented on board in large glass demijohns for regular issue. Of a particularly sour and foul taste that even rum failed to disguise, spillage of any undiluted juice could be guaranteed to burn a hole in the stoutest wooden table if not wiped up fairly smartly. Fresh meat, despite being carried in ice boxes would, after a while, assume a green hue despite the endeavours of the cook to sponge it with vinegar to disguise its state. Tins of condensed milk, once opened, would require the fitting of carefully shaped plugs to prevent invasion of and occupation by cockroaches.

Accommodation standards varied considerably, with the best liner companies providing relatively comfortable, well heated and well ventilated quarters, with perhaps better food than many crew members might have experienced ashore, although tramp ships generally did not fare so well. At the end of May 1911 the *Southampton Times* carried a report from the medical journal *The Lancet* on the '*... crowded, damp, dark and dirty*' living conditions on Britain's merchant ships and the '*crying need of sailors*' for ventilation and proper washing facilities. The *Manchester Guardian* noted '*...on average, seamen and firemen (stokers) are worse paid, worse lodged and probably, even to-day, worse fed than Englishmen doing comparable work ashore*'.

Nearly half a century after the 1854 Act there was still little improvement in accommodation, even on the prestigious passenger ships, as may be seen in the memoirs of a steward on joining a passenger liner for his first trip in 1912:

> The '*glory hole*' [crew quarters] *was a beauty. It was situated just over the rudder, accommodating forty men, and its berths were two high in long rows so that to get in them one had to climb over the foot of the bunk. The sloping bulkheads were also lined with what berths shipbuilding ingenuity had contrived to cram in. The general atmosphere was of suffocation and congestion.*
>
> *My shipmates were beginning to join. They were of all nationalities and in varied degrees of sobriety. Soon the room was filled with the din of ribald songs, drunken quarrels about berths and coarse shouting. The stench of tobacco, foul breaths, stale liquor, the total lack of privacy and the utter vulgarity of my room-mates were revolting to me. Sleep being impossible I dressed and went on deck for fresh air and stayed there till it was time to start work again the following day.*
>
> *Breakfast was a revelation to me. To my timid enquiries as to where the '*Refectory*' was (all hotels have a Refectoire) I was tersely told 'This is a fucking ship, not a fucking monastery'. I meekly followed the rest and with my '*betters*' stood up to my breakfast like a horse at the trough.*[9]

No doubt many a seafarer before and since that revelation has been somewhat disappointed by the standard of accommodation on offer, and by the shipmates with whom he would become intimately associated during the course of the forthcoming voyage. Another account was also given by Hope of a first trip seaman, Alec Gracie, joining his ship, the SS *POPLAR BRANCH*, in Liverpool in 1917. Gracie described his accommodation as a rectangular room where the atmosphere seemed,

---

[9]   Hope: '*Poor Jack*', p.295

at once depressing and claustrophobic … Lining the room were six pairs of wooden bunks, and wooden benches lay alongside the lower ones. A very narrow table filled the centre of the fo'c'sle. This had two holes, one at each end, and the table slid up and down two steel stanchions. It was fixed at the required height by means of wedges.

He described his shipmates joining the ship as a crowd of large men who were all drinking from bottles of beer, smoking heavily and making a lot of noise, when a call came from above for all hands on deck to single up the mooring lines in readiness for departure. This brought about a sudden silence from the fo'c'sle, then,

A sudden silence was broken by 'Oh, go and fill yourself', or something of that ilk, followed by a titter of laughter. This was followed by the sound of someone crashing down the ladder and yet another big man appeared, broad-shouldered, blue-eyed and with a heavy moustache, who shouted, 'Who said that?' 'I did,' replied a sailor and he was immediately struck in the face with a blow that sent him reeling against his mates.

The big man turned out to be the second mate and '*It was astonishing how the "crowd" suddenly changed from a bunch of drunks into efficient seamen*'. Clearly, discipline imposed by violence was still not unknown.

A ship's doctor serving in Cunard passenger ships expressed his concern at the standards of accommodation provided below decks, stating,

I have seen 24 men in the fo'c'sle, 18 trimmers bunked together, and 30 stewards in one 'glory hole'. A couple of benches represented the seating. There was a deal table in the larger quarters. Damp, dirty or drying gear was everywhere. Light was poor and ventilation a joke. Smell varied according to the department. The worst was that of the kitchen and the butcher's staff, whose working gear was impregnated with the odour of fish, rancid fat and stale vegetables.[10]

Women, other than passengers, had no place on board a merchant ship apart

---

[10]   Ibid p.305

from the occasional wife of the master or a stewardess who might be the wife of one of the officers. Stewardesses on passenger ships were few in number and would generally tend to serve the first class passengers only. Some ships, notably the Union Castle liners, also carried women who worked the ships' laundries.

Certainly women at that time were viewed in a very paternalistic and protective light, reflecting the morals of the day whereby women were unable to enjoy the same freedoms as their menfolk. Society's attitude to women in the Victorian era can perhaps be deduced from Tennyson's epic poem 'The Princess', first published in 1847, when he described, perhaps slightly tongue in cheek, women's role;[11]

> *Man for the field, woman for the hearth,*
> *Man for the sword and for the needle she:*
> *Man with the head and woman with the heart,*
> *Man to command and woman to obey.*

General attitudes towards women were however about to change and while the development of Britain during the Victorian years had been marked by industrial growth, the collapse of the great Victorian boom in the late 1860s and early 1870s brought about the beginnings of other changes in society. Inequalities were questioned, bringing about more organised forms of protest, including the suffrage movement. Women were to play a major role in the forthcoming hostilities, bringing about irreversible changes in society throughout and following the end of the war.

The population of Britain had grown from 8.9 million at the turn of the nineteenth century to 35.5 million by the turn of the twentieth century, with life expectancy increasing from 40 to 44 for men and from 42 to 48 for women – population increases that demanded additional overseas trade. Passenger trade was increasing, bolstered by emigration from Europe to America and great prestige could be gained by shipowners from building the largest and fastest passenger liners. A great competitor in this trade was Germany and it was a shock to American and British owners when the four-funnelled Hamburg America Line's *DEUTSCHLAND* won the coveted

---

[11]   Briggs, *A Social History of England*. p.243

Blue Riband for the fastest trans-Atlantic passage from Britain in 1900. Carrying 2,050 passengers she was capable of sustaining a speed of 22 knots and was very much an example of the industrial growth of Germany at that time.

By the turn of the century however there was mounting industrial tension both ashore and afloat, with the period between 1908 and 1914 suffering from a number of major conflicts, particularly those with the miners and the railway workers. Seamen had been demanding what they saw as a proper wage to take account of the deprivations of life at sea compared with work ashore. Paid leave after a voyage was not given, except by a few of the liner companies where it would only be payable to the officers, and that at one day's paid leave for every month served on the voyage. This conflict was compounded by the fact that many British ships were crewed by men of different nationalities and thus pay and conditions tended to follow an international 'norm' rather than the general pay and conditions seen in the more advanced countries of northwest Europe and America. Unions began to make their presence felt, with the founding in July 1887 of the National Amalgamated Sailors' and Firemen's Union of Great Britain and Ireland by Havelock Wilson. Representation of the interests of shipmasters had begun with the Mercantile Marine Service Association in 1862, but after concerns that the views of shipowners through their Marine Superintendents were unduly prominent, Captain Thomas Moore then founded the Imperial Merchant Service Guild in 1893.

A signal point of unrest among the seamen, apart from poor pay and conditions, was resentment of the introduction of the arrangement whereby the engagement and discharge of seamen were held at offices of the Shipping Federation, a representative body of the shipowners, rather than at offices of the Board of Trade as had previously been the practice. This new practice resulted in shipmasters being able to report insubordinate or mutinous conduct which might imperil the ship at sea, whereby the accused seaman could be placed on a Federation blacklist, effectively excluding them from future employment on Federation member ships for given periods of time. This practice, the Federation argued, was instigated as a means of preventing intimidation and indiscipline and had proved to be successful. The seamen had also argued against the compulsory medical examination carried out at Federation offices, the purpose of which, according to the Federation, was to reject men who, by their physical condition, would be unfit for work at sea and who might be likely to make claims upon the shipowner under the Workmen's Compensation Act. Lack of medical care on board was a further specific grievance. Ships without passengers did not carry a doctor and medical knowledge was restricted to that of the master and his officers, whose expertise would generally be limited to the possession of a St John Ambulance Certificate and the *Ship Captain's Medical Guide* – the repository of medical knowledge aboard ship. Available medication was limited and the seaman would be put ashore and left at the first convenient opportunity if seriously ill or injured. He would be provided with pay owing to him but no more. Once that money ran out he would be at the mercy of the nearest Consulate to repatriate him.

By 1911 unrest among seamen was leading towards a strike. The Shipping Federation took little notice of this threat initially, believing the union too weak and its membership too low. The then General Secretary of the National Sailors' and Firemen's Union claimed that the Shipping Federation absolutely refused to admit '*that the men of the British Mercantile Marine have any grievances which require discussion at the present time*' and refused to discuss the matter with anyone claiming to represent the seafarers. A week before the coronation of George V, seafarers at all the large ports responded to a strike call and were joined by dock workers. Of great concern to many shipowners at that time was the Spithead Review to take place on 24 June to celebrate the coronation, with many prestigious passenger ships scheduled to take part in the pageant. As seamen and coal porters ashore were unwilling to participate without some settlement of their grievances, the presence of the merchant ships at the pageant was threatened, apart from which passenger sailings had to be postponed, the cross–Channel service was threatened and cargoes delayed. Threats and counter-threats were made, but by the afternoon prior to the Review some settlement was reached and the strike in Southampton was over by 24th June.

There was also unrest among the officers, an example of which was the move by officers of the Peninsula and Oriental Steamship Company, (P&O) to seek improved pay and conditions. In 1913 the chairman of P&O, Sir Thomas Sutherland, agreed to meet the officers late one morning to hear their grievances but, with little headway being made, he informed the officers that he would be going to lunch and would meet them later. The officers replied that they would also be going to lunch, but would not return. An agreement was reached shortly afterwards.[12]

Against that background of industrial unrest, the then Chancellor of the Exchequer, David Lloyd George, who had introduced legislation regarding shipping and railways, and had supported union recognition, wrote later in his memoirs that '*In the summer of 1914 there was every sign that the autumn would witness a series of industrial disturbances without precedent*' and '*Such was the state of the home front when the nation was plunged into war.*'

---

[12] Course, *The Merchant Navy. A Social History*, p.266.

CHAPTER 2

READY TO GO?

By 1914 the British Mercantile Marine had been steadily transformed, due mainly to implementation of the Merchant Shipping Acts, to become the largest, most efficient and up-to-date of all the merchant fleets. While almost every British family had a member serving in merchant ships, the public perception of the merchant seafarer nevertheless remained less than positive. Bertrand Hayes, later Sir Bertrand, Commodore of the White Star Line, who gave evidence at the *TITANIC* inquiry in 1912, wrote: '*For many years the merchant ship was a matter of small account in the public mind. It was a thing of boys' tales, part of a lower stratum of life than that of everyday doings on land. Sailors, in the popular view, were drunkards and wastrels, and only those who could not fit jobs ashore took jobs afloat.*'[13]

Little thought or organisation had been given to the likely needs of the merchant ships and their manning once in the throes of war, or to the development of any cohesive policy to allow for the fact that merchant ships were disparate in ownership. There was no such thing as a 'navy' under any single banner other than the red ensign. Manning levels varied by ship type and size, with the cargo ships having a total crew of about 60 and the passenger ships usually within the range of anything from 100 to 600 crew members.

From the outset of the war however, crews of merchant ships were rapidly decimated by government requirements to man warships with experienced seamen and even to bolster infantry regiments fighting in the trenches. As Captain David Bone, himself to become a victim of enemy action, reported:[14]

---

[13] Woodman, *More Days, More Dollars*, pp.192, 193.

[14] Bone, *Merchantmen-at-arms*, p.51.

With our entry to the war at sea in 1914, the same indifference [of the Board of Trade] was manifest. There was no mobilisation or registration of merchant seamen to aid a scheme of manning or to control the chaos that was very soon evident. Despite their intimate knowledge of the gap in our ranks made by the calling up of the Naval Reserve – accentuated by the enlistment of the merchant seamen in the navy – the Board of Trade could see no menace to the sea transport service in the military recruitment of our men. It was apparently no concern of theirs that we sailed on our difficult voyages short-handed, or with weak crews of inefficient landsmen, while so many of our skilled seamen and numbers of our sea officers were marking time in the ranks of the infantry.

The adverse effects of the military recruitment of the merchant seafarers were eventually recognised in November 1915, when the then President of the Board of Trade stated '*At the present time the efficient maintenance of our Mercantile Marine is of vital national interest, and captains, officers, engineers, and their crews will be doing as good a service for their country by continuing to man British ships as by joining the army.*' The numbers of qualified watchkeepers on merchant ships had already been reduced, yet it was largely to those men that the recognition of danger to their ships and the necessary immediate responses to such threats would fall. Little did the Board of Trade then realise the significance of the merchant fleets in keeping the supply lines open as the war developed and little did the merchant seafarers realise how little attention would be given to their plights if their ship were to be lost. The Board of Trade made little provision for their rehabilitation, always assuming the seafarer had managed to return to Britain. Captain Bone reports that in certain seaports the Sailors' Homes, provided by philanthropic societies for rehabilitation of merchant seafarers and as a place of rest before joining another ship were permitted, without protest, to be requisitioned by the Admiralty for their own ratings, displacing the unfortunate merchant seafarers.

Merchant seafarers were further disadvantaged compared to those serving in the naval forces, as later reported in *The Times* of 28th January 1915, regarding the behaviour of admiring women towards those who had enlisted. The matter had been causing concern for some while, but,

complaints are still being received from some parts of the trouble caused by the thoughtless conduct of numbers of young girls whose open admiration for the recruits had been finding expression in undesirable ways. In some centres ... the excitement has caused numbers of girls to lose their heads, and in one district where many girls were employed, the nuisance became so great that the military authorities had to consider the alternatives of moving the troops, or taking them on route marches from 8 o'clock to midnight. The presence of the Naval Brigade in training at the Crystal Palace has attracted girls from all the surrounding districts.

To counter this undesirable attention from admiring young girls and the need for late night route marches, the Women's Patrol Committee, with great tact, were able to bring about considerable restraint to the evening activities with their street patrols and the Young Women's Christian Association assisted by encouraging the girls '... *to show their admiration ... in a practical way by making shirts or knitting mufflers, socks and mittens for the soldiers and sailors*'.

The civilian merchant seamen, without the benefit of recruitment centres, naval uniforms and regalia were thus spared the admiration of numbers of girls in undesirable ways and indeed route marches at night. They were also not to be the beneficiaries of the knitted mufflers, socks and mittens by the girls of the Young Women's Christian Association.

As an age of Victorian/Edwardian innocence was to come to a close, confusion and uncertainty affected all in Britain, with rumour and counter-rumour initially rife and severely condemned by the government. The *Daily Mail* of Friday September 4 carried an article about a news-vendor who was probably trying to take advantage of the rumours to increase his sales. The brief article stated: '*Alleged to have shouted "Fall of Paris – Official". James Pearce, 33, news vendor, who denied the charge, was sentenced yesterday to two months hard labour for obtaining one penny by crying false war news.*'

The uncertainties of how to behave in the unfamiliar circumstances of a country at war were not restricted to the civilian population. At the outbreak of war commanders of neither British nor enemy ships had any experience of the application of the various conventions or rules that would apply once a warship encountered a merchant ship. Should a merchant ship regard herself as a body immune from the ravages of war and what protection, if any, could the merchant seafarers expect from any attack by enemy warships? Were international conventions to be faithfully followed, or indeed how might their obligations and responsibilities be interpreted by different parties, not only at the outset of war, but also as the war might progress? Certainly, in 1914, there was the expectation of the belligerent nations that hostilities could last for only a few months with the outcome to be settled mainly by land forces and, perhaps, by battles between the warships built in the arms race prior to 1914.

Britain had by far the largest fleet of merchant ships, with just under 50 per cent of the world tonnage, with long established trade routes and friendly ports of call throughout its worldwide Empire. Sailing ships were still common and accounted for around 20 per cent of the world total of about 20,000 ships and about 10 per cent of world tonnage. Germany, with the second largest fleet at about 12 per cent of the world tonnage, had taken the view that their merchant ships should stay out of the conflict until Germany had won and could then resume their peaceful duties. Both British and German authorities however had considered it necessary to provide a degree of armament to selected larger and faster passenger ships, to act as armed merchant cruisers for the purpose of raiding the merchant shipping of their opponents. The British ships placed under the command of the Admiralty were among those already accredited as Royal Mail Ships which were required to be capable of sustaining a speed of at least 18 knots and equipped with twin engines. In addition to those, by 1915 a number of selected merchant ships were to be equipped with a gun, usually mounted at the stern, but for the specific purpose of self-defence against submarine attack.

Nevertheless, questions arose regarding the likely outcomes of an encounter with a marauding enemy warship. From the British merchant seafarers' viewpoint the questions to be posed were about the protection they could expect, as civilians, from the enemy's adherence to the various internationally accepted rules and conventions; from their government and the Navy, and from their owners. Finally, if they should be involved in conflict, what means would be at their disposal to improve their chances of surviving such an encounter and returning home?

The Hague Peace Conferences of 1889 and 1907 set out the status of merchant ships at the outbreak of hostilities such that any merchant ship in an enemy port at the outbreak of war should be allowed to depart freely. This freedom should also apply to an enemy merchant ship which had left its last port before hostilities had been declared and arrived in an enemy port.

Further, should an enemy merchant ship be encountered on the high seas while ignorant of the outbreak of hostilities it could not be confiscated. The Hague Conferences emphasised the need for the protection of merchant seafarers as non-combatants, an example of which may be seen from the discussion of the legality of laying mines, where the German representative, Baron Marschall von Bieberstein, denied a claim that Germany wished for unlimited use of mines, on the grounds of humanity. The Baron stated that:

> ... *military acts are not governed solely by principles of international law. There are other factors; conscience, good sense, and the sentiments of duty imposed by principles of humanity will be the surest guide for the conduct of sailors, and will constitute the most effective guarantee against abuse. The officers of the German Navy, I emphatically affirm, will always fulfil, in the strictest fashion, the duties which emanate from the unwritten law of humanity and civilisation ... As to the sentiments of humanity and civilisation, I cannot admit that there is any Government or country which is superior in these sentiments to that which I have the honour to represent.*[15]

In London in 1909, following the Hague Conferences, a 'Declaration Concerning the Laws of Naval Warfare', known also as the London Declaration, was initiated as an internationally recognised code of maritime law, providing further humanitarian protection for merchant seafarers in the event that their ship should be captured and taken as a prize or sunk. These protections included the requirement for warships to have good grounds for suspecting the merchant ship to be of a belligerent nation or, if a neutral ship, for the warship commander to have good reason to suppose the merchant ship was carrying contraband, i.e. goods likely to be of value to opposing countries. Of particular interest to the merchant seafarers was that crews were to be taken to a place of safety before their ship was sunk. That Declaration was signed by most of the great maritime powers of the day, including Britain and Germany but, despite the urging of the US for belligerent nations to abide by it once hostilities had broken out, no state ever ratified it.

Nevertheless, both British and German naval authorities subscribed, to varying degrees, to the terms of the London Declaration as a Naval Prize

---

[15] Hurd, *The Merchant Navy*, Vol. 1, p.119.

Code, governing the actions of the stop and search of merchant ships, their capture or indeed sinking by naval vessels.[16] British naval authorities gave instructions that *'During the war, the commanders of His Majesty's ships have the right to stop and search enemy and neutral vessels, and to seize – and in some cases to destroy – the same, together with the enemy and neutral goods found thereon.'* The caveat was placed that any such interventions should only take place when the commander was content that the action would be successful. German naval authorities followed much the same line in their instructions whereby

> *The stoppage and search shall take place only if the commander deems that it will be successful. All acts shall be done in such a manner – even against the enemy – as to be compatible with the honour of the German Empire, and with such regard towards neutrals as may be in conformity with the law of nations and the interests of Germany.*

Indeed Article 116 of the German Naval Prize Regulations stated, *'Before the destruction of a vessel, all persons on board are to be placed in safety, with their goods and chattels, if possible, and all ship's papers and other relevant documents which, in the opinion of the parties interested, are of value for the decision of the Prize Court are to be taken over by the commander'*.[17] The application of these Codes clearly required emphasis to be given to the safety and welfare of seafarers, including the requirement for crews of captured ships to be taken to a place of safety. They were to be released after signing an agreement that they would not participate in any future acts against the interests of an enemy state, on pain of execution should they be recaptured so doing at a later time. Should a merchant ship refuse the instructions of a warship to stop and follow the warship's instructions, or attempt armed resistance, then they would be treated as belligerent participants and subject to *'the usage of war'*. This phrase encompassed the situation whereby the master of a merchant ship who ignored the order to stop but was later captured, would be executed. The belligerent states were also to have regard to ships of a neutral state which would still be engaged in their normal trades. While the

---

[16] Ibid p.132

[17] Huberich and King, *The Prize Code of the German Empire as in force July 1 1915* art.116

German naval authorities had indicated their desire to follow the Codes, it would soon become apparent that the German government would be willing to accept, if not promote, a less humanitarian approach.

From the merchant seafarers' view, these Codes should have provided some comfort in the event of encountering a German warship, although all merchant ships were considered to have the right of resistance to capture. The First Lord of the Admiralty, Winston Churchill, exhorted all masters not to surrender calmly but to do their utmost to escape capture and, should a submarine approach with obvious hostile intentions, the ship should steer straight for it at maximum speed to cause the submarine to submerge to avoid being rammed. Such action would however appear to be in contravention of the Hague Conventions and the London Declaration. The interpretations of these Codes and guides were to vary, usually to the detriment of the merchant ships and their crews. Indeed, the somewhat conflicting sentiments of the international 'rules' and the Admiralty advice placed the shipmaster in an invidious position.

Should a merchant ship find itself the centre of attention from a German warship, the crew could feel they had the protection of the Royal Navy which maintained a worldwide presence without equal. His Majesty's ships could be called to assist by the means of radio, although radio was by no means common on all steamers. While it was certainly the case that the Royal Navy would and did provide assistance, there were far more merchant ships than naval ships traversing the shipping routes worldwide, thus proximity to a naval vessel to call upon for assistance was a rare occurrence away from home waters.

As a last resort, the merchant seafarer would need to resort to the lifeboats, designed primarily to enable a rapid evacuation of the ship in an emergency. When given adequate time and with proper training in the act of releasing and lowering the boats from a motionless and upright ship, boats could be cleared and lowered away in a matter of minutes. Given adverse conditions of weather, ship motion and/or a list, emergency evacuation took on a quite different hue, with many instances of boats being incapable of being launched due to a heavy list and/or being damaged in the act of lowering, with consequential injury and loss of life. The facility of these open boats to provide shelter and provision for any prolonged passage was very limited, particularly in adverse weather, when survival could be anticipated to be no more than a few days, although there were to be some spectacular exceptions.

The numbers of lifeboats provided by the shipowner in accordance with Board of Trade requirements in force in 1914 were specified in the Merchant Shipping (Life Saving Appliances) Act of 1888 and the later Merchant Shipping Act of 1894, whereby the numbers of lifeboats to be provided were dependent upon the gross tonnage of the ship, rather than the numbers of persons carried on a given ship. These requirements also stated that the number of people to be carried in each boat was to be determined by a boat's cubic capacity, but applied only to ships of up to 10,000 gross tons. A recommended scale of provision of boats for larger ships was in force from 1890 onwards with large passenger ships providing liferafts in addition to minimum specifications for the numbers of boats. Further, account was taken in the regulations of the number of watertight bulkheads fitted, on the basis that the greater the number of watertight bulkheads, the less the likelihood of the ship sinking. It was also felt that with the growth in the use of wireless telegraphy assistance, if required, help could be summoned more readily. With the high numbers of merchant ships, if not naval ships, on the major routes expected to be near at hand, it was considered more likely that the lifeboats might only be necessary for the ferrying of passengers between the stricken and the rescue ship.

Some insight into the provision of lifeboats may be derived from the views expressed by senior Board of Trade officials and the Chief Marine Superintendent of the White Star Line at the Wreck Commissioner's Inquiry following the loss of the *TITANIC* in 1912. In response to direct questions regarding the numbers of lifeboats to be provided, both the Board of Trade officials and the Superintendent, all of whom were experienced seamen, expressed the views that it was not only unrealistic to attempt to provide enough boats to accommodate the total ship's complement, but that it would be unsafe to attempt to do so.

The view that it was unrealistic to provide more boats was based on the grounds that enough deck space could not be provided without compromising the comfort and convenience of passengers. In addition, large numbers of otherwise superfluous crew would be needed to launch such a large number of boats and these factors would adversely affect the profitability of a voyage. The claim that having enough boats for all on board was unsafe had been based on the premise that it would '*be putting an undue strain upon the Masters and Officers – that they could never possibly get people into the boats in the case of a disaster'*. With more boats, it was argued, it was likely that some boats would be under-occupied and that an orderly supervision of evacuation would not be possible. Throughout the Wreck Commissioner's Inquiry, the professional officers maintained that had there been fewer boats, there might well have been less loss of life due to the better likelihood of the ship's officers ensuring that all boats had been filled to capacity – indeed many of the boats that did get away from *TITANIC* were not fully occupied. The Wreck Commissioner drew attention to the requirements of German passenger ships to be provided with means for evacuation of the whole of the ship's complement, but the professional officers giving evidence at the Inquiry maintained throughout that they did not consider that to be advantageous and, furthermore, determination of the required numbers of boats was best left to the shipowner.

The Inquiry learned that *TITANIC* carried 20 lifeboats with a capacity of 1,178 persons for a ship capable of carrying 3,330 persons. This was in excess of existing Board of Trade requirements for *TITANIC* whereby lifeboat capacity should provide for 1,060 persons. Folding life rafts were also provided, in addition to some 3,500 lifebelts and 48 life rings, none of which could be of much value in the icy sea conditions. It was also the case that lifeboat drills were not held as it was considered they might unduly alarm passengers. Sir Alfred Chalmers, the most senior professional officer and Nautical Advisor to the Board of Trade until 1911, when asked by the Wreck Commissioner '*Has the TITANIC disaster led you to believe that any single one of the Board of Trade Regulations should be modified?*' responded '*No.*' He went on to say that he did not believe any lessons could be learnt from the *TITANIC* disaster because it was an extraordinary one and that '*The Board of Trade, the Marine Department, guards against ordinary occurrences, not extraordinary.*'

The philosophy of shipowners and the Board of Trade regarding the provision of lifesaving equipment remained unchanged following the loss of *TITANIC* and the earlier loss of 500 lives on the French liner *LA BOURGOGNE*. It was summarised by Captain William Sims of the United States Navy (later Admiral Sims, in command of all US naval forces operating in Europe) in his paper given at the Royal Institution of Naval Architects on passenger ship lifeboats:

> *The truth of the matter is that in case any large passenger steamship sink, by reason of collision or other fatal damage to her floatability, more than half of her*

passengers are doomed to death, even in fair weather, and in case there is a bit of a sea running none of the loaded boats can long remain afloat, even if they succeed in getting away from the side, and one more will be added to the long list of 'the ships that never return.' Most people accept this condition as one of the inevitable perils of the sea, but I believe it can be shown that the terrible loss of life occasioned by such disasters as overtook the BOURGOYNE and the TITANIC and many other ships can be avoided or at least greatly minimised. Moreover, it can be shown that the steamship owners are fully aware of the danger to their passengers; that the laws on the subject of life-saving appliances are wholly inadequate; that the steamship companies comply with the law, though they oppose any changes therein, and that they decline to adopt improved appliances; because there is no public demand for them, the demand being for high schedule speed and luxurious conditions of travel.

Fortunately for the passengers and crews, public demand prevailed for the provision of a sufficient number of lifeboats to accommodate all on board, and was quickly put in hand. This led to the first Safety of Life at Sea Convention in 1914, attended by representatives of 13 countries. It was due to apply from July 1915, but due to the outbreak of war its provisions were never ratified although many nations adopted them, including Article 40 of Chapter VI of the Convention which stated '*At no moment of its voyage may a ship have on board a total number of persons than that for whom accommodation is provided in lifeboats (and the pontoon lifeboats) on board.*'

At the start of the war it was not compulsory for lifeboats to be stocked with any emergency provisions, other than a 10-gallon breaker of drinking water, thus it was up to the individual ship to determine possible needs and stock their boats accordingly. Liferafts provided could be of the collapsible type, constructed of a double lining of canvas, sectioned in two watertight envelopes to provide buoyancy and protection against the canvas being torn. Other rafts were made of wood and supported by four long buoyancy tanks but the boarding of these rafts from the sea proved to be extremely difficult, bearing in mind the boarder would most probably be in a condition of shock, probably very cold, weighed down by clothing and possibly injured. With no provision for shelter, these rafts provided but a very temporary means of survival and provisions and, once on board, were found to be rudimentary at best, if not ruined by seawater. A poster of the time showed five seamen in a raft with the legend, written by a merchant seaman, Edward Osmond, stating that there were faulty storage tanks which rendered the survival rations of food and water useless and faulty flares. The plea was made to makers of lifeboats and liferafts *'For the safety of merchant seamen, do all you can to see that the lifeboat and raft supplies of water, food and signals are properly protected by watertight tanks and tins. They are depending on you.'* No doubt such restrained language would not have matched the emotions of the surviving seaman on his discovery of that which was supposed to aid his survival.

Thus, with the background of the promise of protection and safety from the implementation of measures stemming from international conventions; the protestations of humanity by the German naval authorities; the availability of wireless telegraphy; the worldwide superiority of the Royal Navy; and, as a last resort the provision of lifesaving equipment, the merchant seafarers and their passengers could take a considered view as to the likely chances of surviving an encounter with a German warship.

The merchant seafarer would no doubt have also taken a considered view of Section 158 of the Merchant Shipping Act of 1894 which showed that in the event of the loss of a ship, whether in war or in peace, the service of the seafarer would be deemed to have terminated at the time of the loss and thus wages would cease. This effectively rendered the seafarer immediately unemployed at a moment when his or her life was particularly imperilled. A consequence of this was that the seafarers' allocation of wages paid on his behalf by the shipowner to family or friends would immediately cease and it was sometimes the case that this cessation could be the first the family might know of the loss of their provider. As many crews were drawn from different nationalities and from different parts of the country, families of those lost at sea could draw little comfort in their grief from a shared loss with neighbouring families unlike, in many cases, the families of British service personnel killed in the war.

Should the seafarer survive the loss of the ship and make it ashore, he or she would generally be at the mercy of the nearest Consulate which, in accordance with the Merchant Shipping Act, would seek a berth on a British ship for repatriation to the UK or British possession to which the unfortunate mariner belonged, for which passage the mariner would be designated a 'Distressed British Seaman'. The master of any British ship would be required to provide that seafarer with a berth or 'sleeping place' which '*must be effectively protected against the sea and weather*', with the seafarer being paid an allowance of three shillings a day subsistence if on a steamer, or one shilling and six pence if found a berth on a sailing ship. Where possible, preference would be given in the allocation to a ship with a crew shortage. Once back in his homeland, the survivor would need to provide for himself until he found another berth on another ship and, in many cases, then to repeat the whole process.

By contrast, many British companies whose employees left their services to enlist in the armed forces made considerable provision for their welfare and that of their families. For example, Arthur Guinness and Cadbury augmented the wages paid by the armed forces, pension contributions were paid by the companies, all employees discharged on medical grounds could expect to be taken back into the company on full pay and pensions were paid to widows and children. Additionally, checks were made on the families of employees on active service to enquire as to their well-being and their jobs were kept open for them. Such benevolence by shipowners towards their motley seafarers was unknown.

* * *

As the first verse of Rudyard Kipling's sentient poem 'Big Steamers', first published in 1911 asked,[18]

> *Oh, where are you going to, all you big steamers,*
> *With England's own coal up and down the salt seas?*
> *We are going to fetch you your bread and butter,*
> *Your beef, pork and mutton, eggs, apples and cheese.*

'All you big steamers' were soon to be subject to the most brutal and prolonged attacks on their endeavours, and the ships, and the men and women who crewed them, were to suffer the severest tests of their courage, durability and competence.

And so to war.

---

[18] Briggs, *A Social History of England*. p.222

CHAPTER 3

SETTING THE SCENE

The summer of 1913 had seen particularly good weather, with Britain at the apogee of imperial power and, despite the naval arms race between Britain and Germany, relations between the two countries were better than they had been for some years. In May 1913 the three cousins, King George V, Tsar Nicholas II and Kaiser Wilhelm II had all met in Berlin for the wedding of the Kaiser's daughter, Victoria Louise – the last time the three men would meet. The Kaiser, having spent much of his earlier life in England as the first grandson of Queen Victoria, was particularly fond of English pastimes and country life and very much enjoyed English society. His love for England however had begun to fade after the death of his English mother Princess Victoria in 1901, as his aspirations for a dominant Imperial Germany grew.

On 31 July 1914 the Kaiser announced, in a speech from the balcony of the Royal Palace in Berlin:

> *A momentous hour has struck for Germany. Envious rivals everywhere force us to legitimate defence. The sword has been forced into our hands. I hope that in the event that my efforts to the very last moment do not succeed in bringing our opponents to reason and in preserving peace, we may use the sword, with the help of God, so that we may sheathe it again with honour. War will demand enormous sacrifices by the German people, but we shall show the enemy what it means to attack Germany. And so I commend you to God. Go forth into the churches, kneel down before God, and implore his help for our brave army.*

Again from the Royal Palace in Berlin on 1 August 1914, some three days before war broke out between Britain and Germany, the Kaiser addressed the nation with:

I thank you from the bottom of my heart for your expressions of loyalty and your esteem. When it comes to war, all parties cease and we are all brothers. One or another party has attacked me in peacetime, but now I forgive them wholeheartedly. If our neighbours do not give us peace, then we hope and wish that our good German sword will come victorious out of this war.

As war was declared, Kaiser Wilhelm proclaimed:

I look upon the people and the nation as handed to me as a responsibility conferred upon me by God, and I believe, as it is written in the Bible, that it is my duty to increase this heritage for which one day I shall be called upon to give an account. Whoever tries to interfere with my task I shall crush.

★ ★ ★

On 29 July 1914 the North German Lloyd passenger liner *FRIEDRICH DER GROSSE* left Baltimore with American passengers, bound for Bremen. Built in 1896 and of 10,170 tons, the ship had joined the prestigious fleet of German passenger ships in the trans-Atlantic trade following an earlier career transporting German troops to China. The *New York Sun* printed an alleged passengers' account of the voyage from Baltimore under the heading of '*Heroic Bearing of a Skipper*', as the ship had been called back to New York to the surprise of the passengers when they realised that the ship had turned around in mid–Atlantic. The report of the passengers' account continued:

They then appointed a committee to call on the skipper and asked for an explanation.

The committee found the skipper in tears and his officers looking mournful. He told the committee that the ship had been ordered to New York because of war impending between Germany on the one side and France, England and Russia on the other. Captain Fritz said he feared that a British cruiser might capture his ship and that it would be inadvisable to return to Baltimore, New York being a much nearer port.

Mrs. Preston said that the captain and officers of the ship shed tears in discussing the chances of her getting into New York without being held up, and that at times they acted much like children afraid of the dark. When the cabin

31

passengers went back to their staterooms on Friday night they found that all the ports had been veiled with towels and aprons. The electric lights on the decks were extinguished, and dimly lighted lamps were substituted.

The precautions against capture by British cruisers reached a climax on Saturday night, the saloon passengers said. The ship's orchestra, which had been playing while some of the passengers danced, was ordered to stop. This stopped the dancing and the women naturally wanted to know if shutting off the orchestra was really necessary. One of them said that the skipper even feared the phantom British cruisers might be attracted by the sound of the orchestra.

Thereafter the trip of the liner was melancholy. Officers and stewards were obsessed with the idea that they were in great peril, and sometimes they were seen to embrace when they met on the decks. They were gladder than the passengers when they passed the Ambrose Channel lightship on Sunday evening, safe from cruiser perils of the Atlantic.

It is of course difficult to accept the integrity of the account, if only on the grounds that the master, who was in fact Captain Dierkes, was referred to as Captain Fritz – a pejorative term at that time, although the ship did indeed return to New York after leaving Baltimore. It was however an example of the propaganda to boost morale by suggesting the enemy had no heart for a fight if met with threat of resistance and to support the mistaken belief that the war could therefore last only for a few months. The German High Command had also considered that the war would be over in a few months, in the equally mistaken belief that their superior armies could not be resisted, even though it was assumed that the Allied forces would control the seas. Instructions given to the German merchant ships therefore were to seek a neutral port and resume their activities once the war was won. The USA, as a major trading partner, was the preferred neutral country to seek shelter where it was felt the German liners would be safe.

The day before *FRIEDRICH DER GROSSE* left Baltimore, another large North German Lloyd passenger liner *KRONPRINZESSIN CECILIE* departed from New York shortly after midnight on 28 July, bound for Europe under the command of the highly regarded Captain Karl Polak, well known to many American passengers from his years of trans-Atlantic crossings. He, with many of his passengers, was aware of the reports of imminent war from Europe, but nevertheless his ship left strictly on schedule, with 1,892 passengers on board, including 354 Americans and 667 Germans. Some of the passengers were extremely wealthy and prominent citizens, including members of the United States House of Representatives bound for the International Peace Conference in Stockholm.

When just two days away from the first port of call, Captain Polak received a terse telegraph message from Bremen to open a sealed envelope he had been given a year earlier, when taking command of the *KRONPRINZESSIN CECILIE*. The instructions contained within that envelope were to the effect that Captain Polak should immediately take refuge in a neutral port, preferably New York, as it was felt that waters near Britain and France would be unsafe for German ships. The large liner was slowly turned to head back for New York and Captain Polak gathered his crew and passengers to tell them of the change of plan. It was not well received, particularly by those who had business and pleasure engagements planned. Some of the more wealthy passengers proposed a scheme to buy the ship on the spot and continue the journey to Europe under the American flag. While the proposal was discussed and put to the chairman of the shipping company, Captain Polak had to tell his passengers, apparently with regret, that he must comply with the owner's instructions and return the ship to New York.

Aware that British warships would be on the lookout for him and would be expecting him to return to New York, Captain Polak sent a message to the wireless station at Malin Head, on the northernmost tip of Ireland, suggesting he had changed his route to pass north of Scotland rather than to try and pass through the English Channel to reach Bremerhaven – a deception that proved to be effective. Continuing on the return passage to New York, Captain Polak attempted to disguise his distinctive ship as a Cunard liner in the hope that, if seen at a distance, any British cruiser might mistake her for the *OLYMPIC*, a sister ship to the *TITANIC*, on the basis that both the *KRONPRINZESSIN CECILIE* and the *OLYPMIC* were of a similar size and each had four funnels. Despite the rapid change of funnel markings to the Cunard colours, the Cunard ship had her four funnels equidistantly spaced, whereas the German liner had her funnels in two pairs, separated to provide enough space for the large and elaborate first class dining saloon to be placed amidships where any wave-induced motions affecting the ship would be minimised. Certainly the profiles of the two ships were so dissimilar that it was most unlikely that the disguise could possibly have been effective had a British warship sighted her.

Captain Polak had another problem, which was one of insufficient coal to return to New York at full speed. In the event, with the aid of a passenger, a Mr Clinton Blair, who was an experienced yachtsman with detailed knowledge of the coast of Maine, advised Captain Polak to make for Bar Harbour which was some several steaming hours nearer than New York. The *KRONPRINZESSIN CECILIE* was thus eventually brought to anchor in the tiny harbour, much to the surprise of local inhabitants. Further, unknown to the passengers the *KRONPRINZESSIN CECILIE* was carrying a fortune of $25 million in barrels of gold coins and $3.6 million in silver; the loss of which would have been a double disaster for North German Lloyd.[19]

Churchill, as First Lord of the Admiralty in 1914, expressed the view in his later publication *The World Crisis 1911–1914* that *'It is reasonable to suppose that German merchant ships, other than those armed and commissioned for warlike purposes, will run for neutral harbours as soon as war breaks out, and that very few will attempt under the German flag to return home running the gauntlet of the numerous British fleets operating in the North Sea.'*

At much the same time as Captain Polak was resolving his dichotomy, the 19,524 ton Cunard liner RMS *CARMANIA* had left New York under the command of Captain James Barr, bound for Liverpool with 800 passengers on board and $10 million of bullion in her holds. On the night of 5 August, *CARMANIA* was approached by HMS *BRISTOL*, which signalled, *'War is declared. Darken ship. Maintain wireless silence.'* Captain Barr opened his sealed envelope of secret instructions which ordered him to make all speed for home and hand his ship over to the Royal Navy. Waiting for him on the Liverpool Landing Stage on 7 August was Captain Noel Grant, RN, who took over command, bringing with him as his first lieutenant and gunnery officer a retired lieutenant commander RN of nearly 70 years of age, Eric Lockyer. Captain Grant, with no command experience of a large ship, was 45 years old and Captain Barr, a senior master with Cunard was 58. He was offered a temporary commission as commander, Royal Naval Reserve (RNR) by Grant, provided that Captain Barr would serve under him on the

---

[19]   Putnam, *The Kaiser's Merchant Ships in World War I*, pp.103–108.

ship as a 'special adviser'. Reluctantly, but fearing for the safety of his ship in other's hands, Barr agreed.

Several of Captain Barr's merchant ship officers were offered temporary RNR commissions, with many of his crew, including all of the engine room staff of merchant seafarers, specially enrolled in the RNR for six months, with a number of RN seamen then attached to the ship. By 14 August, just one week after arriving at Liverpool as a luxury Atlantic liner, RMS *CARMANIA* became HMS *CARMANIA*, armed, fitted out and manned as an armed merchant cruiser.[20]

The armed merchant cruisers were to play a significant role as merchant ship raiders, crewed largely by a mixture of Merchant and Royal Navy personnel, who learned to live and work together for the common cause. The Admiralty were concerned that roving German warships would do great damage to British and Allied merchant ships and that a fleet of large and fast British liners should be quickly converted to fighting ships. The protection and preservation of the sea routes to and from the UK as an island nation was vital to maintain the war effort to an extent far greater than those for Germany, as reflected by the sizes of the relative merchant shipping fleets. According to Admiral Jellicoe, when war began there were 915 German merchant ships abroad, of which only 158 were able to return to their ports.[21] When the Franco-German war broke out practically all the German vessels sought neutral harbours, where they stayed until the declaration of peace. Kaiser Wilhelm had given plenty of warning to his military forces and railways to transport troops to the battle lines but had given no preparatory warning to the German merchant fleets until the invasion of Belgium. The result of this was the loss of much of the German merchant fleet to internment at neutral ports and the gift of a substantial fleet of prestigious trans-Atlantic liners into the hands of the Americans for the transport of troops and provisions to Britain, including the *FRIEDRICH DER GROSSE* and the *KRONPRINZESSIN CECILIE*. The lot of the German merchant seaman was to be very different from that of their British counterparts.

Relations between Britain and Germany were becoming increasingly tense, with the German ports uneasy about the status of British ships which

---

[20]   Poolman, *Armed Merchant Cruisers*, pp.14–17.

[21]   Wheeler, *Daring Deeds of Merchant Seamen* ..., p.111.

they began to detain from near the end of July onwards, on a variety of pretexts. This was in direct contravention of the Hague Conferences and the London Declaration, giving a very early indication of how such agreements for the safety and protection of British ships and their crews were to be treated. The usual excuse was that the German ports were undergoing protective works and thus the ship transits of the port areas could both inhibit the works and damage the ships although, despite that argument, inward–bound British ships were not so inconvenienced. By 4 August, 155 British officers with 888 ratings *'were at the mercy of the Germans'*.[22] The crews were eventually taken off their ships and made to sign a declaration that they would not participate in the war against Germany; refusal would result in their being shot as spies. They were removed and many suffered humiliating and violent treatment at the hands of their captors, eventually being placed in concentration camps of varying degrees of harshness for the duration of the war.

On the evening of 2 August, a fleet of U-boats, shepherded by their escort vessels, returned to their base in Helgoland, having spent the day moored in observation positions to give warning of any movements of British warships. That evening, they received orders to prepare for war and seek out the British fleet. On 6 August, just two days after the declaration of war by Britain, 10 U-boats, which were regarded as crude and unreliable and inspiring little German confidence in this new arm of the Imperial Navy, set out to begin their first sortie. Of the 10 boats that set out from Helgoland, only seven returned, having indeed encountered the British fleet. One U-boat had been forced to return to base with mechanical problems, one was lost in unknown circumstances and one destroyed. It was nevertheless a noteworthy expedition in that the first torpedo ever fired in anger from a submarine had been so fired, although it was unsuccessful and the unfortunate attacker, U-15, was subsequently rammed and destroyed. The lack of success of that expedition encouraged a belief in British Allied circles that the submarine perhaps need not be unduly feared as a menace to surface warships. It was known that the German Grand Admiral Tirpitz *'considered submarines to be in an experimental stage, of doubtful utility, and that the German Government was not at all convinced that they would form an essential or conspicuous part of their future naval programmes'*.

---

[22]   Hurd, *The Merchant Navy*, Vol. 3. p.341

That belief was however very short-lived. On 5 September, U-21 made history by sinking the first British warship, HMS *PATHFINDER*, with a torpedo. The sinking by U-21 was the first time any submarine had sunk an enemy warship since the sinking of the Federal States frigate *HOUSATONIC* by the Confederates States' submarine *W.L. HUNLEY* on 17 February 1864, off Charleston during the American Civil War. On 22 September three British cruisers were sunk by one U-boat, U-9, commanded by Otto Weddigen, establishing the submarine indeed as a significant weapon of war.

From the viewpoint of the British merchantmen the submarine was regarded as posing little threat, with their limited range and speed to pursue them on ocean passages; their operational limitations in rough seas; their limited ability to remain submerged; and with little capability for taking prisoners. The smaller submarines, used mainly in North Sea and coastal cruises had a submerged speed of around 6 knots and a surface speed of around 9 knots. The larger boats used primarily in the Atlantic were capable of submerged speeds of around 9 knots and a surface speed of around 16.5 knots.[23] In any event, the submarine was seen as a means for attacking warships with torpedoes and of little concern to an unarmed merchant ship. This viewpoint was also to be short lived.

The distinction of being the first British merchant ship to be taken and sunk by the Germans fell to the Ellerman's cargo steamer *CITY OF WINCHESTER*, of 6,601 tons and under the command of Captain Boyck, when she was captured by the light cruiser SMS *KÖNIGSBERG* on 6 August 1914. The Ellerman ship had departed from Colombo on 23 July, bound for London, and had entered the Gulf of Aden, still unaware of the outbreak of war. Her wireless operator, Alan Lees, was looking out of his wireless room and saw an unfamiliar shape approaching at high speed in the dark. He drew this to the attention of Captain Boyck, who recognised the approaching ship as a cruiser and, as it drew closer, could see the cruiser's guns trained on him. When the cruiser gave the signal to stop, Captain Boyck had no alternative but to comply, although even at that stage he was unaware of the outbreak of hostilities or indeed that it was a German cruiser. The boarding party from *KÖNIGSBERG* was Captain Boyck's introduction to World War I.

---

[23]   Gray, *The U-Boat War*, p.270.

Under the command of the German boarding party, Captain Boyck was ordered to follow the *KÖNIGSBERG* to the bay of Mukalla, where they were joined by two other German merchant ships and then made their way to anchor off the Kuria Muria Islands, where the *CITY OF WINCHESTER* was stripped of her bunkers and provisions as well as her charts and sailing directions. Captain Boyck and much of his crew were eventually put ashore in Mozambique where Boyck recorded that he and his companions '*were treated with every respect and civility by the Germans.*' Meanwhile, the second officer, with the third engineer and the lascar crew were transferred to yet another German ship, the *GOLDENFELS* which returned to the *CITY OF WINCHESTER* at anchor off the Kuria Muria Islands. From that vantage point the second officer and his companions had the unhappy experience of watching the slow sinking of the *CITY OF WINCHESTER*. They were later safely landed by the GOLDENFELS at Sabang.

It is very difficult to imagine the feelings of those who see their ship plundered and sunk before their eyes. Any ship provides an environment unlike any on land – a community isolated from the world of land, often with crews from disparate origins who nevertheless understand that once leaving port the ship provides the boundaries of its occupants' existence and it must, of necessity, be a complete co-operative relying entirely on its on-board resources. The Japanese recognise this by providing the suffix '*Maru*' to each and every ship's name, be it the most magnificent ocean liner or humblest fishing boat. The rough translation of '*Maru*' is wholeness; completeness, a circle of life within given confines. The loss of one's own ship, from whatever cause, is a very profound experience.

The *CITY OF WINCHESTER* was *KÖNIGSBERG*'s first and last British merchant ship victim, as she was blockaded in the Rufiji delta by British warships which eventually destroyed the German cruiser on 11 July 1915 with a loss of 33 of her crew. The *KÖNIGSBERG* had clearly abided strictly by the Prize Code, by ensuring that no harm befell the master or crew of the *CITY OF WINCHESTER*, setting a precedent for the behaviour of German warships towards the British merchant seafarer. The capture of the Ellerman steamer was however in direct contravention of the Hague Peace Conferences of 1889 and 1907, as the ship had left its last port prior to the outbreak of war.

On the same day as *CITY OF WINCHESTER*'s misfortune, the British steamer *DRUMCLIFFE* (4,072 tons), commanded by Captain Evans, was on passage from Buenos Ayres to New York, via Trinidad. As was the case with Captain Boyck, the captain was unaware of the start of hostilities, but that was soon brought to his attention by the presence of the German light cruiser SMS *DRESDEN* commanded by Captain Lüdecke, off the mouth of the Amazon. This had been a chance encounter as *DRESDEN* was on her way to round Cape Horn to join the German Pacific Squadron. Neither commander had anticipated such an encounter nor had either been given specific orders as to the actions to be taken in such a situation. Captain Lüdecke was however conversant with the requirements of the Hague Convention and the German Naval Codes and opted to release *DRUMCLIFFE* on parole, subject to the master and crew signing a declaration not to take any actions or undertake any services contrary to the interests of Germany. Captain Evans had his wife and child on board and, fearing for their safety, agreed to Captain Lüdecke's demands. *DRUMCLIFFE*'s radio was dismantled and the ship soon got underway again.

That same afternoon, the Houlder liner *LYNTON GRANGE* (4,252 tons), under the command of Captain H. Simpson, encountered *DRUMCLIFFE* and *DRESDEN*. Captain Simpson was also advised by *DRESDEN* of the outbreak of hostilities when, almost simultaneously, the Houston liner *HOSTILIUS* (3,325 tons) also arrived at the scene. Captain Lüdecke placed boarding parties on both ships, disabled their radios and demanded that the British crews sign a declaration such that '*We, the Captain, officers and crew of the s.s. LYNTON GRANGE, declare formally that we will not do any service in the British Navy or Army, and will not give any assistance to the British Government against Germany during the present war*'.[24] This demand was followed by the threat that if the declaration was not so signed, the officers and men would be taken on board the cruiser and their ship immediately sunk. If the declaration was signed and subsequently the crew were later found to be breaking the pledge, they would be shot and their ship destroyed. Captain Simpson decided to comply with the demand and his ship was released.

The same demands were made of Captain J. Jones of the *HOSTILIUS*

---

[24] Hurd, *The Merchant Navy*, Vol. 1, p.141.

who, after conferring with his officers, refused to give the required pledge and his crew, after being told of the German demands by the *DRESDEN*'s boarding officer, stated they would stand by their captain. Much to the relief, no doubt, of the men on *HOSTILIUS*, Captain Lüdecke decided to release them and their ship. The German boarding officer, perhaps frustrated by his orders, made an entry in *HOSTILIUS*'s Log, noting her detention by *DRESDEN* and stating '*Let go because her destruction did not seem worthwhile.*'[25]

Continuing on her passage to meet the German Pacific Squadron, *DRESDEN* encountered the *HYADES* (3,352 tons) and sunk her by gunfire and explosives, transferring the crew to her tender *PRUSSIA*. Captain Morrison of *HYADES* and his crew were subsequently landed in Rio de Janeiro where he stated that in his view the gunnery of *DRESDEN* had been poor and that he and his crew had been '*well and kindly treated*' on the *PRUSSIA*. *DRESDEN* later encountered the *SIAMESE PRINCE,* which was boarded and released and the *HOLMWOOD* which was sunk, with her crew transferred to the British ship *KATHERINE PARK*, which was released probably because she was carrying an American cargo. The crew of *HOLMWOOD* was landed at Rio de Janeiro on 30 August without any loss of life.

The almost routine outcomes by then of the encounters between *DRESDEN* and British merchant ships took on a different hue in September when *DRESDEN* encountered the Pacific Steam Navigation Company's *ORTEGA*, of 8,075 tons and commanded by Captain Kinneir. Travelling along the Chilean coast from Valparaiso to Montevideo, about 50 miles off the entrance to the Straits of Magellan and with a valuable cargo and 300 French reservists on board, Captain Kinneir had no intention of surrendering his ship. He ordered all hands to the engine room to stoke up the boilers to increase speed from an otherwise maximum of about 14 knots. *DRESDEN* was capable of speeds in excess of 20 knots and soon began to overhaul the steamer to open fire. *ORTEGA* altered course to present a smaller stern-on aspect and headed for the Nelson Strait. Perhaps the poor gunnery of *DRESDEN*, as suggested earlier by Captain Morrison of *HYADES*, helped *ORTEGA*'s cause, but Captain Kinneir's decision to make for the uncharted Nelson Strait presented too great a hazard for Captain Lüdecke to follow

---

[25]   Ibid p.141

ORTEGA and risk the *DRESDEN*. The Nelson Strait was narrow and rock-strewn, reported in the Pilot Book as being '*Unsuitable for normal navigation*' and used only by sealers but, with courageous and skilful navigation, Captain Kinneir continued, using his own ship's boats to go ahead and make soundings, relying on the age-old navigation methods of 'lookout, line and log'. *ORTEGA* made it through both the Nelson Strait and Smyth's Channel, anchoring at nightfall, and into the Straits of Magellan before arriving safely at Punta Arenas.

In recognition of this feat of navigation the Admiralty received the following letter, dated 3 October 1914, from the Consulate-General in Rio de Janeiro:

Sir, – The Pacific Steam Navigation Company's steamship ORTEGA arrived at Rio de Janeiro upon 1ˢᵗ October. The Master, Douglas Reid Kinneir, in reply to my inquiry as to whether he had anything in particular to report with respect to his voyage from Valparaiso, modestly gave me the following facts:

The ORTEGA sailed from Valparaiso with some 300 French reservists on board. When she had arrived close to the western entrance of the Straits of Magellan, a German cruiser of the "'DRESDEN' class suddenly appeared and gave chase. Be it remarked that the normal speed of the ORTEGA is only some 14 knots per hour [sic], whereas the speed of the German cruiser was at least 21 knots per hour [sic].

Under these circumstances the Master of the ORTEGA took a heroic resolve. He called for volunteers to assist in stoking his vessel. That appeal met with hearty response: firemen, engineers, and volunteers, stripped to the waist and set to work with a will, and the Master assured me that they actually succeeded in whacking the old ship (she was built in 1906) up to a good 18 knots. The Master headed his ship straight for the entrance of a passage known as Nelson's Strait, where the German cruiser did not dare to follow her.

In order to realise the hardihood of this action upon the Master of the ORTEGA it must be remembered that Nelson's Strait is entirely uncharted, and that the narrow, tortuous passage in question constitutes a veritable nightmare for navigators, bristling as it does with reefs and pinnacle rocks, swept by fierce currents and tide rips, and with the cliffs on either side sheer-

to, without any anchorage. I can speak from personal experience as to the terrifying nature of the navigation of Nelson's Strait, having once passed through it many years ago in a small sailing schooner.

However, the Master of the ORTEGA managed to get his vessel safely through this dangerous passage, employing the device of sending boats ahead, to sound every yard of the passage. Eventually, by a miracle of luck and good seamanship, he worked his way into Smyth's Channel without having sustained even a scratch to his plates, and finally brought his vessel to this port.

When it is remembered that, as already stated, Nelson's Strait is absolutely uncharted, and that never before had a vessel of any size attempted that most perilous passage, it will, I think, be admitted that the captain's action in taking an 8,000 ton steamer safely through that passage constitutes a most notable feat of pluck and skilful seamanship; and it is reassuring to know that the old spirit of daring and resource is still alive in our mercantile marine.

I have no doubt that Captain Douglas Reid Kinneir's services will be fully appreciated, not only by the directors of the Pacific Steam Navigation Company for having thus saved the ORTEGA from capture by the enemy, but also by the French Government for having saved from capture the 300 French reservists who happened to be aboard his vessel.

Indeed Captain Kinneir did receive a gold plate and the thanks of the Admiralty for his remarkable feat and the admiration of all in their battle for survival. It was decided that he should be awarded a gallantry medal but, as a civilian he could not be the recipient of such so he was commissioned as an honorary lieutenant, RNR, to receive the award. This was presented to him in person by the King, becoming the first merchant ship master to receive the Distinguished Service Cross. (It may be noted that the rank of lieutenant is a very junior one in the Royal Navy and is usually held by officers in their early twenties. The pay scale for a lieutenant RNR at that time was about £16 per month, equating to a typical salary of a second mate of a cargo liner. Captain Kinneir, born in 1858, was 56 years old, in command of a large passenger ship belonging to a prestigious shipping company and with many years of professional experience to equip him with the skill and confidence to conduct that amazing feat of navigation.) He did not survive the war, dying on Christmas Eve 1916, following complications after surgery to repair an ulcer, leaving his wife and five children.

DRESDEN, having been thwarted by ORTEGA, continued on her mission, encountering the NORTH WALES (3,661 tons) under the command of Captain Griffith Owen on 16 November. After transferring the crew of NORTH WALES with their belongings to the German vessel RHAKOTIS, the vessel was sunk and the crew landed at Callao. Captain Owen and his crew had signed a formal declaration to take no further part in the war, which Captain Owen took seriously to the point of refusing to discuss the matter with the British Consul when he was landed, other than to state that he and his crew had been well treated by the Germans. On 17 February 1915 the final victim claimed by DRESDEN was the CONWAY CASTLE, of 1,694 tons, under the command of Captain J. Williams. His ship was stripped of her stores and provisions and sunk after her crew was transferred to a Peruvian barque and landed later at Valparaiso.

Despite stopping and searching 10 British merchant ships and in some cases sinking them, no seafarers had been killed or injured. Captain Lüdecke had scrupulously followed the spirit of the Hague Convention and the general directions given to German warships in ensuring that all his victims had been removed to a place of safety and treated with courtesy and respect in the interests of humanity. On 14 March 1915, DRESDEN encountered HMS GLASGOW and after a short exchange of fire DRESDEN surrendered but succeeded in scuttling herself. Some of her survivors, including the wounded who were landed at Juan Fernandez by the British transport ORAMA, thanked the British for the care shown to them. DRESDEN's crew were interned in Chile for the rest of the war.

The scene had been set as regards the expected outcome of conflicts between British and Allied merchant ships and the treatment to be accorded to the merchant seafarers by their German tormentors.

★ ★ ★

Captain Owen of the NORTH WALES returned to Britain, where he was given command of another steamer, coincidentally also named the NORTH WALES, by the same owners, Hugh Roberts & Son of Newcastle. On 20 October 1916 his new NORTH WALES was sunk without trace and with the loss of all hands off the Scilly Isles by U-69 (in turn lost with all hands on 11 July 1917). Three months later, his son, Robert Owen, a cadet on the *ARTIST*, survived a torpedo attack on 27 January 1917 by U-55, when 35 were killed and, with just a few other survivors, managed to exist for several days in an open lifeboat in the North Atlantic before being rescued. Robert had to spend several months recovering from hypothermia and exposure but survived the war, eventually becoming a leading consultant at Cardiff Royal Infirmary.

CHAPTER 4

THE EARLY DAYS

The sister ship to *DRESDEN*, SMS *EMDEN* had left her home port of Tsingtao with the German Imperial Asiatic Squadron under the command of Admiral von Spee before the Japanese might try to blockade the port (Japan had declared war on Germany on 23 August.) and was heading towards the German areas of influence in the South Pacific. Captain von Muller suggested to the German admiral that as *EMDEN* had been built for the specific purposes of raiding merchant shipping, he should separate from the German Squadron and seek victims in the Indian Ocean. Von Spee agreed but in doing so was aware, as von Muller was aware, that by entering the Indian Ocean which they regarded as '*an English sea*', it was unlikely that *EMDEN* would survive for long without friendly ports and available supplies, quite apart from the threat from enemy warships.

The reference to '*an English sea*' was hardly an exaggeration, with the Indian Ocean surrounded by the colonies and protectorates of the British Empire, with few ports to provide shelter for the *EMDEN*. The German cruiser would have to rely for survival on her support ship, the collier *MARKOMMANIA*, and the stores and coal from any ships she could capture.

Captain Karl von Muller was, by all accounts, typical of a small band of German naval officers with origins in the Prussian officer class, where chivalry and courage were claimed to have equal value. Well connected and regarded in naval circles, he had been an aide to Grand Admiral Prince Heinrich and was by no means anti-British. His second in command, von Müecke, was a very formal and disciplined officer who had a deep dislike of the English and the British Empire. The gunnery officer was another Prussian, Ernst Gaede, and the torpedo officer was Prince Franz Joseph von Hohenzollern.

EMDEN's entrance to the British trade routes from the Pacific to the

Indian Ocean could only be accessed by passage through the many islands of the Dutch East Indies (now Indonesia). Holland was a neutral nation but international maritime law permitted a neutral state to provide temporary shelter for 24 hours to a ship of a belligerent state, but would not permit the neutral state to pass such information on. *EMDEN* had sought secrecy and anonymity by anchoring in a deserted bay while she took on as much coal and supplies as she could from her supply ship in preparation for her task. At the suggestion of von Muller's first lieutenant, von Müecke, a dummy fourth funnel was built and colours altered so that she would resemble a British cruiser should she be spotted. *EMDEN* entered the Indian Ocean, prepared and disguised – a disguise which proved to be very effective. She had been built in 1909, of 4,268 tons, of 387 feet (118 m) in length and capable of 24.5 knots. Armed with 2 x 18 inch torpedo tubes and 10 x 4.1 inch rapid fire guns, any contest with an unarmed merchant ship could only have one outcome. Nevertheless Captain von Muller had warned his crew: '*Our one reason for existence is to harass and destroy enemy shipping – and we must do so until our means for waging sea warfare is exhausted, until we ourselves are destroyed*'. This was a dramatic, but realistic assessment as *EMDEN* would of course be hunted down once she started her raids on British merchant shipping.

On 7 September 1914, the first steamship built for the Nourse Line and chartered to the India Office, the *INDUS*, left Calcutta bound for Bombay and Liverpool. Of 3,393 tons she was commanded by Captain H.S. Smaridge, with Mr Harry Griffiths as chief officer and Mr George Read as second officer. *INDUS* was to become the first of 22 British merchant ship victims of SMS *EMDEN*.

On 10 September, while in the Bay of Bengal, *INDUS* was approached by a warship resembling the British cruiser HMS *YARMOUTH*. To the surprise of *INDUS*'s crew, the cruiser raised the German battle ensign, fired a round across *INDUS*'s bow, identified herself as the light cruiser SMS *EMDEN* and ordered *INDUS* to stop. *INDUS* was in no position to resist and a German boarding party took command, transferring all officers and crew to *EMDEN*'s supporting collier *MARKOMMANIA* and taking what supplies and stores they felt would be of use to them, making particular note of their delight at finding large quantities of soap on board. *INDUS* was then sunk by scuttling and gunfire from *EMDEN* the same day, watched by her own crew from the decks of the *MARKOMMANIA*.[26]

Sailing under false colours was a common ruse, both for predator and prey. The convention was that a vessel must hoist her true colours before firing the first shot. It was also a convention that a seized ship could be released to ferry home prisoners, if the seized ship offered no value to its captors, and that all prisoners should be treated with courtesy and civility – all of which would have been known by the commander of *EMDEN*.

The sight of what had initially appeared to be a British warship would no doubt have engendered a feeling of relief on board *INDUS*, providing some sense of security and expectation of intelligence on enemy movements. At that time, *INDUS* had been advised in Calcutta that no German warships were in the Indian Ocean. Against that background, as well as initially believing *EMDEN* to be a British warship, it is not surprising that Captain Smaridge submitted so readily to *EMDEN*'s commands. Further, British naval intelligence had announced that *EMDEN* had been sunk in the Pacific some two weeks previously, so the unfortunate Captain Smaridge could have had no inkling of the true identity of the approaching ship.

The account given below of the capture and sinking of *INDUS* is that given by Helmuth von Müecke, first lieutenant and second-in-command of the *EMDEN*:

The EMDEN proceeded cautiously through the openings in the mine field … and very early in the morning of September 11, … with the rising of the sun, a large steamer appeared dead ahead who, thinking we were an English man-of-war, was so overjoyed at our presence that she hoisted a huge British flag while still at a great distance. I do not know what kind of expression came over her captain's face when we hoisted our flag and invited him most graciously to tarry with us awhile. The steamer had left Calcutta and, having been detailed for transport duty between Colombo and France, was fitted out in fine style. Especially were we touched by the fact that she did not disown the English desire for cleanliness and therefore had taken such a big cargo of soap that our small crew, itself in the greatest need of this most necessary assistant to Kultur [culture, civilisation], would have enough to last a whole year. We also found a beautiful racehorse aboard. A bullet

---

[26]   Hoyt, *The Last Cruise of the Emden*, p.88.

behind the ear saved the animal the agonies of a death by drowning. We had less compassion for the numerous built-in, beautifully numbered, horse stalls and gun mounts aboard the ship. A half hour later the sharks could, at closer quarters, occupy their attention with these.

A seaman always has a peculiar feeling when he sees a ship sinking. Even we, accustomed to helping vessels in distress, were affected not a little by the sight of sinking vessels, even those that we had to destroy. The destruction was usually done in the following way: We went into the engine-room and removed the bonnet of a main overboard discharge valve. The water immediately came into the engine room in a stream twice a man's height and more than a man's thickness. The watertight doors to the adjoining fire-room were opened and secured against closing, so that at least two large compartments of the ship would certainly fill up with water. In addition, two smaller compartments were also filled, either by exploding bombs – this at night or by firing shells into them ... Then the Emden would go ahead to meet the next oncoming mast head ...

The *EMDEN*'s torpedo officer, Prince Franz Joseph von Hohenzollern, in his account of the ship's exploits described the capture of *INDUS* with some degree of satisfaction, reporting on the discovery of the British ship: '*As the EMDEN came nearer we could make out a large steamship with a very unusual superstructure. It was an Englishman with the blue ensign waving proudly at her stern. The question was whether she had been chartered by the Admiralty or was being run by the British Government.*'[27]

The boarding party from *EMDEN* soon established *INDUS*'s credentials, advising Captain von Muller that she had been en route from Calcutta to Bombay for the Indian government, equipped to carry troops and horses for the European theatre of war. As von Hohenzollern remarked; '*Not bad! The EMDEN had just caught the fellow in time, before bringing Indian troops to fight against Germany. It was a pity that the soldiers were not already in her as then she would have been more welcome.*' He continued his narrative, describing how the *INDUS*'s provisions and stores were ransacked, '*Our upper deck looked*

---

27 Von Hohenzollern, *Emden. The Story of the Famous German Raider.*

like a colossal warehouse. There were stocks, or at least samples of everything. There were towels, soap, linen, tinned foods, fresh meat, live hens and ducks, drinks, nautical instruments, charts, pencils and some very welcome oilskins with which we could re-equip the cutters' crews and the watches against bad weather.' The description of the sinking of *INDUS* suggests, as perhaps was the case with von Müecke, that this was his first experience of such an event:

> *... too much ammunition could not be wasted, and the ship was bound to sink after the seacocks had been opened. It was an hour, however, before she began to sink, and then slowly, though surely. She slanted to one side, and shipped a good deal of water. Then the bows sank, and all at once she sank gurgling into the depth – an uncanny spectacle. The escaping air made a loud report and scattered a mass of things in the air, the masts sprang several yards out of the water and fell back on to the flat surface with loud reports.*

Von Hohenzollern added that *EMDEN* would stay on the *'fruitful steamship routes ... to capture other ships until the disappearance of the ships that had been announced aroused the enemy and lead to a search for the cause. According to our instructions we meant to use every opportunity to damage the enemy. War is war'*. Documents brought over from the *INDUS* by the boarding party included newspapers, which the German crew

> *... thoroughly laughed over, being full of stories which a baby would scarcely have taken for good coin ... and we were astonished by the lies which the English papers dished out to the Indians. It was of course understandable from the English point of view, for the Indian natives, who had not too much enthusiasm for the British oppressor, had to be won over or at least hindered from rioting.*

The date of *INDUS*'s capture as reported by von Müecke is given as 11 September, conflicting with British sources which record the date of loss as 10 September, as did von Hohenzollern. It is nevertheless of interest to consider the context of the capture of *INDUS* so early in the war, in terms of the tactics of *EMDEN*, the knowledge available at that time to *INDUS* and the behaviour of her master.

EMDEN proceeded with her 'harvesting' of British merchant ships on the well known trade routes without any threat from British warships, while the merchant ships were still being advised that the area was clear of German raiders. It was not until after the *LOVAT, KILLIN, KABINGA, DIPLOMAT* and *TRABBOCH* had been captured that *EMDEN* encountered the Italian liner *LOREDANO* on 14 September, under the command of Captain Giacopolo, and asked the *LOREDANO* to take *EMDEN's* prisoners off to land in a neutral port. Captain Giacopolo refused on the grounds that he had no space on board for numerous passengers and thus, as a neutral, the Italian ship was allowed to continue with her voyage. Captain Giacopolo nevertheless alerted the Indian port authorities of the situation; the first notification received by British authorities of the exploits of the *EMDEN*.

EMDEN had positioned herself off the southwest tip of Ceylon (now Sri Lanka) ready to raid the well established trade routes in the Bay of Bengal, but why was she so successful in capturing 22 British merchant ships in such a short period of time? Certainly von Muller was resourceful and courageous in being able to capture shipping which could provide him with the coal and supplies so necessary to maintain his mission without access to friendly ports. A major contributory factor however must be the inaction of the British Admiralty and the Board of Trade.

While British intelligence was for some while unaware of the presence of *EMDEN* in the Indian Ocean, once they did become aware it took some time for that information to become widely available to the Consulates in the various ports and to the ships. The information that was available could be very misleading and several British ships were wrongly advised regarding their likelihood of encountering *EMDEN*. The loss of so many ships had led many to believe there might be several German warships operating in the area, rather than just one raider. A view in the Board of Trade, for a short while, was that as Britain was so dominant in merchant shipping, the loss of a few ships would make no significant difference to continuing trade.

The Admiralty eventually advised masters not to take the normal routes across the Indian Ocean but to steam, say, 50 miles off the norm and not to leave ports in darkness. Of interest also is the case that the British and Allied warships were searching for *EMDEN* away from the shipping routes when it was abundantly clear that she must be sitting along the routes waiting for the merchant ships to find her. *EMDEN* continued her 'harvest' unmolested until such time as she had to withdraw from the shipping routes for maintenance and reprovisioning, whereupon von Muller transferred all the crews to the captured *KABINGA* and *GRYFEVALE*, (captured on 26 September) and released them to make their own way to Calcutta.

On the arrival in Calcutta of the British crews released by von Muller, it was learned that six German vessels, the Hansa Line steamers *FREIENFELS*, *TROSTBURG, ROTENFELS, FRANKENFELS, PAGENTURM* and the Hamburg-Amerika liner *KURMARK* had been detained by the British authorities in Calcutta at the outbreak of war, as had the Hansa Liner *LINDENFELS* in Aden, all of which were given to the control of the India Office and placed under the command of British officers. Harry Griffiths, the chief officer of the *INDUS*, was despatched to Aden to take command of the captured Hansa liner *LINDENFELS*, which later had a name change to *KINGSMERE*.

Crews and passengers of the captured ships repeatedly spoke of the kindness and courtesy afforded by von Muller and his crew. Generally, crews and passengers were permitted to gather their belongings and personal effects before being made to abandon their ships. Indeed the exploits of *EMDEN* were recorded in the British press at the time almost with some affection and with but a mild rebuke to the Admiralty for its inaction. *The Times* of London, in an editorial of 22 October 1914 under the heading '*The Emden Reappears*' wrote:

The daring little German cruiser Emden has reappeared, this time in the Arabian Sea. While HMS Yarmouth was sinking the Emden's supply ship Markomannia, somewhere off the coast of Sumatra, the Emden was making for the west coast of India. She has had a fine haul, which exceeds in tonnage and value her last series of exploits in the Bay of Bengal. She has sunk five vessels, including a brand-new British India boat, a fine Holt liner crammed with rubber and tin, a Clan boat and an expensive dredger built for the River Tamar in Tasmania, She has also seized Exford, a steamer laden with coal, to replace her lost collier.

Until now the British public has been inclined to regard the cruise of the Emden with amused tolerance, largely because her officers have repeatedly shown themselves to be good sportsmen. The accounts given by the crews of the destroyed steamers invariably bear testimony to the considerate restraint with which the Emden does her deadly work. The time has come, however, to inquire when the Admiralty propose to terminate her audacious career. Her raid at the mouth of the Hoogly and down the Coromandel coast left the province of Burma isolated for a fortnight, paralysed the trade of Calcutta, and must have cost the country over a million pounds. Her reappearance means a loss of at least another million, so that in a few weeks she has wasted for us very nearly the price of a Dreadnought. She is solely responsible for the present high rate of insurance on the Eastern routes, and she may interrupt the Indian mail service. Now that she is back in her old haunts we suppose there will be a further stoppage of Indian trade.

We have no wish to join in the present tendency to disparage sailors in high places, but we are bound to record the growing popular dissatisfaction with the measures taken to deal with this and other and other commerce destroyers. There is a general feeling, which may be right or wrong, that the Admiralty is not devoting sufficient attention to its responsibilities upon the high seas. Amphibious warfare may be attractive, but we prefer to see the Royal Navy preoccupied with blue water.

Certainly the merchant seafaring community would not have regarded the exploits of *EMDEN* with 'amused tolerance' or regarded the sinking of their ships, with the immediate consequence of the loss of most of their belongings, as well as cessation of their wages, as an activity to be described as that of 'sport'. These consequences are completely ignored in the editorial.

When *EMDEN* was eventually discovered after her uninterrupted activities against British merchant ships, she was miles away from the established shipping routes in order to reprovision from her supply ships before returning to the fray. *EMDEN* had sent a landing party ashore at the Cocos Islands, under the command of von Müecke, to silence a radio station that could alert Allied warships to her presence. However, the Australian light cruiser HMAS *SYDNEY*, while trying to link up with British warships, had been alerted by signals from the Cocos radio station and engaged *EMDEN* on 9 November 1914. *EMDEN* was forced to abandon the landing party in order to defend herself, but proved no match for the Australian cruiser and was destroyed with a high loss of life. The extraordinary exploits of von Müecke, who had been stranded on the Cocos Islands with the landing party and who had then escaped by sea and land to return to Germany are separate and remarkable stories of initiative, survival and courage.

On receiving news of the destruction of *EMDEN*, Churchill decreed that von Muller and his surviving officers should be treated with honour and not be forced to give up their swords on their surrender – a rare recognition of their humane actions in a time of war.[28]

Prior to *EMDEN's* early raids on British ships in the Indian Ocean, the Union Castle liner *GALICIAN*, of 6,757 tons and under the command of Captain Day, had left Cape Town for Tenerife, but notification of the outbreak of hostilities had not reached the ship until 8 August. While those on board were discussing the possible ramifications of hostilities as they may affect them, a large four-funnelled passenger liner came into view. This turned out to be the SMS *KAISER WILLIEM DER GROSSE*, built for the North German Lloyd shipping company on the trans-Atlantic run. This ship, at 14,349 tons and one of the largest ships afloat, had held the prestigious Blue Riband for the fastest Atlantic crossing and had been converted into an armed raider. *GALICIAN* received the message to stop and dismantle her wireless under threat of being sunk, to which Captain Day complied. The German ship sent over a boarding party to remove the ship's papers and ensure the dismantling of the wireless, and removed two military passengers in an otherwise cordial exchange. Captain Day reported that members of the German boarding party had been trying to buy cigarettes from the crew of *GALICIAN*, which he forbade, but personally provided some cigarettes and cigars to the boarding officer, who expressed his thanks for the act of courtesy. Several passengers reported that members of the boarding party had offered the opinion that they did not wish to fight and that they had no grudge against English ships. The instruction then given to Captain Day was to prepare the boats for evacuation and proceed as directed with the German raider as escort. However, after further consideration the raider sent the following signal: '*To Captain Day, s.s. Galician. We will not destroy your vessel on account of the women and children on board – you are dismissed. Good-bye. Captain*', to which Captain Day responded '*To German Captain. Most grateful*

---

[28] After the war, von Muller was somewhat at a loss with no navy to employ him. He was elected to the German *Diet*, but never reached high rank. He married and had two daughters, dying of pneumonia and pleurisy on 11 March 1923, aged 50.

thanks from passengers and crew. Good-bye.' In his report to the Union Castle line, Captain Day stated that *'the German officers were most courteous throughout'*.

The encounter of the *ELSINORE*, under the command of Captain J. Roberts, with the German light cruiser SMS *LEIPZIG* on 11 September 1914 was to be somewhat more prolonged and less satisfactory than that experienced by *GALICIAN*. The *LEIPZIG*, stationed off the west coast of Mexico at the outbreak of war, had joined Admiral von Spee's East Asiatic Cruiser Squadron. While on passage in the Pacific Ocean between Corinto and San Luis Obispo, California, the 6,542 ton *ELSINORE* was stopped by the *LEIPZIG* and Captain Roberts taken on board the German ship. There he was instructed to follow *LEIPZIG*'s orders to rendezvous with the German vessel *MARIE*, to which *ELSINORE*'s stores, lifeboats and any other items of interest were transferred, as well as her crew, who were then instructed to transfer coal from the *MARIE* to the *LEIPZIG*. They were paid for this task by the Germans with instructions from the German commander to treat the *ELSINORE*'s crew well. *ELSINORE* was then sunk.

In his later report on the incident, Captain Roberts stated that when first taken prisoner the German commander had promised to set Roberts and his crew off at Cape Corrientes, but later stated he was no longer able to fulfil that promise. He had instead made arrangements for *ELSINORE*'s crew to be landed at the Ecuadorian Chatham Island, as a temporary measure before being shipped to Callao some two weeks later. However, having been landed at Chatham Island and seeing that it provided very little in the way of accommodation or food, Captain Roberts, with his chief officer Mr R. Putt, his signaller and the chief engineer, rode on horseback to find the governor of Chatham Island to ask for a passage to Ecuador to report the loss of the ship. This was arranged, with half of *ELSINORE*'s crew being taken to Guayaquil in a small sloop, accompanied by the governor, Mr Araz, This was despite the protests of a resident German officer, who of course wished the *LEIPZIG* to have as long a time as possible without her whereabouts or actions being known to the Allies. Captain Roberts described his journey on the sloop as *'one of the most monotonous and hardest five days at sea I have ever experienced. The accommodation for the crew was in the hold, where they slept on the hides and dried fish, and the smell at times was somewhat terrible'.*[29] Captain

---

[29]   Hurd, *The Merchant Navy*, Vol. 1, p.184.

Roberts, with half his crew, arrived at Guayaquil on 1 October, with grateful thanks to the governor for all his help and arranged for the remainder of his crew left behind, under the charge of Mr Putt, to be picked up.

In his account of the incident given to the *Weekly Shipping Gazette* of 18 December, Mr Putt stated:

We were landed at Chatham Island, and were told that the Leipzig would not provide us with any stores for living. We therefore had to look around for ourselves. On informing the owner of a sugar plantation of our plight, he very kindly offered to provide for us. The officers, with the exception of two, were supplied with horses and invited to his private residence, where we received the best of attention and treatment, until our departure on Oct. 13th.

On that date we departed in a small smack of 20 tons, having on board 240 bags of sugar. We officers slept in what the captain of the smack termed 'the cabin.' This apartment consisted of two shelves 8 ft. long by 2½ ft. broad. These were the berths, and on each of these two persons had to try and sleep in peace. The remaining crew berthed themselves in the hold upon the cargo of sugar, where they had to make the best of an awkward predicament. We had rather a long passage, packed similar to sardines, for 13 days, and arrived at Guayaquil, Ecuador, on Oct. 25th.

Our first thought was to have a good splash in fresh water. Moreover, we were all looking forward to a change of diet, as we had been feeding on rice and beans, with a little water to digest same. On arriving at Guayaquil we were almost immediately transferred to the Pacific Steam Navigation Company's steamship Ecuador, in which we sailed to Panama.

Whilst no loss of life had been incurred during the adventures of *ELSINORE*'s crew, certainly there had been hardship, which could be contrasted with the treatment given to captives of the one-time trans-Atlantic German Blue Riband holder, *KRONPRINZ WILHELM*. The German liner had left New York on the eve of the outbreak of war, but with no intention of seeking shelter in a neutral port. A large passenger liner of 23,500 tons, with a speed of 23 knots and under the command of Captain Grahn, her purpose was to rendezvous at sea with the cruiser SMS *KARLESRUHE* when, following a transfer of crew and munitions, she became an auxiliary cruiser and commissioned into the Imperial German Navy. (Her serving navigation officer, Paul Thierfelder, who was widely recognised as a humane 'old school' officer and gentleman, was appointed her commander and Captain Grahn had to accept his demotion to chief officer.) After a period of rehearsing gunnery, stop-and-search and boarding party procedures appropriate to her new role as a commerce raider in the South Atlantic, the SMS *KRONPRINZ WILHELM* was ready by 3 September 1914.

Her first victim was the British steamer *INDIAN PRINCE* the very next day, whose crew and passengers, with their belongings, were transferred to the German cruiser. The second victim of her attentions was the *LA CORRENTINA*, of 8,529 tons and owned by the British and Argentine Steam Navigation Company of London. While on route from the River Plate to Liverpool on 7 October 1914 she was captured by *KRONPRINZ WILHELM* and relieved of her coal and cargo of frozen meat. Although fitted with two 4.7 inch guns under the Admiralty scheme of arming selected merchant ships, no ammunition had been provided and thus *LA CORRENTINA* could offer no resistance. An account of her capture and treatment of her crew was given by her third officer Mr C.M. Robertson to the Imperial Merchant Service Guild at Liverpool, as recorded in the *Shipping Gazette*:

> *The Imperial Merchant Service Guild has received a graphic story from Mr C.M. Robertson, late third officer of the meat steamer La Correntina, of the way in which that vessel was captured and sunk at sea by the German commerce destroyer Kronprinz Wilhelm. The cruiser was sighted on Oct 7, at 8 a.m., and Mr Robertson states that some time before her identity was known it was noted as a somewhat remarkable fact that she kept end on to La Correntina in such a way as her four funnels could not be distinguished. Indeed, it was very difficult to tell that she was an armed ship of any kind. Eventually the Kronprinz Wilhelm disclosed her identity, and hoisted signals to La Correntina to stop immediately.*
>
> *Presumably in order to save time, the Kronprinz Wilhelm decided on a most unusual course. Instead of using the boats to transport the passengers she came alongside La Correntina. Strange to relate, little or no damage was done except that part of the upper bridge was carried away when the German cruiser ranged up alongside her. Eventually the passengers and crew were transferred without accident.*

> *Mr Robertson speaks in the highest terms of the general good treatment which was meted out to them while on board the German ship. They were given second class accommodation, the food was good, and there was no shortage of linen, bedding, etc. Altogether 15 days were spent on board the cruiser, when they were transferred to the Sierra Cordoba, acting as a tender to the larger ship. A month was spent on board the Sierra Cordoba, and much to their relief the crew were finally landed at Montevideo, and recently reached home in the Sutherland Grange.*

On 14 January 1915, the Nelson Liner *HIGHLAND BRAE* was off the coast of South America, on the London to Buenos Aires route, with 50 passengers and a ship's complement of 91, carrying a cargo of meat and clothing. Built in 1910 and of 7,634 tons with a speed of 13 knots, she was under the command of Captain R.R. Pond. The chief officer was Mr Samuel R. Hitchin, who maintained a detailed diary of the encounter with the *KRONPRINZ WILHELM*. The large German auxiliary cruiser overhauled *HIGHLAND BRAE* at high speed, firing a shot over the British ship's bow, forcing her to stop and become the fourth victim. The German ship sent over a boarding party and took command, ordering *HIGHLAND BRAE* to follow her German captor. Two days later *HIGHLAND BRAE* was met by the German support ship *HOLGER*, which came alongside and began the transfer of cargo, stores and lifeboats from the British ship which took place intermittently over a period of four weeks. The transfer also included some of the fittings from *HIGHLAND BRAE* to the *HOLGER* to provide more comfortable accommodation for the British prisoners, who were transferred to *HOLGER* on 12 February along with the crews of other victims of *KRONPRINZ WILHELM's* attentions. *HIGHLAND BRAE* was then scuttled.

Samuel Hitchin's diary recorded the event as,

> *Transferred to Holger … first gangway smashed as soon as put out, used Holger's accommodation ladder turned upside down. Commander [of HOLGER] addressed passengers, apologising for inferior accommodation on Holger but begged their pardon and hoped they would get safe on shore, found that much pains had been taken for our comfort. Poop fitted out one compartment for married people and ladies, one for Captains and one for*

officers and Gentleman passengers. Crew berthed in No. 4 Tween Deck. Brae's fittings used, Captain introduced to Captain of Holger who apologised for lack of accommodation. Rather theatrical farewell to Cruiser – flags hoisted and band played Der Wacht am Rhelm and Deutshland Uber Alle – might have spared us that. Speech by Commander through megaphone, some one called for three cheers for Kronprinz Commander and crew which might have been left out and was not universally responded to. Proceeding WNW. Kronprinz following in distance; tea al fresco ascramble.[30]

The final entry in this remarkable diary, made available by Samuel Hitchin's great grandson, Mark Hitchin, referred to the *HOLGER*'s arrival at North Darsena on Wednesday 17 February: '7 a.m. ... *proceeded to No. 4 Dock moored stern on ... 8 p.m. landed no baggage and taken good care of by Company's people, instructed to land baggage at 8 a.m. tomorrow, a nice meal and good bed.'*

While Samuel Hitchin clearly recognised the care that had been taken by his German captors for the safety and comfort of the captives, he was equally clearly less than impressed by the attempts by his captors to require a warm tribute from the captured crews as a farewell to the *KRONPRINZ WILHELM*. *Kapitänleutnant* Paul Thierfelder could nevertheless be satisfied that he had acted in a manner well beyond the Prize Code requirements for the safety of his victims and their 'place of safety'.

The dependence of the converted passenger liners on supporting supply ships was however demonstrated by the fate of *KRONPRINZ WILHELM*. Although undetected by British warships during the raids on commercial ships, she lost her supply ship, *MACEDONIA*, to British warships towards the end of March 1915 and, low on fuel and with the deterioration of the health of the crew from malnutrition, her commander decided to seek the refuge of a neutral port. On 11 April 1915, *KRONPRINZ WILHELM* anchored off Newport News where she was interned by the United States government, with the crew living out the rest of the war in a nearby camp. When the United States eventually declared war on the German Empire, on 6 April 1917, the ship was taken over by the US Navy to be re-named USS *VON STEUBEN* and converted into a troop carrier transporting US forces and equipment to Europe.

---

[30]   Edwards, *War Under the Red Ensign 1914–1918*, pp.38–39.

Although *KRONPRINZ WILHELM*'s career lasted only a few months, during that short period she captured some 15 merchant ships of which 10 were British. Her routine was much the same – stopping and searching with a boarding party, embarking her victims' crews and passengers and taking what stores and coal she could. The German's victims were then usually scuttled by opening sea cocks.

Throughout all the encounters between the German warships and British merchant ships there had been no loss of life and the German commanders and their crews had generally shown a high standard of consideration for the plight of their victims and the recognition of the traditional bonds between mariners. The courtesy and consideration for the safety of the merchant ship crews shown by the German cruisers was widely recognised by the use of the term 'Cruiser Rules' in recognition of their observance of the Prize Code.

CHAPTER 5

THE SUBMARINE MENACE

In the foreword to Hurd's *History of the Great War, The Merchant Navy*, Volume 3, HRH the Prince of Wales wrote:

> *There was nothing surprising or unprecedented in the destruction achieved by the Emden and other German cruisers and armed merchantmen in Eastern waters and elsewhere. Hostilities were conducted in harmony with principles laid down by international law, and, though many valuable ships were sunk, the toll was no greater than might have been expected, and not a single life of the captured crews was sacrificed.*

Indeed that had been the case in the early days of the war, but the merchant ships were also to face attacks by bombs, by mines and by U-boats, which were soon to become the main cause of destruction of British and Allied merchant ships, their passengers and crews.

As the *CITY OF WINCHESTER* had the dubious distinction of being the first British merchant ship to be captured and sunk in World War I, so the *GLITRA* had the distinction of being the first British merchant ship to be captured and sunk by a U-boat – U-17. At around noon on 21 October 1914, *GLITRA*, of 866 tons under the command of Captain L.A. Johnston, was on passage from Grangemouth to Stavanger and approaching the Stavanger pilot station. The pilot cutter initially approached the *GLITRA*, but abruptly turned around and headed back to the port as Captain Johnston became aware, while stopping his ship to embark the pilot, of a U-boat approaching rapidly from astern. Having slowed his ship for the pilot embarkation, Captain Johnston was in a very vulnerable situation as far as running from the U-boat was concerned.

The commander of the U-17, *Oberleutnant zur See* Feldkirchner, had been returning to Kiel after a fruitless wait off the Orkneys for a suitable target, but was unsure of the procedure to adopt. He was aware that two Norwegian patrol craft were in view and did not wish to enter Norway's territorial waters. After circling GLITRA, Feldkirchner fired a warning shot and instructed Captain Johnston to stop. With the U-boats guns trained on GLITRA, a boarding party was sent over and, with one of the boarding party holding a gun to Johnston's head, told him he only had a few minutes to get his crew off his ship into the lifeboats and that no time could be allowed for the collection of any personal possessions. The red ensign was then stripped from GLITRA and destroyed in an act of vandalism by the very aggressive boarding party, with charts, sextants and any other items of interest to the boarding party transferred to the submarine. Unfortunately, these also showed recommended British Admiralty routes, the latest buoyage and locations of minefields which obviously were of considerable interest to the Germans. This treatment of Captain Johnston and his crew was in marked contrast to the courtesies and consideration shown to other British ships by the surface ships of the German Navy and short of the Prize Code that allowed time for the crews of captured ships to collect their belongings.

With the submarine's guns still trained on the GLITRA's crew in their lifeboats, Feldkirchner sent a party over to GLITRA to open the sea valves and scuttle the defenceless and doomed ship in front of her crew. Feldkirchner was uncertain whether leaving the GLITRA's crew in their boats constituted a 'place of safety' according to the Prize Code, so he towed the lifeboats closer to the coastline before casting them off. The pilot boat shortly came to the rescue, towing the lifeboats until the Norwegian patrol boats picked the survivors up and took them to Stavanger.

Feldkirchner was no doubt aware that he had opened a new chapter in the history of war at sea by being responsible for the first capture and sinking of a British merchant ship by a U-boat and was unsure of the reception that might await him on his return to his home port. Subsequent events suggested that the German High Command had been considering a trial sinking to ascertain the ease of accomplishing such action and the response of opinion to that action. The German Commander-in-Chief of the High Seas Fleet, von Ingenohl, thought the action 'uncivilised'[31] and the Chief of the Naval Staff, Admiral von Pohl, considered the action to be unjustified. In the event Feldkirchner was feted on his return as the German High Command realised they had unleashed a highly significant means of imposing German influence on the high seas and were prepared to instruct all U-boats to attack and sink all Allied shipping. This however was subject to the proviso that the Prize Code was followed; in particular the requirement for the crews of captured ships to be taken to a place of safety.

While there had been no pre-war plan for U-boat attacks on merchant ships, it was soon realised that the raiding of commercial ships could endanger the lifeline of supplies to the island nation of Britain. A memorandum of November 1914 from the leaders of the German High Seas Fleet addressed to Admiral von Pohl stated,

> ... there is not the least reason why we should exercise any restraint in our conduct of the war ... We must make use of this weapon and do so in a way most suitable to its peculiarities. Consequently, a U-boat cannot spare the crews of steamers, but must send them to the bottom with their ships. The shipping world can be warned ... and all shipping trade with England should cease within a short time.[32]

The action of U-17 marked a significant and inevitable step change in the conduct of the war against Allied merchant ships.

Prior to and at the outbreak of war, neither the German nor British naval authorities had much regard for the value of U-boats and, although some consideration was given to the potential for U-boats to attack merchant shipping, the concept had been initially disregarded. At the outbreak of war Germany had only 39 boats, compared to 98 in the Royal Navy.[33] The case of the unfortunate *GLITRA* however proved a turning point in the opinions of the German naval authorities who began to swing towards acceptance and promotion of attacking without warning, or unrestricted warfare, without consideration of victims being taken to, or secured in, a 'place of safety'.

---

[31] Gray, *The U-Boat War, 1914–1918*, p.65.

[32] Gibson and Prendergast, *The German Submarine War 1914–1918*, p.26.

[33] Gray, *The U-Boat War, 1914–1918*, p.35.

This swing of opinion gave rise to considerable debate within the German High Command but was blocked by the Kaiser for fear of offending neutral opinion, particularly that of the USA. He was however well aware that many nations were increasingly irritated by Britain's 'board and search' policy, execution of which could involve the ship being escorted to a nearby British port for inspection and the consequent delays. This board and search policy, it was argued, contravened the London Declaration, which Britain had not signed and was thus accused by Germany of making up her own rules. [34] This aspect was much exploited by Germany and later used as justification for U-boat attacks on merchant shipping.

Admiral Reinhard Scheer, who later assumed command of the German High Seas Fleet in 1916 and was to lead the German fleet at the Battle of Jutland, had posed the question regarding U-boats while considering the dictates of humanity in warfare. In his memoirs entitled *Germany's High Fleet in the World War*, he wrote:

> *No State ... thought it against the dictates of humanity to build submarines for war purposes, whose task it should be unexpectedly to attack warships and sink them with all on board. Does it really make any difference, purely from the humane point of view, whether those thousands of men who drown wear naval uniforms or belong to a merchant ship bringing food and munitions to the enemy, thus prolonging the war and augmenting the number of women and children who suffer during the war?*

These sentiments were not initially shared by the German authorities and were in conflict with the earlier declarations by Admiral Tirpitz who considered submarines to be '... *of doubtful utility*' and by von Bieberstein's declaration that Germany would carry the banner for the highest '*sentiments of humanity and civilisation*'.

Nevertheless, the next step change in the escalation of action against merchant shipping came with the audacious attacks by *Kapitanleutnant* Alfred Stoß in command of U-8 on 23 February 1915, when he embarked on a spree in the English Channel by torpedoing, without any warning, the British steamers *OAKBY* and the *BRANKSOME CHINE*, although

---

[34] Ibid., p.59.

fortunately without any loss of life. The following day, 24 February, U-8 claimed the Harrison steamer *HARPALION* under the command of Captain A. Widdes, again without warning and this time with the loss of three lives. Later that day, still in the same vicinity Stoß sank the British steamers *RIO PARANA* and the *WESTERN COAST*, although without any further loss of life. The commander of the *RIO PARANA*, Captain Williams, who hailed from Swansea, initially thought he had struck a mine as he had not been advised of a submarine presence in his vicinity, despite the very recent attacks in that area. He had previously been in command of the *HURSTDALE* when he was captured by the German light cruiser SMS *KARSLRUHE* and transferred to another of the cruiser's captured ships before making it back to Swansea. The redoubtable Captain Williams had returned to sea undaunted, remarking '*Someone has to take command of ships and I am not going to let any Germans afloat frighten me.*' Later the same day as sinking *RIO PARANA*, Alfred Stoß claimed his last victim, the British steamer *WESTERN COAST*, off Beachy Head. Stoß's career was however to be short-lived, as U-8 became trapped in submarine nets and destroyed by British warships on 4 March 1915.

The escalation of the U-boat activity against merchant shipping continued on 26 October 1914, with the torpedoing of an unarmed passenger ship without any warning. The 32-year-old *Kapitänleutnant* Rudolf Schneider, in command of U-24, was lying in ambush off Cap Gris Nez, hoping to ambush one of the troopships carrying reinforcements to France when he spotted the converted French passenger liner *AMIRAL GANTEUME* approaching, her decks crowded with men in uniform. Schneider was obliged by the Prize Code to identify his vessel and give warning to the merchant ship to stop and to ensure that those on board the French troopship had access to a reasonable place of safety before he could attack. Clearly he did not believe adherence to the Prize Code was feasible with the large numbers of troops on board and was aware that British and French warships were in the vicinity. Nevertheless, aware that these additional troops were the enemy, he determined it was his duty to sink the troopship and thus fired two torpedoes, one of which struck his target, causing a huge explosion. Fortunately help was at hand for the French liner in the form of Captain Robert Carey, in command of the cross-channel ferry *THE QUEEN* who, with a considerable feat of seamanship was able to put his vessel directly alongside the stricken troopship and transfer *AMIRAL GANTEAUME*'s complement to his own decks. In total, over 2,000 lives were saved, although some 40 lives were lost from the French ship, mostly women and children among the 30 Belgian refugee passengers, who fell between the two ships. Captain Carey was awarded the MBE for his action and given grateful thanks by the Belgian government.

A vivid account was given by Thomas McClune, an American passenger on board *THE QUEEN* at the time of the rescue:[35]

I was sitting by the taffrail on the starboard side of the Queen, along with a few friends, when I saw a huge volume of smoke, and water rise around the Admiral Ganteaume, which at the moment would be about 360 yards ahead of us. The smoke and water rose to a height of 80 or 100 feet, and immediately it had subsided the Admiral Ganteaume hoisted her signal of distress. Then we heard our captain pipe, 'All hands on deck', and we knew something serious had happened to the Ganteaume. Everyone at once said 'She has struck a mine'. Unable to get near enough on one side, Captain Carey, with superb seamanship, swung his boat right round. As the Queen made her way across the 'nose' of the Ganteaume the steward came to me and asked me if I were willing to help, as the Ganteaume had struck a mine. I replied, 'Yes,' and saw an attempt to lower the Queen's boats. The sea apparently was too heavy and Captain Carey drew his ship alongside the ill-fated vessel. As we did so, five Belgian soldiers dived from the Ganteaume. Four of them immediately sank and did not reappear. The other swam a short distance and then he sank.

The Ganteaume lowered a boat full of people, but as soon as it touched the water it dived straight down and we saw no more of the occupants. The scenes on the French vessel were simply beyond description. Men and women were fighting; others climbing into the rigging and sliding down ropes into the water. As soon as we got close alongside her there was an immediate rush for the Queen. The sea was rather high, and the boats heaved to and fro and it was impossible to run a bridge across. The passengers from the Ganteaume had simply to jump from one boat to the other. Some of them missed their footing or failed to hold the taffrail and they either dropped into the water or were crushed between the boats. I took my stand with the steward and helped

---

[35] Hucknall, *Small Town, Great War 1914–1918.*

him to catch the babies as they were thrown from the Ganteaume. I had a terrible experience in this work. As the last child was thrown the boat heaved away, and I just touched the child's shawl. The little one fell short of the ship and was crushed between the two vessels as they came together again. A man who jumped from the other boat missed his foothold, and though he held the ropes his legs were crushed. The rescue work of Captain Carey and his crew was magnificent, and I do not think there would have been a life lost if there had been no panic.

After the terrified people had all got on board they shrank in horror to the opposite side of our boat with the result that it began to list very seriously. Accordingly they were instructed to distribute themselves more evenly but before they could be induced to do so they had to be dragged apart. They clung to each other in an ecstasy of terror. Then came the most pitiful scene of all. Children had been separated from their parents, husbands from their wives, and our first care was to restore the children to their parents. I shall never forget the spectacle as we conducted the little ones round the boat and one by one they were identified. Nearly all the men, women and children had their faces and hands and clothes blackened by the flying soot from the Ganteaume. Nearly all were soaked with water. The scenes on arrival of the Queen at Folkestone were also indescribable. On all sides people shouted, 'Vive L'Angleterre!' Food was quickly provided for them but no-one who passed through the awful tragedy will ever forget.

Schneider became one of Germany's recognised U-boat 'aces', responsible for sinking 130,000 tons of Allied shipping[36] and was to add to his notoriety, as recorded later in this book, before he was lost overboard from his boat in 1917.

Sinking without warning was not officially condoned by the German High Command at that time, but this further display of a U-boat's ability to sink Allied merchant ships as a means of curtailing the supply chain to Britain and France, with little risk to their own craft, did not go unheeded. As a consequence, and in retaliation, the British government declared the North Sea to be a prohibited zone for all enemy merchant ships, leaving narrow seaways through which Allied and neutral ships could pass to Holland,

[36]   Gibson and Prendergast, *The German Submarine War*, p.378.

Denmark, Norway and the Baltic as well as the east coast of England. These seaways were patrolled and monitored by Allied naval forces, thus effectively closing all access to Germany's ports.

While Admiral Scheer had declared that the sinking of merchant ships by U-boats was foreign to German naval policy, in accordance with the discussion in September 1914, it was not so much on the grounds of humanity but on the basis that there were insufficient submarines available for the task. However, following the successful U-boat attacks on the unarmed merchant ships, opinions began to change as indicated in a memorandum from the leaders of the German fleet in November 1914 which stated that '*As England is trying to destroy our trade it is only fair if we retaliate by carrying on the campaign against her trade by all possible means. Further, as England completely disregards international law in her actions, there is not the least reason why we should exercise any restraint in our conduct of the war.*'

Admiral von Tirpitz proposed that such attacks should now become regarded as an additional arm of war, arguing that the U-boats could starve Britain into submission in a very short time. The Chancellor, Bethman-Hollweg, responded that he could only agree such a course of action if there could be guarantees that Britain's trade would be crippled in six weeks. The Chancellor was concerned about the political consequences of such action which would also mean the sinking of neutral ships carrying supplies to Britain. Should such action be successful in such a short period of time however, he believed the political consequences with neutral states could be overcome with Britain defeated. Nevertheless his view then was that the war on land had first to be successful and at that time British, French and Belgian forces were making their stand against superior German forces near the Belgian town of Ypres, suffering horrendous casualties on all sides.

Pressure on the Chancellor for the wider use of U-boats against merchant shipping was increasing. Count Reventlow, a son of a Danish nobleman who had served in the Imperial German Navy, had become a prominent writer and commentator by 1914. He wrote an article for the German publication *Deutshe Tageszeitung* in support of von Tirpitz, saying:

Great Britain, in order to make her North Sea blockade complete and efficient for starving Germany out, has thrown aside international agreements and stamped them underfoot, both as regards the German Empire and as regards neutrals. *No international law and no respect for 'Kultur' and humanity has for a moment turned British statesmen from their purpose of organising with the utmost refinement the hunger war against Germany for the enrichment of the English. This alone shows that no international considerations against trade war with submarines need to be weighed – quite apart from the fact that Germany is fighting for her very existence against a world of enemies. If the German government were immediately to declare a definite area of the North Atlantic Ocean bounded by the west coasts of the British Isles to be a war area, that would be precisely in accordance with British procedures in the North Sea. All trading ships entering this Atlantic war area would do so at their own risk and expose themselves to destruction by German submarines. 'An eye for an eye' must be the motto.*

On 24 January 1915, von Pohl as Commander-in-Chief of the High Seas Fleet announced that the waters around the British Isles, Ireland and the whole of the English Channel were to be declared a war zone and that from 18 February every merchant ship found in this zone would be destroyed. It was further stated that *'owing to the hazards of war'* neutral ships could not be guaranteed a safe passage in view of the misuse of neutral flags by the British. Admiral von Tirpitz issued a memorandum to commanding officers of all submarines saying that,

> *The first consideration is the safety of the U-boat. Rising to the surface to examine a ship must be avoided for the boat's safety, because, apart from the danger of a possible surprise attack by enemy ships, there is no guarantee that one is not dealing with an enemy ship even if she bears the distinguishing marks of a neutral. The fact that a steamer flies a neutral flag is no guarantee that it is actually a neutral vessel. Its destruction will therefore be justifiable unless other attendant circumstances indicate its neutrality.*

In February 1915, Germany announced the start of unrestricted submarine attacks, namely attacks made without any warning on all merchant shipping within British waters; von Pohl further warned that all Allied merchant ships would be destroyed without it always being possible to avoid danger to crews or passengers, thus formally denying the Prize Code. He drew attention to the not uncommon deceit of Allied ships flying the flags of neutral states despite complaints by those neutral states, particularly from the USA, thus clearly indicating that ships showing neutral state flags could no longer be immune from attack. The German High Command was eventually persuaded that a speedy victory could be won and approval was given for the start of a six-week campaign of unrestricted submarine warfare starting on 22 February. Assurances were however given to the USA that their ships would be spared 'so far as they can be recognised as such'.

Reports of the German vacillation on attacking merchant ships without warning were perhaps not widely promulgated to the merchant seafarers, but Captain John Bell, in command of the 501-ton collier THORDIS, on passage from Blyth to Plymouth on 24 February 1915, had his own views on the submarine threat. Steaming at a sedate 5 knots off Beachy Head in heavy weather he noticed what he thought to be a submarine periscope close on the starboard bow. He gave instructions for full speed and called all hands on deck as an emergency measure. The submarine had crossed his bow, taking up a position on his beam about 30 to 40 yards off, when he saw the track of a torpedo which just missed his stern. Taking exception to this action, Captain Bell ordered maximum speed and turned towards the U-boat, aiming for its conning tower. In his deposition to the Customs officers he later described the incident in a very matter-of-fact manner: 'I then put my helm hard over to starboard and ran over the periscope, when I and all the crew heard and felt the crash under the bottom. I did not see the submarine after, but saw oil floating on the water. I then proceeded on voyage.' Captain Bell was thus accorded the distinction of being the first Allied merchant ship deemed to have rammed a U-boat, for which action he was granted a commission as a lieutenant RNR and awarded a Distinguished Service Cross. He was also awarded a gold stopwatch and money which he shared with his crew. When dry-docked, THORDIS was found to have suffered bottom damage but the submarine, although put out of action, managed to return to its base. The German authorities were however shocked that such action had been taken by an unarmed merchant ship and determined that any shipmaster having been found guilty of such an action, or attempted action, would be executed if subsequently captured.

The early months of the war had shown a certain innocence, naivety and amateurishness; with some affinity between the seamen of the German Imperial Navy and those of the British and Allied merchant ships during their encounters, reflecting the bond between seafarers. Many German seamen had experience of serving on British ships before the war, giving them an advantage of knowledge of British ship operations and of the English language. They were thus often used by the German warships as boarding officers when capturing British merchant ships.

Despite the declaration of unrestricted submarine warfare in February, in practice little changed and while the U-boats were busy around the British coastlines there was little sign of Britain being brought to a state of surrender. The majority of coastal traffic was unaffected, so in August 1915 the Kaiser called off the unrestricted U-boat campaign, by which time 18 U-boats had been lost.[37] The German High Command considered the campaign had caused more ill feeling among the neutral nations, who were also becoming increasingly dismayed at the British 'stop and search' operation on any neutral ship. This had caused particular irritation to the USA, with much resulting diplomatic correspondence about the right of peaceful passage for the ships of non-belligerent states, quite apart from the inconvenience and cost of the 'stop and search' operations.

By the end of March 1915, U-boats had sunk 160 British merchant ships and fishing vessels, thus establishing themselves as a significant and growing menace, with their attacks on merchant shipping according to their commanders' interpretations of the orders given to them. They had gained the reputation mostly as ruthless and skilful men who saw their role simply to sink enemy shipping, although they became frustrated by the limitations on their activities posed by the uncertainties of their leaders regarding unrestricted warfare. To the merchant seafarer, having been advised at the start of the war that submarines could pose little threat to them, with exhortations from the British Admiralty to confront a submarine to force it to dive,[38] it was clear that the U-boats were the cause of the greatest loss of life. The U-boat commanders had shown little evidence of the sentiment expressed by HRH the Prince of Wales that '*Hostilities were conducted in harmony with principles laid down by international law*'.

Churchill, as First Lord of the Admiralty, expanded his view that any merchant ship should confront any threat or demand for its surrender from a

---

[37] Gibson and Prendergast, *The German Submarine War*, p.370.

[38] Ibid., p.36

submarine with four unambiguous and specific actions to be taken,[39], namely:

1. All British merchant ships to paint out their names and port of registry, and when in British waters to fly the flag of a neutral power (preferably the American flag).
2. British vessels are ordered to treat the crews of captured U-boats as 'felons' and not to accord them the status of prisoners of war.
3. Survivors should be taken prisoner or shot whichever is the most convenient.
4. In all actions, white flags would be fired upon with promptitude.

Churchill's view that the master of a merchant ship should not readily surrender his ship gave little comfort to the master who found himself in a situation where he believed that he was likely to lose his ship whether he surrendered or not. It is unlikely that most masters were impressed by the views expressed by Churchill on this matter, bearing in mind the first duty of a master, as a civilian, was that of the safety of his passengers and crew, plus his obligations to his owners and the charterers of his ship. As can be seen, there were numerous displays by masters of courage and exemplary displays of seamanship to thwart the enemy throughout the whole war, but the actions taken depended entirely on the circumstances of each case, as perceived by each master. An interesting contrast can be seen with the capture of two British steamers, *INDIAN CITY* and the *HEADLANDS*.

On 12 March 1915 the 4,645-ton Reardon Smith steamer *INDIAN CITY* was south of the Scilly Isles, bound to Le Havre from Galveston and under the command of Captain John Williams when she was approached by a submarine. This turned out to be U-29, under the command of Otto Weddigen (he who had sunk the three British cruisers *ABOUKIR*, *HOGUE* and *CRESSEY* in one day in September 1914), who surfaced close on the starboard quarter, fired a warning rocket and instructed the steamer to stop. He gave warning that he would sink his prize in 20 minutes to give the crew time to get off in the lifeboats, after which he would take the boats in tow. Once *INDIAN CITY*'s crew were clear, a torpedo was fired into the ship,

---

[39]   Edwards, *War Under the Red Ensign*, p.115

striking in No. 2 hold, blowing the hatches off and setting the ship on fire. Captain Williams' statement, referring to Weddigen, reads:

He then came and took my boats in tow and invited me to come aboard the Submarine. I went aboard and I told the Captain that if I had been further out he would not have had me and he replied 'oh yes I should, I knew you were coming and I have got some more to have today'. He asked me to have a glass of wine and which I accepted. The Captain of the submarine then told me he could do 17 [knots] on the surface and 14 below. I did not go below in the submarine but remained on deck.

I saw 8 men on deck and they were all of the officer class of the mercantile marine and I believe one or two of them were late officers of the Hansa Line. None appeared to be sailors. The men on deck that I saw could all speak good English. They were all well, fit, happy and appeared to be enjoying themselves the same as if they were on a picnic.

The Captain of the submarine said he hoped the war would soon be over and also said that England and Germany should not have been fighting against each other but that if they had been fighting together then we would beat the world in two months. After he had been towing for some little while the Captain of the submarine told me when he had got close to the island he would cast my boats off, and would give me a chart of the Scilly Islands as he had a few spare ones …

When he had towed my boats for about five miles, two steam boats appeared to be coming from apparently inside the Island. The Captain of the submarine then told me to get in my boat and which I did. He then cut our painter and said 'If they are only tug boats I will come back and tow you further in'. He then went away (still on the surface) in the direction of another steamer that was coming up from the southern.[40]

The ship that U-29 went to was the British steamer *HEADLANDS*, of 2,988 tons, under the command of Captain Lugg. In contrast to the *INDIAN CITY*, the order to stop and lower her boats was ignored and *HEADLANDS* turned away from the U-boat and attempted to escape. The pursuit did not last long and U-29 fired a torpedo, striking *HEADLANDS* abaft the engine

---

[40]   The National Archives, ADM 137/1059.

room, at which point Captain Lugg decided to abandon ship, fortunately without any loss of life.

The contrast between the responses of Captains Williams and Lugg to U-boat instructions to surrender was a point of concern with the insurance War Risk Clubs, which felt that some masters gave up their ships too readily, noting that HM Government insured merchant ships to the extent of 80 per cent of their value. Shipowners were contacted on the subject to the effect that rewards should be offered to those who stand by their ships and '*If, however, the practice of instantly abandoning vessels continues, it will be for consideration for the Admiralty to take more direct steps in the matter. The question of compensation for crews for their loss of kit is intimately bound up in this matter ...*' No doubt the civilian merchant seafarers were comforted by the thought that if they disobeyed the instruction of an enemy warship to stop and abandon their ship they could be sure of some compensation for their loss of personal belongings if they survived, even as their wages were stopped.

The views of the Admiralty interviewing officers following the incidents also gave little comfort to the masters of merchant ships under attack from a U-boat. The report on the action of the master of the *INDIAN CITY* read:

> *No doubt the Master was actuated by a desire to avoid risking the lives of any of his crew, which would have been exposed to some risk if the ship had tried to escape and been torpedoed while so doing; but at the same time it is considered that the more correct conduct of a British Master would have been to use his utmost endeavour to escape and not stop his ship or quit it until there was no hope of saving her – more especially as in this case he was only 9 or 10 miles from land.*

The corresponding report on the attack on the *HEADLANDS* stated: '*The action of the Master of the HEADLANDS stands out in pleasing relief. He declined to stop or surrender but apparently kept his course until torpedoed. Suggest Board of Trade be invited to commend him (through his Owners) on his endeavour to save his ship.*'

Kapitänleutnant Weddigen had acted with great consideration and courtesy and had shown it was possible for U-boats to conduct their business with humanity and almost in accordance with the Prize Code, although it could hardly be said that he had left the victims of his attacks *in a place of safety*. His career however had little time to run, as six days after sinking *INDIAN CITY* and *HEADLANDS* he attempted an attack on one of the battle squadrons of the Grand Fleet off the Shetland Islands. On 18 March 1915 Weddigen's U-29 was rammed by HMS *DREADNOUGHT* and '*Picked up on her ram like a winkle on a pin*' as an eyewitness expressed it, before U-29 sank with the loss of all hands. That event, one of the most striking in the history of submarine warfare, was kept secret from the Germans.[41]

Despite the German authorities calling off the trial period of unrestricted submarine warfare, ship and crew losses mounted and it was evident that the conflict between U-boats and merchant ships was to become critical to the outcome of the war. The dreadful losses in the land battles and the increasing shortage of food in both Britain and Germany spotlighted the significance of the maintenance of supplies. Thoughts of humanity and honour rapidly became lost in the intensity of the struggle. While the German authorities had initially emphasised their honour and humanity, the successes of the U-boats were to be encouraged with increasing disregard for the fate of both Allied and neutral shipping. The initial disregard by German authorities of the potential of their submarines soon changed, with a rapid increase in the building of new U-boats and concern for their survival to become the most significant weapon of war at sea.

There was clearly little reason for the merchant seafarers to hope that their lot would improve as the war progressed.

---

[41]   Hurd, *The Merchant Navy*, Vol. 1, pp.300–301.

CHAPTER 6

THE END OF CHIVALRY

By early 1915 it had become abundantly clear that action was sorely needed to reduce, if not negate, the U-boat menace without losing the civilian status of British and Allied merchant shipping. Largely at the behest of Churchill some merchant ships were being armed, with instructions given to masters that any armaments placed on board were solely for defence and to assist the ship in completing its voyage (the *LA CORRENTINA*, referred to earlier, had indeed been fitted with guns, but no ammunition). The Admiralty provided more detailed instructions to masters, based on their perception of the experiences of the past few months, entitled 'The Status of Armed Merchant Ships', which proclaimed: *'The right of a crew of a merchant vessel forcibly to resist visit and search, and to fight in self-defence, is well recognised in International Law, and is expressly admitted by the German Prize Regulations in an addendum issued in June 1914, at a time when it was known that numerous vessels were being armed in self defence.'* The Admiralty issued further instructions with regard to encounters with German submarines:[42]

> *The speed of a German submarine on the surface exceeds that of a merchant ship, but the speed underwater is low. A submarine cannot see under water. When submerged she is obliged at frequent intervals to put up a long tube, known as a periscope, in order to see where she is going. Some submarines are armed with a gun, but this is an inferior weapon, incapable of inflicting serious injury upon an iron steamer manned by a resolute crew.*

---

[42] Instructions for owners and masters of British merchant ships issued with reference to the operations of German submarines against British shipping, 10 February 1915.

> *All submarines carry torpedoes, but their supply is limited, and they will be very averse from firing them at merchant vessels. It is very difficult for a submarine to hit a moving ship with a torpedo, especially if she is kept nearly end on, and experience has shown that a great many torpedoes are fired without any result. In case the ship is struck by a torpedo, there will generally be ample time for the crew to escape in the boats, if the latter are kept ready for service.*

These Admiralty instructions continue with the direction, '*No British merchant vessel should ever tamely surrender to a submarine but should do her utmost to escape*' and then, '*Even should she fail, and be unlucky enough to be struck by one of the enemy's torpedoes, the crew will, in most cases, have ample time to man their boats.*'

The instructions drew attention to the Admiralty advice that a merchant vessel threatened by a submarine should try to place the attacker astern, to proceed at full speed and to make for the nearest land or shallow water, followed by the statement, '*Gunfire from most submarines is not dangerous.*'

In the event of a submarine surfacing ahead of a merchant ship, the Admiralty suggested the following procedure: '*If a submarine comes up suddenly close ahead of you with obvious hostile intention, steer straight for her at your utmost speed, altering course as necessary to keep her ahead. She will probably then dive, in which case you will have ensured your safety, as she will be compelled to come up astern of you.*'

It was this last procedure which offered the greatest scope for ambiguity. Although no mention is made of the intent to ram a submarine or its likely consequences, ramming would be the natural outcome should the submarine not be able to take evasive action in time. Certainly the German authorities regarded this as an instruction to ram and contrary to the rules of war.

It can only be a matter for conjecture what the private thoughts of a merchant shipmaster would have been when in receipt of such banal Admiralty directions which appeared to suggest that U-boats were relatively harmless and, if threatened, would withdraw from conflict.

On the evening of 27 March 1917 the unarmed 2,144-ton steamer *AGUILA* was bound from Liverpool to Lisbon under the command of Captain Bannerman when a U-boat approached and ordered the steamer to stop. While doubtless aware of Churchill's exhortations not to surrender a merchant ship and the Admiralty advice as to what action to take, Captain Bannerman, with passengers on board, chose to put on full speed in an attempt to outrun the U-boat, but the submarine was faster and, when within about 200 to 300 feet of *AGUILA*, opened fire. The ship was brought to a stop with the crew and passengers taking to the lifeboats, but the U-boat continued firing, killing the chief engineer, bosun, donkeyman and a female passenger, while also wounding the master and two others. Under fire from its attacker, one of the lifeboats capsized during its launch, bringing the death toll up to eight.

One of the seamen, Thomas Crawley, had been helping the bosun to launch No. 3 boat when the bosun was hit by shrapnel and had to be left on deck. Crawley later stated *'Shots were flying all around me and I don't know how I escaped. I was the last man to leave AGUILA. Seeing my chance, I caught a lifeline and swung myself off over the side.'* He also stated there was no time to collect any belongings and that he had felt particularly sorry for the women. The third engineer, Mr King, who had received a wound in his side, confirmed that the U-boat had continued firing at the survivors even when they were clear of the ship. The submarine responsible for this act of murder was the U-28, commanded by Baron Georg-Günther von Forstner who, after failing to sink *AGUILA* with gunfire resorted to firing a torpedo to complete the task. No assistance was offered to the survivors who were then some 33 miles off the Cornish coast.

The 'inferior gun' referred to in the Admiralty Instructions had been more than adequate in bringing about the loss of eight lives and its continued action against the crew of *AGUILA* most certainly did not allow the peaceful, ordered lowering of the lifeboats.

A short while later, the steam trawler *OTTILIE* was approached by U-28 and von Forstner told its master, John Randell, *'English ship sunk, west eleven degrees; north four; boats launched.'* Captain Randell asked the U-boat how many survivors there were, but the U-boat responded *'You want to know too much'* and moved away. Captain Randell consulted with his mate about ramming the U-boat and attempted to turn towards the submarine but, possibly anticipating the manoeuvre, the U-boat moved away. The *OTTILIE* made her best speed to the indicated position and two hours later found a boat with Captain Bannerman and 19 others, finally landing them at Fishguard.

It is a matter of some curiosity as to why von Forstner, after his cruel attack on *AGUILA*'s survivors, should show himself to *OTTILIE* close to the English coast to give the position of *AGUILA*, so providing for the rescue of his victims. Perhaps he had second thoughts and felt a pang of guilt for what he had just done. If so, any guilt he may have felt was very short lived when he encountered the unarmed Elder Liner, *FALABA* the next day.

The *FALABA* had left the Mersey on the evening of 27 March 1915, bound for West African ports carrying 147 passengers and general cargo plus 13 tons of cartridges and gunpowder for government use on the West Coast. Of 4,086 tons and with a speed of 13 knots, she was commanded by Captain F.J. Davis with a crew of 94 including four deck officers; thus a total of 242 persons on board. On the morning of 28 March, with Chief Officer Baxter and Third Officer Pengilly on watch, a submarine was seen about three miles away. Captain Davis ordered a course alteration to place the submarine astern and called the engine room for all best speed, in accordance with Admiralty advice, even though he believed the submarine was possibly flying a British ensign. The wireless operator was instructed to send a signal to report the situation, but the ship was soon overhauled by the submarine with its superior speed of 18 knots. Soon the *FALABA* was instructed to stop, but Captain Davis continued to try evasive action until the submarine signalled again to stop or firing would commence and further ordered *FALABA* to abandon ship immediately. On this occasion Captain Davis obeyed the instruction and brought his ship to a stop, having given the order to abandon ship, and commenced swinging out the lifeboats. While trying to do so, the submarine, U-28, fired a torpedo without warning, from a range of about 100–150 yards. As a consequence of this, 104 lives were lost, of which 57 were passengers and 47 crew members. Some passengers and crew members had jumped or fallen into the sea, while others struggled to free and lower those boats still usable after the torpedo attack. The U-boat then steered in their midst with the crew, reportedly led by its commander, von Forstner, jeering and shouting insults without making any attempt to assist, before disappearing. *FALABA*'s survivors claimed that they had only been given about five minutes warning before the torpedo was fired and that the ship listed and sank in about ten minutes following the explosion.

Fortunately for the survivors, the steam trawler *EILEEN EMMA* under the command of George Wright was nearby and picked up 40 persons, six of whom died shortly after. The drifter *WENLOCK*, also soon on the scene, rescued another eight, of whom two died. Captain Davis, who had been seriously injured by the torpedo explosion, had been the last to leave his ship but had been picked out of the sea with a boathook, still clutching his ship's papers, but was one of the six who died soon after.

Among the various incidents reported by survivors were those commending Captain Davis' direction of the evacuation and included that of a female passenger too terrified to get into a lifeboat being picked up bodily by one of the seamen and thrown overboard where she was rescued by one of the lifeboats. Another female passenger and a stewardess refused to leave the ship and both were last seen going down as the ship sank. There was also an account of one of the stewardesses, Louisa Gearle, taking off her lifejacket in the water and giving it to one of the young seamen who was not wearing one. Louisa Gearle, aged 36, drowned. Another stewardess was given a lifejacket by a young officer, but both were drowned.

The chief cook, Mr Marchbanks claimed that the explosion of the torpedo blew one of the lifeboats out of its davits as it was being lowered, tipping it upside down and killing some 18 occupants. There were also reports of some of the lifeboats being unusable due to their being filled with ship's stores or damaged from the explosion. Even though the ship had lifeboat provision for 307 persons, due to FALABA's list it had proved impossible to swing the boats out on their davits. The lack of time available, the listing of the ship and the chaos on deck following the explosion all served to underline the earlier view of the then Captain Sims of the United States Navy, who had criticised the current design of ships' lifeboats and their means of launching as inappropriate means for an emergency ship evacuation. The event also demonstrated the lack of merit in the Admiralty Instructions that 'In case the ship is struck by a torpedo, there will generally be ample time for the crew to escape in boats'. A total of 104 lives were lost, including that of Captain Davis.

The public outrage following the sinking of FALABA was met by a response circulated through German wireless stations from Berlin and dated 6 April referring to a telegram which stated:

No report has been received from the submarine which sank the Falaba. According to trustworthy reports the submarine requested the steamer Falaba to put the passengers and crew in the lifeboats when other ships arrived on the scene. Of late the English merchant ships have been provided with guns by the British Government and have been advised to ram and otherwise attack German submarines. This advice has been repeatedly followed in order to win the promised rewards.

Military necessity, therefore, forced the submarine to act quickly, which *made the granting of a longer space of time and the saving of life impossible. The German Government regrets the sacrifice of human lives, but both British ships and neutral passengers on board of such ships were urgently warned and in good time not to cross the war zone. The responsibility rests with the British Government, which, contrary to international law, has inaugurated a commercial war against Germany, and, contrary to international law, has caused merchant ships to offer resistance.*

When von Forstner was later challenged to account for his actions, he stated that the ship had attempted to escape and had fired rockets to draw the attention of other vessels nearby to summon assistance. This was regarded by von Forstner as constituting active resistance and thus his actions were justified.[43]

The subsequent Wreck Commissioner's Inquiry into the loss of the *FALABA* paid great attention to the time between the *FALABA* being ordered to stop and the firing of the fatal torpedo, bearing in mind the ship was unarmed and '*carried no means of defence or offence*'. In his summing up, the Wreck Commissioner, Lord Mersey, stated he found the warning that the submarine was going to sink *FALABA* in five minutes was given as nearly as he could determine at noon. He wrote:

The Falaba stopped at 12:04 or 12:05, and at 12:10 the submarine fired a torpedo into her. At this moment the submarine was within about 100 yards of the Falaba. The torpedo struck the Falaba on the starboard side by No. 3 hatch aft of No. 1 life-boat and just alongside the Marconi house. The blow was fatal. The Falaba at once took a list to starboard, and in eight minutes (namely at 12:18) she sank. This was within twenty minutes of the notice from the submarine of her intention to sink the ship.

He added:

I do not desire, nor am I in this case required, to find whether the submarine was within her rights as an enemy craft in sinking the Falaba. But I do assume that in any event she was bound to afford the men and women on

---

43   Koerver, *German Submarine War 1914–1918 in the Eyes of British Intelligence*, p.174.

board a reasonable opportunity of getting to the boats and of saving their lives. This, those in charge of the submarine did not do. I am driven to the conclusion that the Captain of the submarine desired and designed not merely to sink the ship but, in doing so, also to sacrifice the lives of passengers and crew.

There was evidence before me of laughing and jeering on board the submarine while the men and women from the Falaba were struggling for their lives in the water; but I prefer to keep silence on this matter in the hope that the witness was mistaken.

There were in fact several survivors of FALABA who drew attention to the extraordinary behaviour of the submarine crew, but perhaps Lord Mersey was reluctant to contemplate the truth of the dreadful lack of humanity shown by von Forstner.

Von Forstner had been having a busy time in British home waters. On 25 March, before encountering the AGUILA, he had sunk the Dutch steamer MEDEA near Beachy Head. On that occasion he had given the crew adequate time to leave their ship and, acting in accordance with the rules regarding survivors to be taken to a place of safety, he towed the survivors in their lifeboats for two hours before inexplicably abandoning them. He also sank the British steamers SOUTH POINT (3,837 tons) and VOSGES (1,295 tons) between sinking AGUILA and FALABA. In total, von Forstner had sunk 27 ships, of which 19 were British, with 154 lives lost. There were no casualties from the 8 non-British ships sunk, suggesting a particular disregard for the British seafarers. Von Forstner, of whom more later in this book, was in command of U-28 from September 1914 to January 1917. He survived the war but was declared a war criminal by the British government.

The response of the German government to the outrage at the sinking of the FALABA added a complaint that as British merchant ships were being equipped with a gun, they should be regarded as warships and as such should not be allowed to stay in neutral, especially American, ports for more than 24 hours. These complaints were met with the response from the British government that '*The vessels are armed only for defence and resistance to capture and are not intended to commit unprovoked acts of hostility. So long as that is the case they remain in exactly the same position as any merchant ship.*'

A gun, if fitted on a merchant ship, was usually placed aft, such that when conforming to the recommended practice of trying to place any threatening U-boat astern and outrunning it, the gun could be used to dissuade the submarine from any further attention. Certainly from the merchant seafarers' viewpoint, the gun was generally, but not universally, welcomed as a means to answer back when threatened by a U-boat as they were not always equipped with ample ammunition or the expertise to use the guns to any great effect. Ideally, the ship's company would be supplemented by trained Admiralty supplied gunners, who would often be embarked at a port prior to entering a known high threat area and disembarked when clear of that area at an appropriate port. The wish to have some means of effective defence was not only to prevent the loss of their ship and the associated perils which immediately followed, but there was also the concern that, should they be captured after resisting the attack and having previously been in the hands of German captors, they ran the risk of being executed as *franc tireurs*. The term *franc tireur* was widely used by the Germans to describe a civilian who had taken up arms against the enemy, contrary to the normal rules of war. It was a tactic adopted to rationalise the harsh retaliation against civilian populations and had been widely used in Belgium.

A full understanding of the term *franc tireur* was all too brutally demonstrated in the later case of Captain Charles Algernon Fryatt. He was born on 2 December 1872 in Southampton, but his family later moved to Harwich where he attended the Corporation School, joining the Great Eastern Railway as a seaman in 1892, rising through the ranks and gaining his first command on the *COLCHESTER* on the Harwich to Hook of Holland ferry route. He was married with seven children.

On 3 March 1915, in command then of the *WREXHAM*, Captain Fryatt thwarted a U-boat attack by altering course to place the submarine astern and calling on all hands to man the stokehold to gain as much speed as possible. His crew matched his demands and the ferry was able to increase from its normal 14 knots to 16, eventually outrunning the submarine after a 40 mile chase. *WREXHAM* arrived safely in Rotterdam, with only burnt funnels to show for her submarine encounter. Captain Fryatt was awarded a gold watch by the Great Eastern Railway in appreciation of his courage and seamanship and, in an interview with a local paper he commented, '*The old ship did wonders; sixteen knots is some going! It shows what can be done when it's up to you. "Bully off and go" is my advice to all British skippers with German submarines on the beam. In nine times out of ten the luck is with you.*' Later that month, when in command again of *COLCHESTER*, Captain Fryatt was able to avoid another U-boat attack and became known locally as 'The Pirate Dodger'.

Later still, on 28 March, in command this time of the *BRUSSELS* and approaching the Maas Light ship, Captain Fryatt's lookouts reported a large submarine on the starboard bow. As the two vessels closed, the submarine began to cross the bow and signalled the ferry to stop. Captain Fryatt considered his options, including the exhortations of Churchill to try and head towards an attacking U-boat. This he decided to try and, as he later related to Great Eastern Railway: [44]

> *I could see there was no use trying to get away from him as … he could easily have torpedoed me and his speed was much greater than mine. He hoisted two flags for me to stop but I did not like the idea of giving up my ship so I decide to ram him.*

When the submarine realised the intent, it began to submerge but, as Captain Fryatt continued,

> *He was approximately twenty yards ahead of me when he submerged and I steered straight for the place where he submerged and when I considered that I was on top of him I then gave the order 'hard-a-port' to sweep over his periscope. His periscope came up under our bottom abreast of the gangway doors about two feet out of the water and came close along our port side. I could not feel the ship strike her but one of the firemen felt a bumping sensation under the bottom. I think I must have damaged him if I have not sunk him as I consider it was impossible for him to get clear according to the position of his periscope when it came to the surface.*

Indeed, when *BRUSSELS* reached her destination, a drydock examination confirmed bottom damage consistent with striking a submerged object and it was later confirmed that *BRUSSELS* probably had struck U-33 but did not sink the submarine. The U-33 commander, *Kapitänleutnant* Gansser, in

---

[44] Edwards, War Under the Red Ensign 1914–1918, pp.118,119.

his war diary reported that he had hailed *BRUSSELS* at a distance of about four miles, instructing her to stop immediately or be fired upon, which instruction was ignored. The war diary stated:

> *At a distance of one mile I cleared one tube for action. The steamer neither altered course or speed. U-33 making direct for the steamer. At a distance of 500 metres and only a few seconds before the shot was to have been fired, the steamer put her helm over with the manifest intention of ramming us … As observed through the periscope, the steamer passed us at a distance of twenty to thirty metres, after which she resumed her course at high speed … came to the surface.*

Although U-33 had not been sunk by *BRUSSELS*, there was nevertheless outrage in Germany that a British merchant ship had attempted to ram one of their submarines. Captain Fryatt was branded by the Germans as a dangerous pirate who could expect no mercy should he be caught. From that time on, knowing that Captain Fryatt was regularly commanding Great Eastern Railway ships on the Harwich to Hook of Holland shuttle, German warships were very much on the lookout to capture him. Instead he was awarded two more gold watches; one from the Admiralty congratulating him on his heroic action and one from the Mayor of Harwich.[45] Furthermore, Captain Fryatt's name was mentioned in the House of Commons, as it was to be again, as described later in this book. Holland, as a neutral nation would not allow armed ships of the belligerent nations in her ports, therefore none of the Great Eastern Railway ships carried a gun.

Captain Fryatt was perhaps fortunate on that occasion that he had managed to drive off Gansser in U-33. Gansser's later exploits resulted in him being listed as a war criminal by the British.

In February 1915 Germany had given notice that waters around the British Isles would be treated as a war zone, within which any merchant ship would be sunk. In response, with the British armed merchant cruisers of the Cruiser Squadron stepping up their 'stop and search' of neutral merchant ships and their battle with the U-boats, a new British Order in Council was announced on 11 March. This decreed that no neutral ships should go to

---

[45] These watches can be seen at the Imperial War Museum, London.

German ports on pain of seizure by Britain and their cargoes confiscated. Further, that any neutral ship with goods loaded in a German port for export would also be taken to a British port where goods could be unloaded and confiscated. Unsurprisingly, this increased activity by Britain caused many complaints from the neutral nations, not least from the Americans when, even if their ships were not deemed to be carrying contraband, the disruption to their voyages incurred delays and costs.

Apart from the British 'stop and search' activities, this was a time when Germany's reputation was at a very low ebb due largely to reported atrocities committed in Belgium and questions were being asked in Italy why a number of prominent people believed that Germany had so many enemies. An article from *The Times*' correspondent in Rome published the following response from Germany's Field Marshal Reiger on 8 April 1915: '*Germany has so many enemies because she is the nation which excels others. The world, as Schiller said, loves to darken that which is on high. Socrates had to drink hemlock, Christopher Columbus was cast into prison, Jesus Christ was crucified.*' The Rome correspondent offered his own comments on the Field Marshal's explanation. '*There have been many assertions of the intimacy between the Kaiser and the God of Battles, but this latest utterance is surely unique in the likening of modern Germans to the Saviour of the World.*'

It was very clear by this time that despite the advice given by the British Admiralty to merchant ships about the relative harmlessness of the U-boats, it was still the U-boats that provided the greatest threat to the life of the merchant seafarer. The U-boat commanders were seen to be disregarding any bonds which had been forged over centuries between seafarers of all nationalities, although those bonds had been embraced by the surface ships of the German Navy. The term 'pirate' became common parlance for the U-boat crews, reflecting perhaps the definition of pirates by the Roman philosopher and lawyer Cicero as *hostes humani generi*, or enemies of the human race.

Lack of chivalry and threats to the well-being of the merchant seafarer were however not limited to the enemy afloat, with particular and surprising harshness shown by those responsible for imprisoning their captives ashore. This began towards the end of July 1914, before war was declared, when British merchant ships that wished to leave German ports were prevented on the grounds that due to harbour works their departures might be unsafe.

The same harbour works however did not restrict the entry of British ships to those ports and, by 4 August some 155 British merchant officers and 888 ratings were being held in German ports.[46]

Initially the crews of ships being held in the ports were permitted to go ashore but they were forced to sign documents to the effect that they would not take part in a war against Germany and refusal to do so would be deemed to admittance of spying, for which the penalty was execution. In the port of Hamburg the officers and crews were taken off their ships and placed in prison hulks within the harbour, subjected to beatings by the harbour police guards should any form of disobedience be suspected and provided with what was described as 'rotten and putrid' food. Merchant seafarer prisoners at other ports were similarly abused, in some instances billeted in disused stables and made to undertake manual work.

A particularly unfortunate group of British fishermen who had been captured at sea towards the end of August were subjected to humiliation and ridicule by German civilians while being marched to the naval prison in Wilhelmshaven, where they were jeered and spat at, had missiles thrown at them and were kicked and abused by their guards. They were eventually put into cattle trucks and taken to a prison camp in Emden, after an extremely unpleasant stay at Wilhelmshaven, with little clothing and little more than cabbage soup for food. One of their number was a black seaman called William Savory from Barbados, who was singled out for particular humiliation and dragged out of the truck at every stop to be exhibited for further insult and abuse.[47]

There were many prison camps throughout Germany and Austria-Hungary, but the principal camp was at Ruhleben in Germany which was an old race track with stables and a grandstand, where the captured crews from merchant ships and British civilians were interned in inhumane and insanitary conditions. Many passed the first few months lying on cement floors, with the more fortunate among them obtaining straw as a covering, but none had beds or blankets. The prisoners suffered acute hardship without bedding, heating or adequate food for the early days of their incarceration, but conditions gradually improved as their plight became known to authorities

---

[46]   Hurd, *The Merchant Navy*, Vol. 3, p.841.

[47]   Ibid., p.344.

in Britain who, initially, seemed to have forgotten them and/or disregarded the information from the camps as gross exaggeration of their plight. As with their colleagues still at sea, these merchant seafarers had to draw upon their resources of courage, patience and fortitude.

By the latter stages of the war conditions for the prisoners at Ruhleben had gradually improved to the stage where the prisoners effectively managed themselves, elected a camp captain and organised education classes and entertainment. Those at the prison camp at Brandenburg fared much worse, with the camp guards earning a reputation for brutality, where food and sanitation was deplorable, the camp riddled with vermin and, until almost the end of the war unheated. Prisoners were set to work felling trees, making railway trucks, manufacturing torpedoes and other manual tasks, starting work at 5:00 a.m and working through until 7:00 p.m. for which they were paid a pittance, if at all. Little regard was given by the Germans for ill health, disability or age of their civilian captives. A description of freezing conditions in the huts was given by one British master: '*We formed parties to scrape refuse heaps for anything that would burn, but this became such filthy business we were bound to give it up and freeze. In summer the heat was intolerable; flies and mosquitoes very trying.*'[48] 'Propaganda marches' were held every week or so, whereby British prisoners were paraded through the streets of Berlin as evidence of German victories at sea.

The concentration camp at Cottbus was divided into two sections, with one for British prisoners and the other largely for Russians, who were treated in an even more inhumane fashion with terrible suffering. One account by a British prisoner described the brutal treatment of the Russian prisoners:

The unfortunate wretches were lashed to the strafing posts for two hours a day, and in November, when the cold weather set in, it was pitiful to see these world-abandoned creatures fall limp in their lashings, where they would remain an hour; when untied they would fall on the ground in a limp bundle of rags. I have also seen these Russians pass in pairs as many as ten lines of barbed wire, one holding up the lower wire for the other to pass, and so on, until they came to the British compounds, where they were given the German soup; our men by this time were getting parcels from home. It seems incredible

---

[48] Ibid. p.350.

that any human being would risk his life for a basin of German pig-swill soup, yet men were shot in attempting to pass from one compound to another with that object.[49]

Atrocities were committed on prisoners at other camps, including being made to sleep in open fields without any cover; prisoners on arrival being stripped in the streets; dogs being set on prisoners; and, at the Sennelager camp, to humiliate and distinguish British prisoners from others, having their heads and faces shaved on just one side. Lack of sanitation and washing facilities resulted in many of the men suffering from infestations of vermin, with many bizarre methods of ill treatment by the German guards. Degrading and inhumane treatment was common throughout the camps, where the merchant seafarers at Hameln were held for an initial period adjacent to a barracks holding British troops. The troops were not permitted to mix with the seafarers but, when an opportunity allowed, they would throw additional food over to them. The attitude of the Germans towards the British seafarers continued to be inhumane and cruel and not just restricted to the camp guards, but also by the civilians in the streets before whom many were paraded.

One account of imprisonment was given by Captain Brooks of the British India passenger steamer *MASHOBRA* which was torpedoed and sunk in the Mediterranean by the Austro-Hungarian U–29 on 15 April 1917, with the loss of eight lives. Captain Brooks was taken prisoner and held in the submarine during which time U–29 was subject to three attacks by Allied vessels. He was landed at Castelnuovo eight days after being captured and was imprisoned for three days, giving the following account of his ordeal: '*I was imprisoned for three days and nights in the cell of the fortress, with a reeking wet floor, no bed or bedding, and, for covering, a few blankets alive with vermin. The nights were bitterly cold, I was all the time hungry, without money, with very little clothing and no food except scraps from the guard's rations.*' Captain Brooks was then sent to Graz, travelling in a cattle truck, on a journey lasting four days and nights during which he was allowed one small meal a day consisting solely of a little bread. His account continued, '*On arrival at Graz I was placed in a room, without ventilation, for 31 days in solitary confinement and not allowed to take any exercise; food of the most horrible kind was served out twice a day and was hopelessly insufficient.*

---

[49] Ibid. p.351.

At the end of the 31 days I could scarcely walk, being half starved and very weak.'
From Graz, he was moved to a prison camp at Salzerbad where he stayed
for 18 months, enduring disgusting food and conditions and complaining
that the parcels sent to him and others from the Red Cross and from the
British India Company were pillaged by the guards. In some cases, the guards
handed over the parcels having replaced the food and clothing with rubbish
and bricks. Although the prison guards eventually deserted their posts in view
of the Austro-Italian armistice, Captain Brooks had still to find his way back
to the UK. In company with 70 other British fellow British prisoners they
made their way by rail, by bribing engine drivers and railway officials with
what little money or few possessions they had retained, and after four days
managed to reach Trieste, where they were able to board an Italian destroyer
which took them to Venice. Not only was Captain Brook's experience an
example of dreadful and inhumane treatment of the imprisoned merchant
seafarers, it was also an example of the difficulties and lack of support in
being repatriated.

The lot of the imprisoned seafarer was indeed an unhappy one. Having
lost their ship through enemy action, their wages had been stopped and,
additionally having endured capture and captivity, they found that a House
of Lords ruling that owners of ships captured or sunk by the enemy could
not be held legally responsible for the wages of those taken prisoner,[50] thus
they could make no provision for their dependants and family during their
internment. There seemed little evidence of chivalry or honour from their
own country in their predicament.

Fortunately the plight of the merchant seafarer was acknowledged by
the Imperial Merchant Service Guild which started a war fund to provide
parcels for all imprisoned merchant seafarers. This action accelerated with
the help and support of many charities and a few shipowners, such as the
British India Steam Navigation Company, which had been paying some
allowances to their crews' dependants and sending parcels of food and
clothing direct to the prisoners. Following discussions between the Board
of Trade and shipowners, it was agreed that a 'subsistence' payment would
be paid to all the prisoners by the British government and this was further
formalised such that the Merchant Navy officers be recognised by Germany

---

[50]   Ibid., p.361.

with equivalent ranks to those of the armed services, although the Germans were initially reluctant to accept this. Having taken any identification papers away from their prisoners, they were unable to make that distinction until the shipowners were able to show evidence of the qualifications and ranks of their imprisoned officers. The system then allowed for parcels of food and clothing to be sent from Britain to the prisoners; living conditions in the concentration camps generally improved and the prisoners' dependants were able to receive modest allowances.

Some seafarers who had been interned at the outbreak of war were repatriated by Germany, but those captured after the start of the submarine campaign were viewed quite differently and remained in captivity until the war's end. Other merchant seafarers who were ill or infirm were released from Germany, but sent for internment in Holland or Switzerland, during which time their treatment was paid for by the British government. At the end of the war, returning seafarers could claim one month's wages from the Board of Trade where their ships had been lost to enemy action and they had then been interned, although this did not apply to those who had been in German ports at the outbreak of war. An allowance was also paid to those who had lost their personal effects when their ship had been lost and were subsequently interned.

CHAPTER 7

A DANGEROUS GAME

In early April 1915 two young brothers, Leslie and John Morton of Birkenhead, sailed together from Liverpool on the three-masted *NAIAD* bound for New York. Leslie, as the older brother, was second mate despite being only 18 years of age and his brother John was just completing his apprenticeship indentures. By the time they reached New York they had deeply regretted their choice of ship and were facing a long and unwelcome voyage to Australia. They therefore decided to ask their father for funds to buy tickets as passengers back to Britain and were fortunate that their father responded by forwarding the sum of £37 10s to pay for both of his sons to return to Liverpool. The brothers were, however, committed to the *NAIAD* and would have to desert, losing their wages and personal effects, apart from suffering the disgrace of jumping ship. They were aware of the presence of a large Cunard liner in New York, about to depart for Liverpool and with their fare secure, they approached an officer on the Cunarder to book their passage for the return home. The officer however offered them positions as able seamen as several of their own seamen had deserted during the stay in New York.

Encouraged by the prospect of a quick return to Britain, the two brothers needed to make a discreet departure from the *NAIAD* so, donning as much clothing as they could wear with as many of their belongings as they could secrete in their clothing, they sneaked off the ship with two other crew members. No longer needing the £37 10s for passage, they decided to celebrate their escape from the *NAIAD* and spent their father's gift on a full night of entertainment on Broadway. They reported for duty on board the Cunard liner *LUSITANIA* the following morning at 08:00, Friday 30 April, prior to departure the following day.

The two brothers may or may not have been aware that Germany had declared that '... *on and after February 18th 1915, every enemy merchant ship found in the said War Zone will be destroyed without it being always possible to avoid the dangers threatening the crew and passengers on that account*'.[51] Additionally a widely promulgated announcement was made by the Imperial German Embassy in Washington on 22 April 1915, emphasising the risks to be taken by trans-Atlantic passengers on British ships:

> *Travellers intending to embark on the Atlantic voyage are reminded that a state of war exists between Germany and her allies and Great Britain and her allies; that the zone of war includes the waters adjacent to the British Isles; that, in accordance with formal notice given by the Imperial German Government, vessels flying the flag of Great Britain or of any of her allies, are liable to destruction in those waters and that travellers sailing in the war zone on ships of Great Britain or her allies do so at their own risk.*

LUSITANIA, along with another large Cunard liner, the MAURITANIA, had been built with government subsidies to enable them readily to be converted into armed merchant cruisers. In the event however, on the grounds that their heavy fuel consumption of 1,200 tons of coal a day would have made them unsuitable as cruisers, neither liner was in fact converted. Although *LUSITANIA* was unarmed, she had nevertheless been listed as an auxiliary cruiser in the authoritative publication *Jane's Fighting Ships* and in *The Naval Annual* of 1914 – both of which would have been available to German warships.[52]

The prestigious holder of the Blue Riband for the fastest Atlantic crossing, RMS *LUSITANIA* had left New York on 1 May with 1,959 souls on board for her 202nd Atlantic crossing, bound for Liverpool with Captain William Turner in command. Of 30,393 tons and briefly the world's biggest ship when she was built in 1907, she was capable of a speed of 25 knots. Her passengers, including a large number of Americans, paid little heed to the warnings on the basis that *LUSITANIA*, as a passenger ship without valuable cargo for the war effort and carrying many neutrals, could be of

---

[51]   Hurd, *The Merchant Navy*, Vol. 1, p.410.

[52]   Poolman, *Armed Merchant Cruisers*, p.36.

little interest to German U-boats and too fast for a U-boat attack.

The passage was uneventful until approaching the Irish coast when Captain Turner received notification from Admiral Sir Charles Henry Coke to divert to Queenstown rather than go directly to Liverpool and was warned that there may be U-boats in the vicinity. Admiral Coke however had not advised Captain Turner that that the cruiser HMS *JUNO*, which had been detailed to escort *LUSITANIA*, had been recalled to Queenstown as she had been considered to be unfit for such a task. No substitute escort was offered. On 6 May, all lifeboats under davits were swung out ready for lowering and watertight doors shut, lookouts doubled and port holes covered as a precaution with the liner entering a known danger area.

On 7 May, *Kapitanleutnant* Walter Schweiger in U-20 was patrolling off the coast of Ireland where the morning had been very calm and misty with reduced visibility. By afternoon, the mist had cleared and at around 2 p.m. Schweiger sighted what, as he said later, he thought to be the topsides of warships which, when coming closer, resolved to be a single, large four-funnelled passenger liner. Without disclosing his position or giving any warning, he fired a single torpedo which struck the liner amidships. It was only then, claimed Schweiger, that he realised he had hit the *LUSITANIA*. The effect was devastating and within 20 minutes the huge liner had sunk, leaving the sea crowded with struggling men, women and children. Schweiger noted in his war diary: '*It looks as if the ship will stay afloat for a very short time. I gave the order to dive to 25 metres and leave the area seawards. I couldn't have fired another torpedo into this mass of humans trying to save themselves.*' He later stated that he was appalled at the carnage he had caused and disappeared from the scene '*moved by mixed feelings*'.[53]

A second explosion on *LUSITANIA* had occurred, which was initially thought to have been a second torpedo, but which may have been the ship's boilers exploding or indeed from the ignition of her part cargo of cartridges. The sighting of the torpedo approaching the liner is best described by an American passenger, Mr James Brooks of Connecticut:

None of my fellow passengers regarded a submarine attack as a serious possibility, and we had a very comfortable voyage, favoured by pleasant weather. A good

---

[53] Hurd, *The Merchant Navy*, Vol. 1, p.418.

many passengers were still at lunch when, on Friday afternoon, the attack came in reality. I had just finished a run on deck, and had reached the Marconi deck, when I glanced out over the water. It was perfectly smooth. My eyes alighted on a white streak making its way with lightning-like rapidity towards the ship. I was so high, in that position, above the surface of the water that I could make out the outline of the torpedo. It appeared to be about twelve feet long, and came along possibly three feet below the surface, its sides white with bubbles of foam. I watched its passage, fascinated, until it passed out of sight behind the bridge, and in another moment came the explosion. The ship recoiling under the force of the blow was jarred and lifted, as if it had struck an immovable object. A column of water shot up to the bridge deck, carrying with it a lot of debris, and, despite the fact that I must have been twenty yards from the spot at which the torpedo struck, I was knocked off my feet. Before I could recover myself, the iron forepart of the ship was enveloped in a blinding cloud of steam, due, not, I think, to the explosion of a second torpedo, as some thought, but to the fact that the two forehold boilers had been jammed close together and 'jack-knifed upwards'.

It is worth noting the description of the ship being 'lifted', bearing in mind that *LUSITANIA* was one of the biggest ships in the world with a weight in the water, or displacement, of over 44,000 tons, which provides some insight into the dreadful explosive power of a torpedo. Following the explosion, *LUSITANIA* took a rapid list to starboard, severely limiting the attempts to launch lifeboats on the port side of the ship. Mr Brooks continued:

All the boats on the ship had been swung out the day previous, and the work of launching them was at once commissioned. The attempt in the case of the first boat was a tragic failure. The women and children were taken first, and the boat was practically filled with them, there being only a few men. The boat was lowered until within its own length of the water, when the forward tackle jammed, and the whole of its occupants, with the exception of three, were thrown into the water. The LUSITANIA was then on an even keel. On the decks of the doomed vessel absolute coolness prevailed. There was no rushing about, and nothing remotely resembling a panic.

A different account emerged from another American passenger, a Mr Isaac Lehmann from New York, who claimed that the crew were not doing enough to launch the boats after having witnessed one failed launching. Concerned with what he had just witnessed he went to his cabin and, in his words, *'I don't know whatever possessed me, but I looked into my dress suit case and got hold of my revolver, as I figured this would come in handy in case there was anybody not doing the proper thing.'* Returning to the boat deck, Mr Lehmann saw one boat ready for launching with 30 to 40 persons on board and crew members standing by the falls. He demanded of one of the seamen why the boat was not being launched and received the reply that the captain had yet to order the launching of the boats. Mr Lehmann stated, *'My reply was, "To hell with the Captain!' Don't you see the boat is sinking? And the first man that disobeys my orders to launch this boat I shoot to kill.'"* The seamen responded to this threat by beginning to launch the lifeboat when the ship lurched, smashing the lifeboat against the ship's side and, according to Mr Lehmann, *'... killing pretty much all of them.'*

Mr Lehmann clearly survived, having been rescued by one of the other lifeboats after spending about four hours in the water wearing his life preserver. He was transferred to HMS *WANDERER* and taken to the Queens Hotel in Queenstown, after which he stated that he had received no assistance or food from that point on and made his own way to London despite having sustained a wound to his leg. His concluding observations on the disaster were:

> *I would say that on board the steamer when she was sinking there was very little panic; everybody seemed to be resigned, but there was no real direction on the part of the officers or men who had charge of the boats, no one to command them and no one to give orders ... The greatest life-saving apparatus on the boat was the life preservers. People ran around looking for them, but none could be found. Then the lifeboats were so heavy that it took ten men to handle one boat, and those who are not experienced in this work cannot very well get them out."*

Mr Lehmann did not seem to consider his rush to his cabin to find and then threaten to use his pistol as a panic action. He had been on his way to Paris to negotiate the sale of a large quantity of cloth to the French government for military uniforms and the delay caused by the sinking and recovery from his injury in getting to Paris resulted in his failure to negotiate the contract.

He brought this case to the Mixed Claims Commission and while the Court deemed his claim that the sinking of *LUSITANIA* had caused him to lose the contract was speculative, he was nevertheless awarded $6,000.

The Formal Report of the Board of Trade to both houses of Parliament stated: '*Some of the passengers attempted to assist in launching the boats and, in my opinion, did more harm than good. It is, however, quite impossible to impute any blame to them. They were all working for the best.*'[54]

While the crew of *LUSITANIA* had been drilled in the lowering of the lifeboats, no boat drill, or allocations of passengers to boat stations, had been carried out on the basis that passengers might be unduly alarmed by such an exercise. Similarly, passengers had not been shown how to use their life preservers, with reports of some passengers wearing them upside down or even with their heads through the arm holes. Against that background it is perhaps surprising that, given the short time available to evacuate the ship combined with the increasing list of the ship, plus injuries to passengers and crew, there was not more mishap and confusion in escaping from the sinking ship. Many witnesses provided testimony to the effect that *LUSITANIA* had gone down with many people on deck and lifeboats with passengers on board still in their davits.

On the bridge of the stricken ship, the deserter from the *NAIAD*, Leslie Morton, had the 14:00–16:00 watch as lookout on the starboard side of the bridge, with his ex-*NAIAD* shipmate, Arthur Elliot on the port side. Leslie was credited as being the first to spot the torpedo, although he always maintained there were two of them, and called out the warning to the officers on the bridge. He then left the bridge to seek out his brother and warn him to get his life preserver on before going to his boat station. Once there he assisted passengers to climb into the lifeboat, stepping across the gap between the boat and the ship's side due to the list. An officer gave the order to lower away and the boat was successfully lowered. *LUSITANIA* was however still moving forward and as soon as the boat reached the water it was pulled astern but still held by the lifeboat falls. Leslie decided to climb down the falls to release the boat from the ship's side, but before he could reach the boat, another lifeboat fell on top of the one just launched, spilling

---

[54] Koerver, (ed.) *German Submarine Warfare in the Eyes of British Intelligence*, p.262.

its passengers into the sea and crushing those remaining in the boat just launched underneath it, with an understandably high loss of life. In Leslie Morton's account he says that he helped other boats to be lowered and then, with his brother, jumped into the sea and *'just swam for it'*. He found a collapsible liferaft, which he managed to set up by erecting the sides of the raft and helped others to board. He and another seaman, Joseph Parry, picked up a number of passengers in the water, after first diving out of the raft to find some oars, and rowed the survivors to a small fishing vessel. After that they returned to the scene to pick more survivors out of the water and to rescue some from a sinking lifeboat. Eventually they were all picked up by the minesweeper HMS *INDIAN EMPIRE*, after rescuing some 70 to 80 survivors, and landed at Queenstown. John Morton also survived but their ex-*NAIAD* shipmate, Arthur Elliott, did not. Leslie, who became a witness at the Wreck Commissioner's Inquiry was congratulated for his bravery and was awarded the Silver Board of Trade Medal for Gallantry in Saving Lives at Sea.

Another notable hero of the day was First Officer Arthur Jones who successfully lowered two lifeboats, boarding the last one himself as *LUSITANIA* sank. He managed to get all passengers to a small fishing vessel, the *BLUEBELL*, which had rushed to help. He returned to the scene of the sinking, picking up more survivors and ferrying them to *BLUEBELL* and to a nearby trawler. He made many return journeys to the site of the sinking to find more survivors, by which time he and his boat crew were close to exhaustion, but he was able to transfer them to a Queenstown tender, the *FLYING FOX*, finally landing at Queenstown some nine hours after the loss of *LUSITANIA*.

Out of the 1,959 souls on board, 1,257 passengers and 702 crew, a total of 1,198 lives were lost, making the sinking of *LUSITANIA* the worst maritime disaster of the war, with only 289 bodies recovered, many of which were unidentifiable. The ship's complement included 440 women and children, of whom 95 died. There were 25 women among the crew, 21 of whom were stewardesses, with only 8 of them having survived.[55] That loss was considered so great that Cunard forbade the employment of women on their ships for the rest of the war. Among the dead were 140 American citizens and 94

[55] Ibid., pp.261–262.

children.[56] (Another source records 128 American citizens lost.)[57]

There were many accounts of the carnage and despair of people in the water, including references to bodies observed floating upside down because the life preservers had been incorrectly worn. One passenger, Miss Alice Middleton, recounted that as *LUSITANIA* listed, '... *we had to cling to the side* [rail] *to keep us from rolling* [about], *then she exploded and down came a funnel, so I jumped over. I had a terrible time in the water; four and a half hours bashing about among the wreckage and dead bodies.*' She was unconscious when picked out of the water and landed at Qeenstown, and '*In fact they piled me with a boat of dead and it was only when they were carrying the dead bodies to the mortuary that they discovered there was life in me, and ran* [me] *in a motor to the hospital, so with the good attentions of the doctor and nurses they managed to get life into me.*'[58]

Among the crew losses were boys of 16 and 17, George Ronnan, Paul Wiencke, George Bates and Thomas Quinn. There were also boys of 15 working as stewards' boys, and for some it was not even their first voyage. Perhaps the most despairing and heart-rending reported sight of all, among the chaos and carnage, with dead and dying people in the darkening water as evening descended, was that of a poor woman, alone, actually giving birth among the waves.[59]

Admiralty guidelines for merchant ships included the advice to '*Avoid headlands near which submarines routinely lurked and found their best hunting*' but it was known that the Admiralty codes had recently been broken by the Germans, who were therefore well aware of that advice. In turn, British codebreakers in Room 40 in Whitehall were aware of German submarine positions. Captain Turner received a message informing him that a U-boat was active well to the south of the Irish coast, so he altered course to pass about 12 miles off the Old Head of Kinsale to avoid that submarine position. That message was sent and received on 7 May but, unknown to Captain Turner, that message in fact referred to the previous day's position of the U-boat. Believing that *LUSITANIA* was now clear of the U-boat threat and safely within the protection of the Royal Navy, Captain Turner did not carry

---

[56] Thompson, *The War at Sea 1914–1918*, p.192.

[57] Hough, *The Great War at Sea 1914–1918*, p.175.

[58] Thompson, *The War at Sea 1914–1918*, p.194.

[59] Bridgland, *Outrage at Sea*, p.8.

out zigzag manoeuvres and had reduced speed, at Cunard's instructions, to arrive at Liverpool to avoid anchoring to await the tide.

The Admiralty was most concerned that no blame for the loss of this prestigious ship should be laid at their door, with Churchill and Admiral Fisher deciding that Captain Turner should be held to blame; that he had disobeyed orders and should face charges of gross negligence and of deliberately putting his ship in harm's way. The wish of both Churchill and Fisher was that Captain Turner should be arrested immediately after the Inquiry 'whatever the verdict'. The orders that Captain Turner was charged with disobeying related to measures to protect liners against submarine attack, and were not issued until *after* the incident and, further, survivors were invited to claim that *LUSITANIA* had been struck by *two* torpedoes and not one, to explain the massive second explosion which occurred. This second explosion, which caused more damage than the torpedo strike, in fact may have been caused by the on-board munitions, which the Admiralty denied were on board or, more likely, by the ship's own boilers. The Admiralty's concern was that the public would not believe that such a large ship could be destroyed by a single torpedo and that further questions would be asked. Churchill had earlier expressed the view that that it was '*most important to attract neutral shipping to our shores, in the hope especially of embroiling the United States with Germany.*' It also transpired that Cunard had asked specifically for a naval escort for the *LUSITANIA*, which had been refused, and that Captain Turner's request to sail north around Ireland to approach Liverpool had been denied by the Admiralty. (Later that afternoon the log of Schweiger records that other large steamers had been sighted, noting, '*It is remarkable, that there being so much traffic on this particular day, although a day before south of the St. George Channel two big steamers have been sunk. Also that the LUSITANIA has not been sent through the North Channel is inexplicable.*')[60]

The full story and the claims of a conspiracy to see a large liner being sunk with American citizens on board to hasten the United States' participation in the war may never be fully known as the communications between the *LUSITANIA* and the Admiralty in the two days leading up to the sinking remain a mystery.[61]

---

[60] Koerver, (ed), *German Submarine Warfare in the Eyes of British Intelligence*, p.271.

[61] 'Secrets of the Lusitania', *The Week*, 9 May 2015.

At the Wreck Commissioner's Inquiry, led by Lord Mersey (who had previously presided over the *TITANIC* Inquiry), it became clear that the Admiralty case was unsound, with significant errors and omissions of fact. Lord Mersey was reputed to be enraged by the Admiralty case and cleared Captain Turner of all charges. In a carefully worded statement to avoid reference to the charges made by the Admiralty, after expert advice, Lord Mersey wrote:

> *The conclusion at which I have arrived is that blame should not be imputed to the Captain. The advice given to him, although meant for his most serious and careful consideration was not intended to deprive him of the right to exercise his skilled judgement in the difficult questions that might arise from time to time in the navigation of his ship … The whole blame for the cruel destruction of life in this catastrophe must rest solely with those who plotted and with those who committed the crime.*

After the publication of the Inquiry Report, Lord Mersey stated, '*The LUSITANIA case was a damned dirty business.*' He refused to accept his fees and resigned immediately.

Captain Turner was the Commodore Captain of Cunard with a long history of distinguished service and personal bravery in various previous rescues at sea. He retained the full confidence of Cunard and returned to sea when, in command of the troop-carrying *IVERNIA*, he survived the sinking of his ship by UB-47 with the loss of 125 lives on New Year's Day 1917 in the Mediterranean. The stigma of the allegations made against Captain Turner remained with him for the rest of his life, with the case reignited by the publication in 1921 of Churchill's four-volume tome *The World Crisis*, where allegations were again made against him. His wife, Alice, had left him after the *LUSITANIA* Inquiry in 1915, emigrating to Australia with their two sons, Percy and Norman. In the mid-1920s, after his retirement, Turner went to Australia to find them and discovered that they had moved to Canada – he never saw them again. (The eldest son, Percy, followed his father's footsteps and went to sea, but was later killed in a torpedo attack by a German U-boat in 1941.) Captain Turner was awarded an OBE in 1918 and died in Liverpool in 1933 at the age of 77, as a virtual recluse in the shadow of the false Admiralty allegations.

The sinking of the *LUSITANIA*, as an unarmed passenger ship was met with outrage and condemnation by the Allies and the neutral nations. Washington delivered a strongly worded protest to Berlin and demanded that attacks on all passenger ships should cease. Theodore Roosevelt stated the act was one of piracy '*on a vaster scale of murder than any old-time pirate ever practised*'. A Dutch newspaper called the outrage '*an act opposed to every law and every sentiment of humanity*'; a Swedish paper regarded it as '*an unpardonable crime against humanity*' and a Norwegian paper described the sinking as '*a mad and reckless action*' on which '*The whole world looks with horror and detestation of the event.*'

The American Ambassador in Berlin, mistakenly believing he may be recalled as a protest against the sinking, asked a leading German banker to take care of his valuables for safekeeping, to which the banker replied, through a secretary, '*Tell Judge Gerard I will take care of his valuables for him, but tell him also that if the MAURITANIA comes out tomorrow, we shall sink her too.*'[62]

The German response to the sinking was generally one of great approval as an outstanding victory against British sea power. The German press claimed the sinking of *LUSITANIA* was a great demonstration of Germany's determination to win the war and those who had supported unrestricted submarine warfare proclaimed this to be vindication of their support. Press claims were also made that the success of U-20 '*must be placed beside the greatest achievements of the naval war*'. German cities set out to honour the crew of U-20 and a medal was struck in Munich in commemoration of the act. Admiral von Tirpitz supported the action taken by Schweiger and was much in favour of the continuation of such sinkings. The German Centre Party wrote, in their *Kölnische Volkszeitung* paper,

> *The sinking of the giant English steamship is a success of moral significance which is still greater than material success. With joyful pride we contemplate this latest deed of our Navy. It will not be the last. The English wish to abandon the German people to death by starvation. We are more humane. We simply sank an English ship with passengers, who, at their own risk and responsibility, entered the zone of operations.*[63]

---

[62] Gilbert, *First World War*, p.157.

[63] Ibid., pp.157–158.

The German press professed indignation over the 'slanderous' remarks in the British and American press concerning the *LUSITANIA*'s destruction. They claimed the German Navy had informed them that the ship had been a powerful, armed auxiliary cruiser and argued that Schweiger had achieved a remarkable success simply doing his duty. (The German government had also suspected that *LUSITANIA* may have been carrying armaments and indeed later examination of the wreck showed evidence of large quantities of ammunition carried in the cargo holds.)

The question as to whether Schweiger had been specifically instructed by High Command to sink *LUSITANIA* can be answered partially by statements obtained later from German prisoners of war claiming that U-20 had received positive orders to do so, as the ship was carrying munitions of war, arguing that the commanding officer was placed in a very difficult situation. The informant, a submarine *Kapitänleutnant*, added, '*The* [commanding] *officer was placed in a very difficult position, and I myself would probably have acted in the same way under the circumstances, but I should have been very sorry indeed to do it.*'[64] There was anecdotal evidence circulating in German naval circles that Schweiger had been ordered to lie in wait for *LUSITANIA*. Although hailed as a hero in Germany and despite being lauded and presented with the prestigious House Order of the Hohenzollern [*an award for outstanding chivalry*], he appeared to be anything but proud of his feat.[65]

On the other side of the world, in Shanghai, German and British expatriates, with others, had shared social activities and maintained scrupulous impartiality in their dealings with each other, on the basis that they were not responsible for the actions of their respective governments. That all changed when several Germans publicly drank a toast '*To the Loss of the LUSITANIA and the success of the German Navy*' in a Shanghai club. The cordial relations which had hitherto existed between the Germans and the British were, unsurprisingly, rapidly severed and the committees of the Shanghai Club, the Race Club and the Country Club demanded that their German members should cease the use of the clubs' facilities until further notice.

The U-boat activities and the international outcry over their actions in sinking merchant ships without warning were nevertheless becoming

---

64   The National Archives, ADM 137/3872 and ADM 116/1513.

65   Koerver,(ed), *German Submarine Warfare in the Eyes of British Intelligence*, p.174.

increasingly troublesome to the German authorities, both in the matters of internal and external relationships. Although Germany had given orders on 6 June that large passenger ships should not be sunk, there appeared to be little constraint on U-boat activities. The Imperial Chancellor, Bethmann-Hollweg, considered that submarine warfare should be restricted but the naval authorities, supported by the Kaiser, stood firm and told the Chancellor that the campaign must continue unless he would accept sole responsibility for the outcome of a cessation. Some compromise was reached whereby only British ships would continue to be sunk without warning and, eventually, there should be a direction that no passenger ships at all should be sunk without warning. The Chancellor was concerned that the patience and tolerance of America was being sorely tried with the loss of American lives on *LUSITANIA*, following so soon, despite American protests, after the loss of the *FALABA*.

Despite the early celebrations of the German 'victory' over *LUSITANIA*, it soon became clear to the German Navy that the sinking had been a major political error such that the wanton act could have grave consequences for Germany in terms of relationships with neutral countries, particularly America.

The German Chancellor's concerns about the sinking of passenger ships without warning and American tolerance were soon to be tested. On the afternoon of 18 August, the White Star liner *ARABIC*, with a crew of 248 and 186 passengers, including 26 Americans, had left Liverpool bound for New York. A medium-sized passenger liner of 15,801 tons she was commanded by Captain William Finch who, conscious of the fact that he was in an area frequented by German submarines, had taken due precautions by preparing lifeboats for immediate launching, closing watertight bulkheads and posting additional lookouts. In the morning of 19 August, when about 50 miles off the Old Head of Kinsale, not far from *LUSITANIA*'s grave, Captain Finch had his attention drawn to a ship ahead of him in a sinking condition which turned out to be the British steamer *DUNSLEY*, with two lifeboats near her with sails set. Radio messages were sent from *ARABIC* to notify the Admiralty of the situation and, aware of Admiralty instructions not to go to the aid of a sinking ship in that area on the basis that there could still be a U-boat in the vicinity, he turned away from the *DUNSLEY* and called for maximum speed. At this point U-24 appeared from behind the sinking *DUNSLEY* and fired a single torpedo without any warning at *ARABIC*. The torpedo was seen by Second Officer F.F. Steele who ordered '*hard a'starboard*' and Captain Finch called for emergency full speed but to no avail as the torpedo struck aft. Captain Finch then immediately called for '*full speed astern*' to take the way off the ship to enable lifeboats to be lowered, but the effect of the explosion was instantaneous and devastating, with the stricken ship taking an immediate initial list to port before lurching over and taking a heavier list to starboard, sinking some eight minutes after the torpedo struck.

The order was given to abandon ship and, even though there was so little time available, with the operation exacerbated by the list, the lowering of boats was carried out in an orderly fashion. Despite that, No. 16 boat, with over 40 persons on board was capsized by the suction caused by the sinking of *ARABIC* and then struck by a falling davit resulting in the loss of most of those in the boat.[66] As usual, there were many reports of selflessness and courage, including the actions of Captain Finch who remained on the bridge directing operations until his ship sank, stern first, with Captain Finch going down with his charge. He fortunately re-surfaced and managed to cling to a raft before swimming to a boat where he was able to help others into it before boarding it himself. He then managed to rescue several others out of the wreckage. The chief officer, Mr Bowen, and first officer, Mr Oliver, had stayed on the bridge with their captain, finally diving into the sea to be picked up by one of the boats. In the engine room, a junior engineer, Mr P.G. Logan, had stayed by his post until he could serve no useful purpose and climbed up on deck just in time to help a quartermaster release the falls of a boat before the ship went down. As the ship was sinking, Mr Logan saw a collapsible boat with six or seven persons in it having great difficulty in controlling it so, removing his heavy protective engine-room boots, he dived into the sea and swam to the collapsible, taking charge and, rowing towards the wreckage strewn across the sea, he was able to rescue some 14 other persons from the water. Other acts of outstanding courage were shown by the carpenter, Mr. N. MacAuley, seamen, firemen and stewards, as well as passengers. The survivors were rescued and taken to Queenstown, where *ARABIC*'s surviving lifeboats were later collected and put on public display.

---

[66] Hurd, *The Merchant Navy*, Vol. 2, p.28.

The *ARABIC* had been equipped with 16 lifeboats and 22 collapsible boats, all of which had their lashings loosened as a precaution against emergency release and indeed the collapsibles and rafts floated clear when the ship sank. Out of a total crew of 248 and 186 passengers, including 26 Americans, many of whom were showbusiness people, 44 lives were lost. It is a tribute to Captain Finch and his officers and crew that the loss of life was not higher, given the circumstances of the torpedo attack. A Mr Thomas Scott, Secretary of the Merchant Marine Association, in a letter to the Secretary of the Admiralty dated 27 August 1915 wrote:

Dear Sir,

I am desired by the Council of this Association to invite the attention of my Lords Commissioners of the Admiralty to the qualities of seamanship displayed by Captain W. Finch, Master of the White Star Steamer ARABIC, which was sunk by a German Submarine when the courage and discipline evinced proved to be of the finest character thus accounting for the comparatively very small loss of life which ensued.

The submarine which had sunk both the *DUNSLEY* and *ARABIC* was the U-24, under the command of *Kapitänleutnant* Rudolf Schneider, who had already achieved the distinction of committing the first submarine atrocity of the war when he sank the French steamer *AMIRAL GANTEAUME* on 26 October 1914 with a loss of 40 lives. Although the German authorities had stated on 16 June that no more passenger ships would be sunk without warning, Schneider claimed that he thought *ARABIC* was a troop ship carrying armaments. The unlikely scenario of a British ship carrying armaments *away* from Britain to America suggests this was but a poor excuse to disregard his instructions.

The further loss of American lives soon after the loss of the *LUSITANIA* brought even further outcries from the American public about German brutality. Germany was already under considerable political pressure to curb U-boat actions against passenger ships and was forced to make a promise that in future no passenger liners would be attacked if not engaged in a hostile act. Indeed, secret orders were sent to all submarines to stop all activities on the west coast of Britain and the English Channel on 18 September and to confine their activities to the North Sea, acting within the Prize Code restrictions.

The Australian newspaper, the *Argus of Melbourne* on 23 August wrote '*It is time to have done with a nation which repudiates every scrap of international law. Germany has adopted a policy which is a challenge to humanity and a negation of all that civilisation means.*' The *New York Journal of Commerce* wrote, '*Does there exist no power in the civilised world to keep this arrogant barbarianism within bounds?*'

The sinking of *ARABIC* was additionally embarrassing to Germany politically in terms of the increasing rift between the German Foreign Ministry and the Naval High Command in Berlin. Following the sinking of *LUSITANIA* the United States expressly invited the German government publicly to state disapproval of that sinking and advised that any further actions resulting in the death of US citizens would be regarded as a '*deliberately unfriendly action*'. Following the *ARABIC* sinking, both the German Chancellor and the German Foreign Secretary, Gottlieb von Jagow, sought the Kaiser's approval to spare all passenger ships from U-boat attacks, bypassing the authority of the German Admiralty. Admiral von Tirpitz was sufficiently angered by being bypassed that he offered to resign, but his resignation was not accepted and the Kaiser continued to support his Chancellor's view on the matter.

The German Ambassador to the United States, von Bernstorff, had been given the somewhat difficult task of pacifying American feelings and was still in the midst of diplomatic entreaties regarding the *LUSITANIA* when *ARABIC* was sunk. On 5 October 1915, von Bernstorff sent the following letter to the US Secretary of State Robert Lancing:

> *Dear Mr. Secretary,*
>
> *Prompted by the desire to reach a satisfactory agreement with regard to the Arabic incident, my Government has given me the following instructions.*
>
> *The orders issued by His Majesty the Emperor to the commanders of the German submarines – of which I notified you on a previous occasion – have been made so stringent that the recurrence of incidents similar to the Arabic case is considered out of the question.*
>
> *According to the report of Commander Schneider of the submarine that sank the Arabic, and his affidavit as well as those of his men, Commander Schneider was convinced that the Arabic intended to ram the submarine. On the other hand, The Imperial Government does not doubt the good faith of the affidavits of the British officers of the Arabic, according to which Arabic did*

not intend to ram the submarine. The attack of the submarine, therefore, was undertaken against the instructions issued to the commander. The Imperial Government regrets and disavows this act and has notified Commander Schneider accordingly.

Under these circumstances my Government is prepared to pay an indemnity for the American lives which, to its deep regret, have been lost on the Arabic. I am authorized to negotiate with you about the amount of this indemnity.

I remain (etc)

J. von Bernstorff

Needless to say, the US government was not particularly impressed by this letter, but recognised the diplomatic implications of this apology. Nevertheless, the *LUSITANIA* and *ARABIC* sinkings brought about a step change in the opinions of the American public and increased pressure on the American government about the retention of their neutral status. The testing of America's resolve to protect its citizens yet remain neutral in the war was a very dangerous game to play.

There was of course nothing the merchant seafarers could do about this situation, even if they were aware of the political dimensions of the US/German negotiations. In practice all it meant was that the seafarer stood a greater likelihood of being murdered if serving on a cargo ship or a fishing boat than on a passenger liner.

The Admiralty view of the action of the *ARABIC* was that while the action and courage displayed by Captain Finch saved many lives, '*No ocean-going British Merchant Vessel is permitted to go to the assistance of a ship which has been torpedoed by a submarine*' and, with regard to the master of *DUNSLEY*, '*A ship which is pursued by, or escaping from, a Submarine should fly the largest ensign half mast at the foremast head or triatic stay. This, so far as can be ascertained, he does not seem to have done.*'[67] This Admiralty comment could be regarded by the merchant seafarers in much the same light as the earlier banal Admiralty advice that submarines provided little hazard to a merchant ship.

On 25 December 1917, the perpetrator of the *ARABIC* sinking, Rudolph Schneider, was in command of U-87 when the boat was lost with

---

[67]   The National Archives, ADM 137/1131.

all hands, initially rammed and then sunk by the Royal Navy.

In the meantime, away from the publicity and outcry about the brutal attacks on passenger ships, on American Independence Day, 4 July 1915, the 7,333-ton British horse transport steamer *ANGLO CALIFORNIAN*, under the command of Captain Frederick Parslow, was some 70 miles off Fastnet on her return from Montreal when she was sighted by *Kapitänleutnant* Walter Forstmann in U-39.

Captain Parslow was on the bridge of his ship as the watch was changing at 08:00 and looking forward shortly to coming under the protective umbrella of British coastal patrol warships when U-39 broke surface on the streamer's port beam. Captain Parslow responded by altering course to place the U-boat astern and ordered the engine room to give all maximum speed. At the normal speed of 12 knots, he hoped that emergency full speed might enable him to outrun the U-boat, at least until assistance could arrive in the form of the destroyers HMS *MENTOR* and HMS *MIRANDA* which had been alerted to his predicament by his wireless operator. The U-boat however was capable of 16.5 knots and soon began to overhaul the steamer, firing warning shots, but Captain Parslow kept going. His ship was unarmed but he was determined not to surrender until and unless all hope of escape was lost. He was joined on the bridge by one of his sons, Frederick Junior, who was the second officer, and together they manoeuvred the *ANGLO CALIFORNIAN* the best they could to avoid the shells now being firing at increased intensity and finding their mark on the steamer. By 10:30 the U-boat had almost overhauled the steamer and Forstmann signalled to stop the ship. With his ship by this time badly damaged Captain Parslow considered he could do no more and was unnecessarily risking the lives of his crew, including that of his son. He stopped his ship and began lowering his boats, with U-39 by now close at hand.

At that moment the radio officer handed Captain Parslow a message indicating that the British warships were nearby to deal with the U-boat and offering encouragement to hold on. Parslow needed no encouragement and took the decision that if he could hold off the U-boat for even a short period, he might save his ship. He ordered full speed and all hands, other than his son, below decks where they would not be so exposed to gunfire. His son took the helm and, on the exposed bridge, father and son attempted to elude the gunfire, but the situation soon became hopeless when the chief officer,

Harold Read, reported heavy damage and fire in one of the holds. Captain Parslow felt they could survive under fire no longer and again gave the order to abandon ship, spurred by the signal from U-39 that if he did not feel he needed his lifeboats then the U-boat would shoot them away. Under Chief Officer Read's guidance four boats were cleared away, but coming under fire from the submarine many of the ship's crew were killed. Second Officer Parslow remained on the bridge and was witness to his father being killed alongside him. Captain Parslow did not survive long enough to see the arrival of the destroyers, at which time Forstmann decided he should vacate the scene.

The *ANGLO CALIFORNIAN* was saved, eventually reaching Queenstown harbour under the command of Mr Read, with Frederick Junior unharmed. Captain Parslow was buried at Queenstown with eight members of his crew but a further 11 had only the Atlantic as their grave. After the war, Captain Parslow was posthumously appointed as a lieutenant in the RNR and awarded the Victoria Cross [*it could not have been awarded to a civilian*]. His citation included the words '*Throughout the attack Lt. Parslow remained on the bridge on which the enemy fire was concentrated entirely without protection and by his magnificent heroism succeeded, at the cost of his own life, in saving a valuable ship and cargo for his own country. He set a splendid example to the officers and men of the Merchant Marine.*'[68] Frederick Junior was commissioned as a sub-lieutenant and awarded the Distinguished Service Cross for his gallantry.

Captain Parslow had three sons. At the time of the action he was aware that one son had been killed in France and another lay wounded in a field hospital. It can only be a matter of conjecture whether that had any bearing on his reluctance to surrender his ship to the Germans. His son Frederick remained in the Merchant Navy, eventually gaining command with the same shipowners, Lawther, Latte & Co. of London. In March 1938, his ship the *ANGLO AUSTRALIAN* passed the Azores on her way to Panama. The last message, from Captain Parslow to the owners read, '*Passed Fayal this afternoon. Rough weather. All well.*' It was the last heard from Captain Parslow or the *ANGLO AUSTRALIAN*.

A commemorative paving stone as a tribute to Captain Parslow [*senior*] marking the centenary of the *ANGLO CALIFORNIAN* action is at the Islington Green War Memorial in London.

---

[68] Second Supplement to the *London Gazette* of Friday 23 May 1919.

CHAPTER 8

A BREATHING SPACE?

As more men were joining the armed forces, so women were increasingly being employed in jobs which had previously been the preserve of men. Trade unions were generally responding to the government's plea for peace during the war years and anti-war movements were discouraged, both within Britain and in Germany. An attempt by British women to participate in the International Women's Peace Congress in neutral Holland, on 18 April 1915, was curtailed by the simple expediency of the British government suspending the ferry service between Britain and Holland.

The first year of the war had seen a rapid descent from the generally honourable and chivalrous conduct of the German surface raiders to the barbarity shown by some U-boats, notwithstanding the practical limitations imposed on them in terms of their ability to take prisoners on board and their vulnerability to attack when on the surface. Against all expectations on both the German and British sides, the war had not finished in a few months and indeed seemed set to become a prolonged and vicious affair. Total British shipping losses from the start of the war to the end of August 1915 due to surface warships, mines and submarines, amounted to 470 vessels with the loss of 2,095 souls. Corresponding U-boat losses during the same period amounted to 20, although four of these were recorded as being lost from unknown causes.[69] During the month of August alone, a total of 126 merchant vessels were lost to U-boats, of which 78 were British,[70] at the cost of three U-boats.

The short-term period of unrestricted submarine warfare had not made

---

[69] Koerver, (ed.) *German Submarine Warfare in the Eyes of British Intelligence*, p.697.

[70] Ibid., p.693.

the catastrophic inroads into British imports as had been hoped for by various factions within Germany and U-boat losses had been higher than expected. The main effect was the loss of worldwide support for Germany due to the horror of the U-boat activities and the risk of drawing America into the war. From the end of September 1915 until March 1916, there was only one U-boat hunting in the Atlantic, the U-24, which nevertheless managed to sink four merchant ships in December 1915, albeit in accordance with the Prize Code.[71] While the Kaiser had supported calling off the six-week unrestricted submarine campaign in August 1915, there was still the increasing dispute between Britain and the United States on the 'stop and search' contraband control exercised by British warships.

The United States was facing other problems nearer to home when, on 19 January 1916 the newly appointed German Foreign Minister, Dr Alfred von Zimmermann, sent a telegram to the Mexican government outlining a plan whereby should the submarine activities bring the United States into the war, then Germany could win active support from Mexico by giving 'generous' financial assistance to Mexico to win back some of their lost territories from the USA. A few days later, on 23 January, the German Ambassador in Washington, Count Bernstorff, asked Berlin for $50,000 to influence members of the US Congress to keep the United States out of the war. Needless to say, the 'Zimmermann Plan' caused outrage in America once it was discovered.

On 3 February *Kapitänleutnant* Hans Rose, in command of U-53, sank the US steamer *HOUSATONIC* off the Isles of Scilly and bound for Liverpool, in accordance with the Prize Code, on the grounds that it was carrying grain of use to the enemy. In Berlin, Zimmermann told the American Ambassador, *'Everything will be alright. America will do nothing, for President Wilson is for peace and nothing else. Everything will go on as before.'*[72]

The sinking of the *HOUSATONIC* had come at a very difficult time for President Wilson who had recently been elected on the platform of keeping the US out of the war. Zimmerman had seriously misjudged the mood in the US and President Wilson broke off diplomatic relations with Germany, following which he published the Zimmerman Plan to expose Germany's attempt to bring Mexico into the war.

---

[71] Ibid., p.xxv.

[72] Gilbert, *First World War,* p.308.

In the light of those disputes, and despite the soured relations with the US, German authorities took the view that the cessation of the unrestricted attacks would improve relations with the United States and that American hostility to U-boat attacks might be lessened if the U-boats were to give prior warning of an attack on an individual ship. A dichotomy arose however that if merchant ships were equipped with guns, it became a hazardous operation for a U-boat to surface and reveal itself to warn the merchant ship of an impending attack. This was also viewed against the background of the German view that the Allied blockade of German ports was becoming a stranglehold.[73]

Ironically, fear from U-boat attack was not restricted to the Allies, as indicated by a plea made by the Austro-Hungarian governments, through the United States' Ambassadors in London and Vienna, with regard to the safe repatriation of their subjects from India. As reported in *The Times* of 20 March 1916, a petition in the previous December had been received from the married Austrian and Hungarian men interned at Ahmednagar, India, on behalf of their wives and children about to be repatriated on the *GOLCONDA*, a ship of the British India Steam Navigation Company. This petition, to be brought to the attention of the British government, announced that '... *the Imperial and Royal Government will hold them* [the British government] *responsible for the lives and wellbeing of these passengers – the majority of whom are better class people – who are being forcibly repatriated in wartime and against the will of their husbands and fathers'*. The petition also requested that '... *all belligerent nations be duly advised of the ship's departure and her route, and that she should be distinctly marked and that everything should be done to secure the safety of the passengers'*. Sir Edward Grey, on behalf of the British government, replied that he was astonished that the Austrian Government, which was one of the authors of the danger from submarine attacks, should have thought it seemly to endorse such a request and that he was unable to take any special precautions. No special acknowledgement was made of the claimed '*better class people*' but Grey observed that the proper precaution was '... *that Austria-Hungary and Germany should observe ordinary rules of humanity in their methods of warfare.*'

On the home front there had been initial panic buying and hoarding

---

73   Gray, *The U-Boat War 1914–1918*, pp.136–137.

of food at the outbreak of war, although that soon settled into a more disciplined awareness of likely shortages, with prices soaring. Queues at food shops increased but a newly formed government committee, acting under the Defence of the Realm Act, set prices for basic foodstuffs, although many felt these to be too high. A four-pound loaf of bread was to cost fivepence halfpenny and a pound of cheese ninepence per pound, at a time when wages stood at around £11 per month for an able bodied merchant seaman; about the same wage as a postal worker. Britain continued to import most of her foodstuffs, increasingly so as agricultural output fell as a consequence of men joining the armed services. Supplies of fuel were restricted and street lights dimmed. New laws required all windows to be fitted with blinds to be drawn at night, with severe penalties for contravention of these laws, which could be as much as £100 or six months imprisonment, at a time when there were genuine concerns about the bombing raids of the German Zeppelins which had begun in January 1915. Coal shortages brought about claims of profiteering and hoarding as the price of coal rose each month, with coal queues becoming as common as food queues. Plenty of advice was given in the popular newspapers of the day about how to save food, including government exhortations to keep warm so that less food would be needed, somewhat forgetting that there were coal shortages. On the few occasions that the merchant seafarer could return home for leave, conditions could be seen to have changed and worsened as shortages continued.

Although there was to be a relative lull in the U-boat activities, threat to and loss of life was still very much evident, with growing public hostility towards the German U-boat crews. The atrocity of the murder of the passengers and crew of *ARABIC* on 19 August had immediate consequences for the enemy. On the same day of *ARABIC*'s sinking, the British steamer *NICOSIAN* was on passage to Avonmouth under the command of Captain Manning, carrying passengers, mules and materials for the war effort. A Leyland liner of 6,379 tons, she was about 80 miles south of Queenstown when she was spotted by U-27 under the command of *Kapitänleutnant* Bernard Wegener. U-27 signalled *NICOSIAN* to stop and abandon the ship, and sent a boarding party over to be satisfied that the British steamer was carrying goods for the war campaign. U-27 then began shelling *NICOSIAN* once her boats were clear of the ship, much in accordance with the Prize Code.

At that time another steamer came into view, so Wegener decided to investigate the new arrival and moved between the then burning *NICOSIAN* and the escaping lifeboats, momentarily losing sight of the newcomer behind the *NICOSIAN*. The newcomer had been seen flying an American ensign and a flag signal to denote her request to rescue the survivors of *NICOSIAN* but, when she reappeared from behind *NICOSIAN*, she lowered the American flag, replacing it with the white ensign and revealing herself as the British Q-ship HMS *BARALONG*. The Q-ship immediately began shelling U-27, quickly sinking the surprised German submarine, with only a small number of survivors who had been on deck, including Wegener, jumping into the sea and swimming towards the nearby *NICOSIAN*. At that point the marines on board *BARALONG* were ordered to fire on the German survivors, despite their attempts to surrender. Some managed to swim to their latest victim and began to climb the boat ladders left hanging when *NICOSIAN* was evacuated. The marines continued firing, but when it was seen that a few Germans had managed to clamber up the boat ladders and get on board *NICOSIAN*, a party of marines was despatched to follow them and, in the reported words of their commander, '*take no prisoners*'. The Germans fled to the engine room in a desperate attempt to hide amongst the machinery but were soon found and killed.

HMS *BARALONG* was a converted merchant ship equipped with guns to act as a decoy to attract U-boats – a ploy adopted by both Allied and German naval forces. An ex-Ellerman and Bucknall steamer built in 1901, she was of around 4,000 tons, capable of 12 knots at full speed and looked a typical example of an ageing tramp steamer, although destined never to appear in the official Navy List. She was under the command of Lieutenant Commander Godfrey Herbert, who had been bitterly disappointed in not being able to assist the *ARABIC*, sunk earlier that day and only a few months after the *LUSITANIA* massacre. Indeed he later claimed that he thought he had found the U-boat responsible for the atrocity against the *ARABIC* and the party he sent out to find and kill the remaining German survivors was congratulated by Herbert on their achievement when they returned. The survivors from *NICOSIAN*, still in their lifeboats, then reboarded their damaged ship which, initially having been taken in tow by *BARALONG*, was able to make it back to Avonmouth under her own steam.

In Herbert's report, his description of the killing of the Germans who had made it to *NICOSIAN*'s engine room was, '*A thorough search was made which resulted in six of the enemy being found, but they succumbed to the injuries they had received ... and were buried at once.*'[74] The report also stated '*The recapture of the* NICOSIAN *by an armed party was a perfectly legitimate act of war, and the party put on board to do this could not afford to take risks, especially with people who it was thought had a few hours previously just sunk the defenceless* ARABIC.'[75]

Unsurprisingly, accounts of an incident such as this gained many variations as to what really happened to the few German sailors who made it to the *NICOSIAN*. Some of the crew of *NICOSIAN* who had yet to evacuate their damaged ship before the German survivors clambered on board gave accounts of extreme brutality meted out to the Germans by the marines from *BARALONG*. These included the act of 'furnace dipping' whereby the Germans were suspended over the open furnaces for the boilers before being beaten to death or even thrown alive into the furnaces, although such versions of events were never corroborated.[76] Other versions suggested that the muleteers still on board *NICOSIAN* had contributed to the capture and murder of the Germans and still other accounts suggested that the bodies of the Germans had been reviled before being thrown into the sea.[77] What is common to all accounts however is the considerable hatred and violence shown to the initial survivors of U-27 and that no trial or court martial of Herbert was ever held. At a later stage Herbert had stated that '*certain things were done in hot blood, which a calmer judgement might regret*'.[78]

News of the murder was received with horror and outrage in Germany and a strongly worded protest was sent from Germany, via the American Ambassador in London, demanding a war crimes trial for Lieutenant Commander Herbert. Sir Edward Grey, in reply, agreed that Herbert should be tried in a neutral court, but along with German submarine commanders who had committed similar atrocities, although that suggestion was not pursued by the German government. *BARALONG*'s name was changed as

---

[74] Koerver, (Ed.) 'German Submarine Warfare 1914-1918 in the Eyes of British Intelligence.' p.295

[75] Ibid p.297

[76] Coles, 'Slaughter at Sea.' p.168

[77] Ibid p.169

[78] Ibid., p.175.

were the names of her crew members, many of whom had been merchant seafarers, who then signed on later ships under different names for fear of reprisals should they be captured.

The Admiralty indeed made great efforts to conceal Commander Herbert's identity, including measures to falsify his war records. In his study of the *BARALONG* incident, Coles wrote, '*This shielding of Herbert might have been necessary at the time, but later the concealment of the truth virtually condemned his actions and was tantamount to finding him guilty without trial.*'[79] He was decorated with the DSO for sinking U-27.

Kapitänleutnant Bernard Wegener of U-27 had previously seen considerable action and had been responsible for sinking 12 ships, including a British submarine, E-3 with the loss of 28 men; HMS *HERMES* with the loss of 22 men; and HMS *BAYANO* with a loss of 200 lives. Altogether Wegener had been responsible for the loss of 240 British lives, plus 23 from the Spanish steamer *PENA CASTILLO*.

The lull in U-boat activity and the scarcity of German surface raiders at the beginning of 1916 had brought about a feeling of relief for British merchant shipping, especially if outside the declared war zone, although by no means was the danger from enemy activity removed. The newly built Clan Line steamer *CLAN MACTAVISH* had left Fremantle for London on 9 December 1915, calling at Durban and Cape Town and thence to Dakar to have a six-pounder gun fitted on her port quarter. Under the command of Captain W.N. Oliver and of 5,816 tons, she was passing off the Canary Islands in the early evening of 16 January 1916 when she spotted a ship on her port bow, with another vessel showing up shortly after. As the ships drew closer, Captain Oliver signalled the closing ship to identify herself and received the response that she was the British Harrison Line steamer *TRADER*, a ship known to Captain Oliver and, satisfied with that identification, he responded with his identity. The two ships were on converging courses, with *CLAN MACTAVISH* as the 'stand on' vessel and the *TRADER* to give way under international collision rules. As the two ships were steaming almost side by side, Captain Oliver began to feel uneasy as the other ship showed no signs of giving way, so he altered course to avoid a close quarters situation. At that point, the other vessel suddenly signalled, '*Stop at once. I am a German cruiser.*'

---

[79]   Ibid., p.160.

Captain Oliver did not know it at the time, but the threat was from the converted German merchant ship *MÖEWE*, fitted with significantly more powerful armament than his newly fitted six-pounder. However, with his newly built ship capable of better than 13 knots, Captain Oliver resolved not to surrender and ordered emergency full speed, sending his gun crew to their station. He immediately despatched a radio signal for help. He hoped that a British warship would be in the vicinity and gave his position, stating he was in imminent danger from an enemy ship. The *MÖEWE*, seeing that her order to stop was being ignored, opened fire on the Clan liner, with one shot landing on the foredeck and killing the lookout. The *CLAN MACTAVISH* responded with her single gun, which could only fire at a target on her port side and was soon suffering from the superior fire power of the German cruiser, whose shells wrecked the officers' accommodation, damaged the bridge and killed seven Lascar firemen in the stokehold, before bursting a main steam pipe. With his ship disabled and 18 men killed with five more wounded, Captain Oliver had little option but to cease fire and surrender his ship.

The *MÖEWE,* commanded by *Korvettenkapitän* Count Dohna-Schlodien, signalled to Captain Oliver to ask if he had any wounded on board and immediately sent a boat across to the *CLAN MACTAVISH* at the same time as the Clan liner was lowering her own boats. The German boarding party placed bombs on the British ship to sink her quickly and took Captain Oliver with his chief engineer and radio operator to the *MÖEWE* in the German's boarding party boat. The remaining survivors were escorted in their own boats back to the German raider, from which vantage point they witnessed the destruction of their ship.

Captain Oliver had destroyed all confidential documents and ensured his gun had been disabled. He noted as he boarded the *MÖEWE* that the bodies of a number of German sailors were being taken aft for burial before he was led to be interviewed by the German commander who wrote of that interview in his log:

When the Master reports to me, I take him severely to task for his criminal behaviour. The Master states that he disclaims all personal responsibility – he had received orders from his Government to get his ship through to England. Furthermore he had been provided with a gun, and he regarded it as his obvious duty to use it … I must own that I appreciate the loyalty with which this old Scottish seadog stuck to his principles, and I shook him warmly by the hand.[80]

An account of the capture and sinking of the *CLAN MACTAVISH* was later written by an officer of the *MÖEWE*, who had seemed to have regarded the Clan liner as a British warship;

The Clan Mactavish – as we later found out the ship was named – had cleared her deck for action and was aiming a heavy gunfire at us, of course, without any result. This was sufficient for Count Dohna to proceed again parallel to the steamer and rake her, not caring where our shots landed. Every salvo hit the mark. Soon we heard explosions on board and the ship was in a helpless position. Then her captain morsed; 'We stop', at the same time ceasing fire. The Möewe's guns were also silenced, and our prize crew went aboard the ship. The men were taken off her, and a Captain and two sailors of the British Navy, who were in civilian clothes, added to the numbers of our prisoners of war.[81]

Captain Oliver was taken back to Germany on the *MÖEWE*, spending the rest of the war in a German prisoner of war camp. He was not to know that his radio signal stating he was in danger of being captured by a German ship had in fact been received by the wireless operators of the nearby HMS *EXETER* but had not been passed up to the bridge. He was awarded a DSO and a Lloyd's Silver Medal for his action against the *MÖEWE* and became Marine Superintendent of the Clan Line before retiring. He died, in 1933 aged 66, while on a train journey in Scotland.

Count Dohna-Schlodien treated his prisoners well and the *MÖEWE* (or *SEAGULL*), in various guises also as *PUNGO* and *VINETTA*, had a long and successful career as a cruiser, maintaining a reputation for compassion in the observance of the Prize Code, so blatantly disregarded by so many of the submarine colleagues. *MÖEWE* was eventually captured and after the war served under the red ensign as the *GREENBRIER*, engaged in the fruit

---

[80]   Edwards, *'War Under the Red Ensign 1914-1918'*. p.87
[81]   Ibid., p.87.

trade between Bristol and the West Indies. The count retired from the Navy in 1919, becoming a merchant working in Hamburg. He died in 1956 at the age of 77.

Not only did the merchant ships have to suffer enemy warships and mines on the surface of the sea and submarines below, they also had to suffer attacks from above, in the form of the Zeppelins. These were giant airships, about 540 feet in length, capable of up to about 75 knots and carrying 4,000 lb bomb loads. By the beginning of 1916 the sporadic raids on London and the east coast ports had become more sinister and they were extending their scope to attack Liverpool. On 31 January 1916 a fleet of nine Zeppelins took off from northern Germany with their target the port and city of Liverpool on the most audacious raid yet planned. While the weather had been favourable for the raid in terms of wind and visibility, it became very cold to the extent that instruments were freezing up and the high cloud precluded navigation fixes. Navigation was therefore reduced to dead reckoning and, with no radio communication permitted between the airships, the fleet had to remain in visual contact. In the event the airships became disorientated but eventually believing they were over Liverpool, released their bomb loads. In fact they had mistaken the industrial centre of Derby for Liverpool, which had no anti-aircraft defences and thus suffered considerable damage and loss of life.

The last Zeppelin of the fleet to make its bombing run was L-19, under the command of *Kapitänleutnant* Odo Loewe, who had been experiencing engine problems from the time the airship had crossed the North Sea. He was unable to complete his mission and, losing speed and height, became separated from the rest of the Zeppelin fleet and set course for home on his own. When over the North Sea the loss of height was becoming a matter of great concern, by which time he had jettisoned nearly all his ballast, leaving only his incomplete bomb load on board to jettison to enable him to retain the necessary height. With three of his four engines failing he decided to release his remaining bombs in the belief that they would fall harmlessly into the sea. The date was 1 February 1916.

At that time, an ex-German collier, the *FRANZ FISCHER* had decided to anchor south of the Kentish Knock over the hours of darkness, heeding the warning of a naval patrol craft of mines in the area. Having secured the anchor and stopped the engines, the master and his chief engineer were settling down for a nightcap when they became aware of the unfamiliar sounds of engines overhead. The men went back up on deck, by which time the sound of the engines had stopped but they were suddenly hit by a great explosion of a bomb striking amidships on the port side. Initially it was thought the *FRANZ FISCHER* had not been fatally struck, but the lifeboats were quickly freed and lowered. There was however difficulty in releasing the falls, at which point the collier very suddenly turned over on her port side, sinking rapidly and throwing all the men on deck into the freezing sea. The chief engineer, Mr John H. Birch, surfaced in the darkness and though he could see nothing, he could hear voices around him. Sensing a dark object in the waves he swam towards what turned out to be a lifebelt box with handropes which he grabbed and was soon joined by seven other survivors. They tried to climb on top of the box to get out of the water, but each time that was attempted the box rolled over and the man trying to climb on was thrown off and disappeared into the darkness. John Birch decided to find other means of support and located a lifebelt, leaving the others to the lifeboat box. Eventually only one man was left on the box, Able Seaman Albert Hillier.

Also anchored south of the Kentish Knock was a small Belgian steamer, the *PAUL*, which had heard the explosion but seen nothing. Fortunately they were alerted to the sound of cries in the water and sent a boat away to investigate, eventually finding John Birch, Alfred Hillier and a steward in the darkness, all of whom were by that time close to death. John Birch had lost consciousness in the water and awoke to find himself in the *PAUL*'s lifeboat. With the three men hauled into the *PAUL*'s boat it soon became clear that the ebbing tide was carrying the boat away from the *PAUL* and it was almost by chance that the master of the *PAUL*, suspecting that all might not be well had raised anchor to look for them, despite being aware that they might be moving into a minefield. He eventually found the three men in the darkness although Alfred Hillier did not survive the ordeal, contributing to the total loss of the 13 lives. The *FRANZ FISCHER* therefore had the sad distinction of being the first British merchant ship to be lost from an airborne attack.

Perhaps unaware of the devastation caused by his jettisoning of his bombs, Otto Loewe was having his own problems trying to keep L-19 airborne. He had met with a strong headwind once clear of the Thames Estuary and ran into mist over the North Sea. During the early hours of the morning of 2 February, some three days after setting off on the bombing raid over Liverpool, Loewe broke radio silence and sent a message to his base reporting that his radio was operating only intermittently and that three of his engines were malfunctioning. He also reported his position as being off Borkum, aiming to cross the Belgian coast near Antwerp Island, when in fact he was lost, passing over the Dutch island of Ameland. There he came under heavy fire from Dutch gunners and was last seen by the gunners on fire and drifting before a strong southeasterly breeze.

A little later that morning, the mate of British trawler *KING STEPHEN*, George Denny, who was in the wheelhouse, saw a distress rocket in the sky. The trawler was approaching the Dogger Bank fishing grounds, with the trawl down and the sky beginning to lighten with dawn. George Denny called his skipper, George Martin, to the wheelhouse and as daylight came saw the wreckage of a Zeppelin in the sea. They approached carefully to see if there were any survivors and soon saw at least 20 uniformed Germans clinging to the wreckage, with one man perched on top of the great balloon, lashed to a rail with a signalling lamp. It was the wreckage of L-19, but the *KING STEPHEN*'s crew would have been unaware of L-19's mission or of her destruction of the *FRANZ FISCHER*.

George Martin was very wary of the Germans, many of whom, he suspected, might be armed, and also thinking of the situation where he had a crew of nine unarmed men. He considered that taking these men on board would be a very risky business as he and his crew could without doubt be easily overpowered, if not killed by their prisoners. A German officer appeared in uniform, possibly Otto Loewe, who was sporting an Iron Cross, who pleaded to be taken on board the trawler, offering payment for rescue and promising that they would not attempt to take over the trawler. George Martin was in a dilemma; should he risk his trawler and his men by taking the German L-19 survivors on board, or should he leave the Germans to their fate?

George Denny, in summing up their dilemma, stated later:

We had a confab about affairs. We looked at the position like this. There were about twenty or twenty five of them and only nine of us. They would all have revolvers and we had nothing but sticks. So we thought it was not safe to tackle them on our trawler which their Kaiser called an 'insignificant little ship'. What do you think would have happened if we had invited them on board? They could easily have overpowered us and taken our ship to Germany with us as prisoners — that is if they didn't pitch us overboard at first. So the skipper shouted to them that he could not take them off and then they started shouting and saying that they would not touch us if only we would save them. They screeched for us to save them but the skipper did the right thing when he said he could not do it. What would their Kaiser said have said if he got to know that nine of us had been able to overpower twenty-five of them and bring them prisoners to Germany? Why, he would have taken all their Iron Crosses from them.[82]

George Martin spoke directly to Loewe but, despite Loewe's protestations and promises, the trawler shipper felt he was not to be trusted. In a later statement to the press he confirmed the sentiments expressed by his mate, George Denny, with the caveat that if there had been another ship close by, he might have taken the risk. In the event, he backed away from the collapsing L-19 and its German survivors, this time with their cries ringing in his ears, noting the calm sea conditions, and made for the nearest port, Harwich, to inform the naval authorities of the situation. The *PAUL*, like most other vessels of her type, was not equipped with radio. Some hours later the L-19, with all her crew, sank before the trawler reached Harwich.

A few days later a Norwegian fisherman picked up a bottle at sea containing a dispatch from Otto Loewe in which was written: '*With fifteen men on the platform and no gondola, L-19 is going very slowly. I am unable to save the airship. In foggy weather, we, on our return from England, passed Holland and were bombarded by Dutch sentinels. At the same moment three motors failed. 1 p.m.*'[83] The bottle also contained letters from each member of the L-19 crew to their relatives, as the only trace of the Zeppelin and the men who manned her.

George Martin was unable to forgive himself for the action he had taken, which was not without some opposition from his own crew, although he had been fully supported by his mate. He was full of remorse for the outcome and died just a few days after reaching Harwich. The action was condemned

---

[82]   Bridgland, *Outrage at Sea*, p.70.

[83]   Edwards, *War Under the Red Ensign 1914–1918*, p.109.

by Germany and by a number of British voices too. The *KING STEPHEN* was never to go back to sea as a trawler and was taken over by the Admiralty and converted into a 'Q' ship.

The historian Martin Gilbert wrote that the war at sea was in many ways the forgotten war with the merchant seamen in daily danger and many of course put in positions they could not have imagined in peacetime. Perhaps the most forgotten of all were the unsung heroes of the crews of the many small trawlers, often working in very precarious conditions with many converted to fish for the lethal mines in order to protect their larger cousins in the merchant and naval fleets. One of their wartime chroniclers, E. Hilton Young wrote,

> *We sift the drifting sea,*
> *and blindly grope beneath;*
> *obscure and toilsome we,*
> *the fishermen of death.*[84]

The circumstances in which seafarers found themselves were indeed varied and their lot so often depended crucially on the humanity of those who attacked them. On 6 February 1916 the British cargo steamer *FLAMENCO*, of 4,629 tons and under the command of Captain Norman Martorell, was on passage from Newport to Valparaiso with a cargo of coal. When at some distance from the coast of Brazil, Captain Martorell watched a cargo steamer approaching and, thinking it was on a closing bearing, altered course. At that point the approaching steamer signalled '*Stop immediately*', followed by '*Do not telegraph*' and the raising of the German naval ensign. Captain Martorell chose to ignore the signal, immediately sending out a wireless message to which the approaching ship responded with gunfire, holing *FLAMENCO* amidships and hitting beneath the bridge and in the wireless cabin. With his ship by then on fire Captain Martorell gave the order to take to the boats, but in swinging the boats clear for lowering, one of them capsized, killing a fireman.

The German raider turned out to be the *MÖEWE*, still commanded by *Korvettenkapitän* Count Dohna-Schlodien, who sent his boats out with

---

[84]   Gilbert, *First World War*, p.279.

a boarding party to finish off his victim, when they noticed men from *FLAMENCO* in the water being attacked by sharks. *MÖEWE*'s men immediately went to their defence and hauled the British survivors to safety, with none being lost to the shark attack. As on other numerous occasions Count Dohna-Schlodien had shown compassion and humanity to his British victims.

Compassion was however singularly absent in the treatment of Captain Charles Algernon Fryatt, who had earlier proved to be the scourge of U-boats by outmanoeuvring and outrunning them when in command of the Great Eastern Railway's Harwich to Holland ferries. As mentioned earlier, he had gained the reputation for great skill and courage and for good reason was hailed as 'The Pirate Dodger'. With several more near encounters in his ship, the *BRUSSELS*, his luck continued to hold, as did the luck of the other ferries on that run until the late evening of 22 June 1916.

While departing from Rotterdam with general cargo and Belgian and Russian refugees, with confidential documents handed to Captain Fryatt by the British Consul General, a white rocket was seen fired from the coastline, which was later argued as either being a signal to warn *BRUSSELS* of waiting German warships or to alert waiting warships that *BRUSSELS* was leaving. In the darkness, with no navigation lights showing, it was not possible to see if any other vessels were about so, for fear of risk of collision, Captain Fryatt briefly showed his navigation lights to see if there was any response. No response was forthcoming so full speed was ordered for the dash to England, but it gradually became clear that the unarmed *BRUSSELS* was not alone and she was soon surrounded by a fleet of nine German destroyers, which made any resistance or escape impossible. Reluctantly Captain Fryatt brought his ship to a stop and was soon boarded by a number of armed German naval personnel, although not before he had taken the confidential papers to the stokehold for incineration, leaving his chief officer, Bill Hartnell, temporarily in charge. Captain Fryatt had no option but to surrender his ship. It is a matter of conjecture whether the prime purpose of the capture of the *BRUSSELS* was to seize Captain Fryatt in revenge for his earlier actions, or whether it was to seize the confidential documents that had been handed to his care.

The ship's company were however taken on board the destroyers and later loaded into cattle trucks and transported to a camp in Ruhleben in Germany. After a few days Captain Fryatt and Mr Hartnell were separated from the rest and taken to a prison in Bruges, arriving on 2 July, where they were subjected to interrogation. Captain Fryatt made no secret of his earlier encounters with U-boats and his attempted ramming of U-33, for which event he was to be tried by court martial. The British government protested strongly at this treatment and the American government entreated their German counterparts to at least ensure that Captain Fryatt would be competently defended, but were not able to receive any such assurances. No doubt at some time during those proceedings he gave thought to the exhortations of Winston Churchill that British merchant ships had a 'duty' to try and ram any German submarine.

On 27 July the court martial, set up by Admiral Ludwig von Schröder, took place in Bruges, with Captain Fryatt represented by a Major Naumann of the German Army Reserve. At the start of the trial, a telegram just received from the Foreign Office in Berlin was read to the court by Dr Zäpfel, the court president and an experienced barrister, asking for the trial to be postponed in the light of the public outcry from neutral nations, many of which, particularly the Americans, were taking a great interest in the proceedings. After a short break to consider the telegram from Berlin the court continued with the trial as Admiral Schröder, who apparently had control over the proceedings, informed Berlin that the trial must proceed. Shortly after 16:00 the court found Captain Fryatt guilty and ordered that he should be executed without delay. He was taken from the court to an army barracks and, just two hours after sentence had been passed, was taken into a yard, tied to a post, blindfolded and shot. Half an hour later a telegram arrived from Berlin ordering the execution to be postponed.[85] His date of execution was one day short of the anniversary of his encounter with U-33.

The priest who was allocated to Captain Fryatt for his few remaining hours later wrote a sympathetic letter to the widow stating that Fryatt had been calm in facing his execution, firmly believing he had correctly carried out his duties in the protection of his passengers, crew and ship. Chief Officer Bill Hartnell was allowed a brief meeting with Captain Fryatt and reported that certainly Fryatt had shown great courage but was outraged that he had not been allowed a proper defence.

There was condemnation worldwide, igniting an outburst of anti-German

---

[85] Brigland, *Outrage at Sea*, p.109.

feeling. The House of Commons condemned the barbarity of the act; the King wrote to Captain Fryatt's widow expressing his indignation; there was a call to ban all German ships from British ports for five years following the end of the war; the British Workers' League held a rally in Trafalgar Square; and British troops in the trenches wrote *'This one's for Capt. Fryatt'* on the shells of their big guns. The Prime Minister declared that after the war's end, diplomatic relations with Germany could not be resumed until reparation was made for Captain Fryatt's murder. The German authorities and press, aware of the outrage caused, responded by claiming that their submarine crews must be protected from such illegal acts by British merchant ships; an illegal act that had been sanctioned by the British government.

After the war, Captain Fryatt's body was brought back to Dover, escorted by Royal Naval vessels and placed on a gun carriage, to be taken by train to a memorial service at Saint Paul's cathedral. The streets were lined with those mourning the atrocity that had been committed in that yard in Bruges on 27 July 1916. Captain Fryatt was finally buried in Harwich, his home port, and a memorial plaque in his honour can be seen at Liverpool Street Station.

Arthur Balfour, the then First Lord of the Admiralty and former Prime Minister, expressed his disgust at the German attitude to British merchant seafarers and wrote:

> *Small is their knowledge of our merchant seamen. Their trade is not war – they live by the arts of peace. But in no case does patriotism burn with a purer flame, or show itself in deeds of higher courage and self-devotion. It means that the German Navy is to behaviour at sea as the German Army behaves on land. It means that neither enemy civilians or neutrals are to possess rights against militant Germans; that those who do not resist will be drowned, and those who do will be shot.*

CHAPTER 9

A MEDITERRANEAN INTERLUDE

The Mediterranean theatre was also seeing high losses of life among British merchant seafarers, with the month of December 1915 proving particularly disturbing. While the cessation of unrestricted warfare had largely brought about a lull in the U-boat attacks in the North Sea and British home waters, more U-boats were sent to the Adriatic from where there were richer pickings. Shipping routes were readily identified, weather conditions were more suitable for submarine attacks in the relatively benign Mediterranean and there were less effective U-boat counter measures. There was also a lower probability of the U-boats encountering American ships and American passengers.

On 1 December the 4,796 ton unarmed cargo steamer *CLAN MACLEOD*, under the command of Captain H.S. Southward, was on passage from Chittagong to London and about 100 miles to the southeast of Malta. Attacked by a U-boat without warning, Captain Southward immediately altered course to place the submarine astern and ordered emergency full speed to try and outrun the attacker. The submarine continued firing, with shells falling ahead of the steamer, but Captain Southward continued to manoeuvre his ship to avoid the shells. However, it soon became apparent the submarine had the advantage of speed and, after suffering a direct hit, Southward decided that escape was not possible and thus stopped his ship, and signalled his surrender. The submarine continued firing, hitting the bridge and wounding the captain and destroying the starboard lifeboats. Nine men were killed and three more fatally wounded but, despite this and the continued shelling, two boats on the port side were successfully lowered.

Southward was ordered to board the submarine although he had been seriously wounded. His attacker turned out to be U-33 under the command of *Kapitänleutnant* Konrad Gansser, who subjected the wounded captain to a tirade of invective, an account of which was issued by the Press Bureau on 26 April 1916:

> ... *I was ordered to go on board. I did so and found the Commander and Lieutenant in a furious rage with me because I had not stopped sooner. The commander rushed down from the conning tower, shook his fist in my face, and said, 'Why did you not stop?' I replied that I wanted to save my ship. His next remark was 'I can shoot you as a franc-tireur'. I said 'I don't think so'. He said 'You are assisting my enemy'. I replied 'I am your enemy'. The Commander then said 'Had you stopped when I fired three shots you would not have had this', pointing to a wound in my hand. I replied that it was my misfortune. I was then ordered back into the boat, and the submarine at once proceeded to sink the steamer by shell fire. After firing a couple of shots into every compartment he returned to the boats, and I was again ordered on board. I was asked for my instructions, which I said I had destroyed. I was also asked for the register and I told him it was on board the steamer. The Lieutenant dressed my hand, pointed out my foot was wounded, and gave me packets of dressing for my foot and some for the wounded. Before I left the submarine he told me to inform all captains that I met that they would be fired upon if they tried to escape. I told him that that would be their business and had nothing to do with me. He also asked me the position and I said I had not had a position for some time. We then parted company, and after I had picked up two wounded men who had evidently stowed themselves away, the two boats set sail for Malta, the Chief Officer having charge of the cutter with nineteen men on board and myself in charge of the lifeboat with fifty men on board. The submarine kept about half a mile astern of the boats with only the periscope showing for three or four hours, then disappeared.*

The following day Captain Southward's boat was picked up by a passing steamer, the *LORD CROMER*, but the other boat with the chief officer was not picked up until 4 December by a French warship. *Kapitänleutnant* Konrad Gansser would have been well aware that the lifeboats were faced with significant hazards, being some 100 miles from the nearest land, offering no assistance to the survivors other than the few dressings referred to by Captain Southward. Gansser was listed as a war criminal by Great Britain for his action against the *CLAN MACLEOD*, among others, but survived the war.

After several months of hospital treatment for his wounds, Captain Southward returned to sea in command of Clan Line steamers but, on 15 March 1918, when in command of *CLAN MACDOUGALL* he lost his life, along with 32 others, when his ship was torpedoed off the Italian coast by UB-49.

On Christmas Day 1915 the 7,974 ton P&O luxury liner *PERSIA*, under the command of Captain W.H. Selby Hall and with a distinguished passenger list, left Marseille after a well advertised schedule, steaming towards Malta to take on more passengers and to take on coal. On 30 December, as lunch on board was coming to an end Captain Selby Hall, who also held the rank of Commander RNR, was on the bridge and was just taking charge of the watch from Second Officer Geoffrey Wood, who was the first to see a torpedo approaching and who sounded the emergency signal for boat stations. The torpedo struck on the port side and the ship immediately began to list to port, rendering the starboard lifeboats useless as they would have simply swung inboard should there have been an attempt to release them from their davits. The torpedo explosion had smashed the engine controls such that it was not possible to stop the ship which, increasingly listing to port, began circling with the bow digging deeper into the water. While the ship carried enough boats and rafts for more than double the number of persons on board, many passengers were trapped within the restaurant and the rapidly increasing angle of list made movement around the ship extremely difficult as the crew began lowering the port lifeboats. Under these circumstances it was a great credit to Captain Selby Hall and the crew of *PERSIA*, and in particular to Chief Officer Clark, that five boats were cleared away. Other boats were not so fortunate, with two boats being dragged under with their occupants when the *PERSIA*, still with way on her, sank within 10 minutes of being struck. In total, Captain Selby Hall and 334 others lost their lives, out of a total of 519 persons board.

Among the passengers were Lord Montagu of Beaulieu and his mistress Eleanor Thornton, reputedly the model for the Rolls-Royce Spirit of Ecstasy. As the ship was sinking, Lord Montagu, dragging Eleanor with him, tried to clamber up the sloping deck to reach a rail on the starboard side when the wall of water hit them and swept his mistress from his grasp, never to be seen again. He eventually managed to find a lifeboat, albeit a badly damaged and upturned one, where he joined about six other Europeans and about 20 Lascar crew members hanging on to whatever they could. For a while, the boat was righted by a wave and they all managed to clamber in, itself a difficult task, but the boat was capsized several more times. Their hopes were raised when they sighted a 'large Cunarder' but, despite their attempts to attract its attention to their plight by letting off the lifeboat's flares the ship passed by. By sunset the next day Montagu found himself in company with two passengers and 15 Lascars when, after 30 hours in the boat they were eventually rescued by the Blue Funnel steamer *NING CHOW*.[86] The previous day other boats had been picked up by HMS *MALLOW*, but three of the six boats, including No. 3 boat with Captain Selby Hall on board, were never found. Although the boats were lashed together initially, the increasingly heavy seas had separated them.

A surviving French passenger, Monsieur de Teuquin, later recounted his experiences:

> *Of the twenty-five or thirty people who had been around me on the upturned hull of a lifeboat, not one was alive. I caught hold of a beam, then a barrel; I was vomiting water and coal dust; the great ship had disappeared. I was holding on to a barrel with my left hand; with my right I was fending off chairs, the tables and all the wreckage which was eddying around and which held the risk of wounding me if it had been thrown against me. At that moment, I saw some heads out of the water, screaming for help with terror in their eyes – then disappearing.*
>
> *I shall never forget – and above all, a voice which came from I know not where, a far-off voice of a woman or child or a young man who was shouting 'Mother! Mother!' I then raised myself up to look for the voice, to hold out a hand or an oar to it, to save it – but I saw nothing. A-ah! That voice – the shout 'Mother! Mother!' How heartrending it was. These wretched people, once in the lifeboats, remained for thirty-two hours without anything to eat, without clothing, soaked, so squeezed they could not sit down and for the first hour coughing up all the coal-dust and salt water they had swallowed.*[87]

---

[86] Woodman, *More Days, More Dollars*, p.278.

[87] Brigland, *Outrage at Sea*, p.125.

The sinking of the *PERSIA* caused international outrage as the submarine had attacked without warning and had made no attempt to assist the survivors; this during a period when the German authorities had banned unrestricted attacks on passenger ships. Initially, Germany claimed that it might have been an Austrian submarine responsible for the attack, which was hotly denied by the Austria-Hungarian authorities. It was later revealed that the attack was carried out by the German submarine U–38 under the command of Max Valentiner, who became the third ranking 'ace' of the U-boat fleet, having plied his trade in both the North Sea and Mediterranean theatres.

Max Valentiner had not yet finished his day's work as he was to provide the last loss of a British merchant ship in 1915. Only a few hours after sinking the *PERSIA*, he came across the Clan Line steamer *CLAN MACFARLANE* under the command of Captain James Swanston. The steamer, of 4,823 tons and with 75 souls on board had left Birkenhead on 16 December bound for Bombay and had had an uneventful voyage until the afternoon of 30 December. At around 4 p.m. as Chief Officer F.J. Hawley was going on watch and unaware of the fate of the *PERSIA*, a terrific explosion shook the ship in No. 5 hold. After ascertaining that his ship could not be saved and checking that all his crew were accounted for, Captain Swanston ordered the boats to be lowered and it is a tribute to the skill of the crew, mainly Indians, that all six boats were quickly and safely lowered. Within an hour of the explosion all six boats were being rowed to the north to keep clear of the sinking ship, during which time the culprit, U–38, commanded by Max Valentiner surfaced, made the usual enquiries of the survivors and then shelled the ship to hasten her sinking, again without offering any assistance.

An account of the ordeal which followed is given by Hurd,[88] based on the full and detailed information supplied by Chief Officer Hawley, extracts of which are given below.

As the darkness of night fell around him, Captain Swanston, undismayed by his misfortune, ordered all boats to be placed in line and made fast astern his own boat, in order to ensure their keeping together during the oncoming night. Fortunately they had all been provided with sails and each man had a lifebelt. So masts were stepped and a course was set for Crete, upwards of

---

[88] Hurd, *The Merchant Navy*, Vol. 2, pp.198–202.

sixty miles distant. With the wind blowing from the west, the little boats
continued to sail throughout that night and during the succeeding day, the sea
happily remaining comparatively calm.

During the afternoon land was sighted and, as the wind dropped Captain
Swanston, with his officers, decided to revert to rowing, alternating between
rowing and sailing dependent upon the wind. On the morning of 2 January
a glimpse was seen of Crete, but the wind was picking up and the seas
becoming rough so the small flotilla attempted to sail along the coast until
a landing could be effected once the sea conditions improved. The narrative
continued:

> *By this time the unfortunate men had become exhausted by exposure, and to*
> *add to their troubles a tow-rope parted, with the result that the Third Officer's*
> *and Second Engineer's boats went adrift. The Captain, seized with a high*
> *sense of duty, cast off his boat to go in search of the missing craft. It was an*
> *almost hopeless task in the darkness which prevailed. Mr. Hawley, the Chief*
> *Officer, lay to with the other boats throughout the night. The weather, far*
> *from improving, became increasingly bad, and weary and dispirited as they*
> *were, the men had to bail continually. In the meantime death claimed five of*
> *the natives in the Chief Officer's boat and one died in the Second Engineer's*
> *boat.*

On 3 January the captain's boat was seen but his search for the other boats had
failed and three more of the seamen died from exposure. One of the boats
became unseaworthy so its occupants were transferred to the chief officer's
and the captain's boats, but no sooner had this transfer been completed when
the rudder of the captain's boat was carried away. Captain Swanston cast
off from the head of his convoy and, using an oar in place of the rudder he
secured to the stern of the second officer's boat, becoming the last in the
convoy. The heavy weather required the crews to continue bailing through
the night but by morning the captain's boat was missing and, although briefly
sighted later during that day, they could not reach it again. As darkness again
fell, all sighting of it was lost and it was never seen again. As Hurd comments
'… *it will never be known how this undaunted seaman and his companions, adrift in*
their rudderless boat on a distressed sea, met their end'.

By the morning of 5 January Mr Hawley, by this time the senior surviving officer, had to abandon another boat and make the hazardous transfer of its occupants in a heavy sea to his own boat, in the process of which his boat's rudder broke. In these desperate circumstances the smoke of a steamer was seen on the horizon but the dwindling little convoy of boats were not seen. Another day and night passed.

The following morning of 6 January, three more of the crew died in Mr Hawley's boat and later during the day the wind and sea conditions eased. Mr Hawley then decided to abandon the aim of making a landing on Crete and to try and make for Alexandria which, although some 250 miles away, was in a direction such that the boats could ride more easily in the seas and would cross the shipping lanes. Two more of the boat's occupants died, just before another steamer was sighted, which also failed to see them. Their rescue eventually came with the arrival on the scene of the CROWN OF ARAGON to take them to Malta but their troubles were not yet over, as a submarine was sighted. Fortunately their rescuer, armed with a 12-pounder, was able to escape although not before two more of the Clan Line steamer's crew had succumbed to their ordeal. Of the 76 souls on the CLAN MACFARLANE, 52 experienced and competent merchant seafarers had perished from the exposure and ordeal of seven days and seven nights in small, ill-provisioned open boats.

Max Valentiner, in one day, had caused the loss of 386 lives from the two British merchant ships in callous contravention of the Prize Code. He was declared a war criminal by Great Britain for his murderous attacks and is referred to again later in this book. Germany took its usual stance of denying responsibility for the attack on PERSIA, as indeed did Austria, refusing to be Germany's scapegoat for the atrocity. However in January 1916, Germany gave a pledge to America that its submarines in the Mediterranean were only allowed to sink merchant ships once the passengers and crew had been safely disembarked and, with few exceptions, this pledge was honoured in the Mediterranean until the later unrestricted U-boat campaign.

Somewhat less glamorous perhaps than the prestigious PERSIA and the Clan liner, was the COQUET, built for the Mercantile Steamship Company in 1904. At 4,398 tons she was bound from Torrevieja to Rangoon with a cargo of salt and under the command of 35-year-old Captain Arnold Groom, with Mr A. Griffiths as his chief officer with, apart from other Britons, crew members from Italy, Greece, Spain, Norway and the West Indies. The perils of the sea alone had already claimed one of the crew, a young apprentice called Alfred Ballard, who had been washed overboard in heavy weather on 11 November.

Usual precautions were adopted for passages through the Mediterranean, with both lifeboats swung out ready for an emergency evacuation, an extra lookout and a state of constant alertness. What followed on the morning of 4 January 1916 was a precursor to one of the more notorious actions of the war in the Mediterranean. Captain Groom's own account, published by the *New York Times* on 30 March 1916, described the scene.

> *About 10:45 a.m. I was writing in the saloon when I heard a gun fired. On my reaching the bridge the Third Mate told me it was fired across our bow. Then another was fired across the bow, one over the bridge and one under the stern from a submarine on the port quarter. I stopped the engines and indicated that I had done so by flag signals. The firing stopped and the submarine was soon close to us with signals flying 'Abandon ship.' Immediately I took the chronometer, sextant and chart in the starboard boat and we left the ship. The other boat left a little before us. We had no sooner got clear of the ship than the submarine started firing at her … They stopped firing and coming close to the boats ordered us alongside. This was a dangerous proceeding as the submarine's deck was just awash and there was a big swell. I was ordered aboard the submarine and then some Austrians armed with revolvers and cutlasses were sent in our boats and the two boats returned to the COQUET. All hands were given twenty minutes to get what they wanted from the ship. At the same time the Austrians looted whatever they could in the time given. They lowered one of the small boats to take them and their loot back to the submarine.*

Captain Groom watched as the submarine's boarding party, having placed time-fuse bombs within his ship, left *COQUET*, shortly after which there were two explosions. '*Four or five minutes after the explosions the COQUET lifted her stern high in the air. Something hit the whistle lanyard, and with a pitiful scream the COQUET disappeared.*' Captain Groom's account continued with his description of his discussion with the submarine's commander.

> *While all this was happening the commander of the submarine asked me a good many questions. The two lifeboats were near the submarine again now,*

and bailing was in full progress in each boat with two or three buckets. I
pointed this out to the commander of the submarine, and the fact that both of
the bilge planks of the boats had most likely been sprung alongside his awash
decks. I told him it was nothing short of murder to send thirty one men away
like that in the middle of winter, too, so far from land. He laughed and said
he would save the next ship and send her to look for us ... The boats were
alongside by this time and the Austrians searched them for anything valuable,
taking chronometers, sextants, and charts, and also every scrap of paper they
could find. They ordered me back into my boat, and then left us.

Captain Groom was therefore left with two damaged and leaking boats,
about 200 miles from the nearest land, which was to the northeast, and no
means for navigation. He, and his crew of 31 men, in two damaged lifeboats,
were about to embark on a further chapter of a harrowing experience.

With the winds from the northwest quadrant Captain Groom realised
that it would not be possible to head for the nearest land so, in consultation
with Mr Griffiths it was agreed to set the sails and run before the wind to
make for the North African coast, even though they knew the reputation
of that coastline for its hostile inhabitants. They hoped that as they were to
cross the shipping lanes between Egypt and Malta their chances of being
seen and rescued would be greater. Initial progress was good and hopes were
raised when a steamer was spotted, but those hopes were dashed when it
continued past them. This was a further example of the difficulties for a
ship to spot a small boat in the open sea, as had been the case with the
CLAN MACFARLANE survivors, even during times of alertness to watch
for enemy submarines.

Soon the weather had deteriorated such that sails had to be brought
down and the boats' sea anchors deployed. These were found to be inefficient
so the boats laid their masts out as well. The boats' occupants were very
cold and wet, having no shelter and were suffering the same Mediterranean
winter weather at the same time as the surviving boats of the CLAN
MACFARLANE. Captain Groom's account continued:

With a heavy sea running we were soon all wet through, and remained so,
particularly for the next six days. All the time we were in the boats all the
able-bodied men had to take turns at bailing, two at a time. The steward, who

was old and ill, I exempted from this work, also four boys who were very young, also seasick and somewhat frightened, I fancy. The boat was overloaded with seventeen in it, and was ankle deep in water, in spite of the vigorous bailing with two buckets.

The two boats had lost sight of each other, but on the night of 6 January Captain Groom saw a dark object which he thought might be a small steamer running without lights so he fired a red flare. To his delight a red flare was fired in response, but it turned out not to be a rescuing steamer, but Mr Griffiths' boat. Nevertheless they were very pleased to see each other but Captain Groom considered their chances of being seen and rescued would be improved if they kept some distance apart to increase their range of view. The boats drifted apart and Mr Griffiths and his boat were never seen again, also to suffer an unknown fate, at much the same time and in much the same seas as the ill-fated Captain Swanson of the *CLAN MACFARLANE*.

The weather deteriorated further that night and continued the next day, 7 January. Captain Groom noted that they were all chilled to the bone and all suffered excruciating pains in their ankles, knees and wrists. On the morning of the 8th, the weather moderated and the sail was set, heading to the south towards the African coast, with land eventually sighted on the 10th. However the wind direction had changed making it extremely difficult to make any headway, with an unpleasant swell adding to the difficulty in controlling the boat. After mustering his exhausted men to make a desperate effort to man the oars, they finally managed to beach the boat despite being nearly swamped in a small bay surrounded by uninhabited small caves. The situation was described by Captain Groom.

We slept on the sands that night, after having slaked our thirst with some well water and eaten a quantity of limpets from the rocks with our biscuits. There were a quantity of cave-dwellings around the bay; but they were all so damp and smelly that we deemed it wiser to sleep in the open on the sandy beach, thinking that sand would have retained some of the sun's heat. This conjecture proved faulty, however; there was a chill dampness which struck up through the sand, and, having only our wet clothes to cover us, we woke up chilled through and through, with every bone aching; we slept, owing to the fact it was the first opportunity we had had of sleeping since leaving the ship.

The buildings we had seen from the sea proved to be long-deserted ruins, and there was no sign of life anywhere. The two engineers, the second mate, and I kept watch by turns during the night.[89]

Captain Groom reviewed the situation on the following morning of 11 January and, while the beach was uncomfortable, he judged that as there was plenty of water available and shellfish they could all survive there for the time being. He contemplated re-launching the boat for reconnaissance to find habitation as the weather had abated but resolved first to try and ascertain where they were before setting off again, apart from which they were by then all too exhausted for such endeavours. Nevertheless, Captain Groom took three men with him for a reconnaissance, including a fireman who could speak some Arabic, in the hope of finding some sign of life. He described their trek as extremely difficult and uncomfortable, walking over large stones and hills with ankle-deep sand. After several hours of walking they came across an Arab who went back to the beach with them and offered to pilot their boat to the nearest port but, despite the efforts of the second mate, William Sayer and the carpenter, Alexander Wiklund, who together had been charged with trying to make the boat more seaworthy, the boat was effectively beyond repair. The Arab suggested that they walk to the nearest town, but by this time Captain Groom was too exhausted so he sent two Greek firemen, Nicola Sikeris and Cristo Ralides to go with the Arab to try and arrange for some boats to take them to the nearest port. That night the remaining 13 survivors slept in one of the caves, with a fire for warmth and to dry out their clothing, believing that their ordeal would soon be over.

In the morning, Captain Groom was trying to have a wash in an adjacent muddy pool when he heard rifle shots and saw two Arab men yelling at them. He and the others with him took some refuge in a trench alongside one of the old deserted buildings, shortly after which the two Arab men disappeared. Half an hour later a party of about 15 Arab men appeared, all armed with rifles and shouting loudly and this time with a more serious intent. From Captain Groom's own account:

I held up my hands to indicate I was unarmed; one of them still jabbered at

---

[89]   Ibid., p.221.

me but the other took careful aim at my head; I ducked forward and to one side a little at just about at the same instant that he pulled the trigger, so the bullet took a track through the flesh across the back of my shoulders, instead of hitting my head. The Arab was only about six feet away when he fired; the force of the shock knocked me backwards. I remember falling and my head hitting the sand. After that I must have lost consciousness, as when I awoke everything was quiet except for the groaning of the carpenter, who was rolling between me and the edge of the water, about six feet. I found he was horribly mutilated but still alive. He asked me to drag him away from the sea; I tried to, but he was a big man and my wound was very painful. A little way out in the water the steward was floating face downwards; whether he was shot or drowned or both, I do not know. Further up the beach the little Italian messroom boy was lying dead. I could see nothing of anybody else, and was afraid to go out of the trench, thinking that if the Bedouins saw me alive they would come back to finish me off.

Captain Groom was certainly due some good fortune and soon a small Italian steamer appeared, as the result of the two Greek firemen sent for help having managed to reach the Italian fort of Marsa Susa and persuade the authorities to send a ship. A boat landed with an Italian officer and Arab soldiers who took Captain Groom, the fatally wounded carpenter Alexander Wiklund and the bodies of the steward, Alfred Lloyd and the Italian messroom boy, George Livonis (also recorded as Livanos in the *COQUET*'s documents), back to the ship. They found one of *COQUET*'s seamen, named Alexander Lord, lying wounded on the beach having been both shot and bayoneted, who was able to tell Captain Groom that the remaining 10 crew members had been taken away by the Arabs. Nineteen men who had survived the sea and made it to the beach had been killed.

Captain Groom reported to the Italian commander that he was convinced he had been sunk by an Austrian submarine as he had noticed the insignia of a crown on the cap badges. In fact his tormentor had been U-34 under the command of Claus Rücker.

The 10 men seized by the Arabs faced yet a further ordeal. They had been forced, at bayonet point, to make a three-week odyssey over very rough ground; an expedition for which they were ill equipped following their nightmare lifeboat voyage. They were marched throughout the daylight hours, fed only on rice and goat meat, reaching a destination at an abandoned and ruined fort at Jedabiah exactly one month after their ship had been torpedoed.

Their stay in the fort was initially a little less fraught than their cross-country trek and they were joined after a few days by a party of Italian prisoners and placed in a compound. An Arab guard then took them all out to form a working party, mainly to make some restoration of the buildings at Jedabiah and an account was given of what followed by one of the British survivors.

The same evening two Italians prevailed upon our Greek sailor to try to escape, to which he agreed. So about midnight they all climbed the wall of the compound, which was right on the outskirts of the fortified blockhouse of Jedabia. They climbed to the top all right, with much puffing and blowing, and the first man to drop down on the other side fell on some rusty tins and rubbish, making a frightful row, and we all thought the whole lot would be caught but nothing stirred, so they set off on foot. Of course the next day the Arabs discovered the escape, and some of them set off in pursuit on fast racing camels, and soon caught up with the fugitives and brought them back.

Then all we prisoners, British and Italian, were lined up and given a lecture by the Commandant of Jedabia upon the evils of trying to escape. He asked who was the instigator of the attempt and all the blame put on the poor Greek sailor. The two Italians were given twenty lashes with the kurbash and the Greek was given fifty lashes and condemned to be chained to a six-foot chain pegged into the ground, for six months, and he was also handcuffed. Whenever he wanted to move about, the Second Mate had to take a turn around his [the Greek's] neck with the chain and keep hold of the peg, and peg him securely when he came back. The Commandant also warned that the person or persons attempting to escape would be shot.

The prisoners continued their work under the direction of their Arab guards and were made to build a corrugated iron prison to which they were confined when not working, with food provided and cooked for them by their guards. One morning in April they were surprised to see Europeans encamped nearby and learned that they were German officers from a nearby submarine, who turned out to be very cordial and expressed sympathy for the prisoners' plight. It turned out that the Germans were visiting the Turkish leader Nuri Bey, who later provided the prisoners with some tobacco and payment for their work, which he said had been undertaken for the Turkish government.

The loss of *COQUET* was not immediately known and it was some time before any news became available of the fate of the survivors. On 10 February the ship's owners declared that *COQUET* had been sunk on 4 January with the crew having got away in two boats, one of which had landed on the Tripoli coast. That news would have been relayed following the success of the two Greek firemen who had been despatched on 11 January to seek help and raised the alarm at the port of Marsa Susa. A statement from the Foreign Office dated 24 April 1916, over three months after the sinking, referred to the failure of attempts so far made by the Italian government to ascertain the whereabouts and welfare of the survivors. They were however known to be in the hands of their Bedouin captors and every attempt was being made to locate them. A further statement from the Foreign Office, dated 21 June, to the Mercantile Marine Office read:

> *The Under Secretary of State for Foreign Affairs presents his compliments to the Mercantile Marine Office and is directed by Secretary Sir E. Grey to state that he learns from His Majesty's Ambassador at Rome that there are eight British believed to belong to the 'COQUET' at Gedabia. They are doing masons' work and one known as the engineer is working with a sewing machine. The labour is not severe. They enjoy relative freedom and are in good health and are well treated and well fed. Their clothes are in bad condition but the Bedouins are trying to remedy this.*

The Italian Minister of the Colonies has instructed the local authorities by telegraph to endeavour to ascertain the mens' names.[90]

On 1 July, Sir Edward Grey was able to state that:

> *... he learns from His Majesty's High Commissioner for Egypt that the following nine British subjects are in the hands of the Natives in Tripoli:-*
> *William F. Sayer, Edgar G. Hogg, Jos. Johnson, Nicolas Hartley, Sten Johnson,*

---

[90]   The National Archives, BT99/3231/120479 C619737.

Nicola André, John H. William, Chris Hill, Sid Taylor. The Prisoners are stated to be in good health. His Majesty's Representatives at Rome and Cairo have been asked by telegraph to take such steps as they can to obtain their release.[91]

Shortly after, the survivors were summoned by the Turks and informed that they were to be released. They were provided with Arab clothes and set off on camels to an Italian blockhouse where they were well treated for a few days before being put on a Maltese coastal vessel and taken to Malta where they were handed to the British Consul and transferred to a ship bound for London. All ten survivors of *COQUET*'s crew arrived in London on 29 August 1916, nearly eight months after the sinking of their ship.

The survival of the *COQUET*'s crew is a ringing testament to their toughness and resilience, providing a further example of the character and courage of British merchant seafarers, as unarmed civilians, in the face of the brutality of their captors.

Not all submarine encounters, fortunately, had such horrific consequences and there were many instances of submarines making unsuccessful attacks. The months of June and July for example had 10 and 7 attacks respectively against British ships. Two of these involved a torpedo fired without warning, which missed and were not repeated, with the rest being subject to limited gunnery attacks or indeed chased for a period of time without any guns or torpedo being fired.

One such example was the attack on 17 July 1916 on the *KINGSMERE*, 5,476 tons and formerly the Hansa Line *LINDENFELS*. She had been captured by the British in Aden and placed under the command of Captain Harry Griffiths, himself formerly the chief officer of the *INDUS*, sunk by the German raider *EMDEN* in 1914. *KINGSMERE* was not carrying any passengers but had a crew of 95 consisting of 17 British and 78 Indians.

KINGSMERE was bound from Bombay to Marseille and Liverpool at a speed of 10 knots in rough seas but clear visibility. A submarine appeared on the port quarter and, at a range of 500 yards, fired two rounds at 30-second intervals at about 07:35 hrs. Captain Griffiths ordered his gun crew consisting of RNR Petty Officer Felix La Fontaine and RNR Seaman James McQuirk

---

[91] Ibid.

aft to reply with the stern mounted 12-pounder. No hits were recorded on the *KINGSMERE* or the submarine, which immediately dived after the response from *KINGSMERE* and did not give chase. The steamer had not, at that time of the morning being flying her ensign, but quickly raised it to half mast as a distress signal, with full speed being called for by her master. The submarine was not identified '*Owing to the sun being just behind the S/M details not discernible. S/M had piece of canvas reaching from stem to stern triced up vertically to disguise her silhouette.*'

In response to the question about his crew's behaviour, Captain Griffiths stated, '*All behaved very well, with exception of native firemen on duty below, who attempted to leave the stokehold but soon returned to their duty and no steam was lost.*'[92] The *KINGSMERE* was indeed fortunate that the submarine did not give chase as had there been any delay in the firemen returning to their duty and a loss of steam, the submarine could have quickly overhauled the steamer. Further, as with many other steamers of her time, while fitted with a gun for protection *KINGSMERE* was not fitted with a wireless transmitter and could thus not call for assistance or alert other ships of her encounter.

Where possible, in every case the master, or senior surviving officer, was interviewed by an Admiralty official and his responses entered on a form entitled 'Particulars of Attacks on Merchant Vessels by Enemy Submarines'. The last entry on the form was a summary of the interviewing officer's view as to whether he considered the master had complied with Admiralty and local instructions and did all in his power to avoid capture. The somewhat patronising view on Captain Griffith's action was '*Master appears to have carried out the best procedure possible under the circumstances.*'[93]

---

[92]   The National Archives ADM137/4023 C619737

[93]   Ibid.

CHAPTER 10

THE SUSSEX PLEDGE

While there had been comparatively little U-boat activity throughout the winter of 1915/16, there were still disputes in the German government regarding the reintroduction of unrestricted U-boat warfare. There were also disagreements between the Allies and Germany regarding the status of armed merchant ships.

The British government's position on the arming of merchant ships had been made clear from the start of the war, namely that the character of a peaceful merchant ship is not changed by virtue of it being supplied with a gun for defensive purposes only, although in fact few ships were so provided. The suggestion therefore was that guns should never be fired unless the merchant ship was fired upon first. Paradoxically perhaps, the British government had adopted the principle that armed vessels of other flags should be treated as war vessels. An Order in Council of August 1914 expressly provides that a *'ship of war shall include an armed ship'*.

The German position was unequivocal in that any merchant ship equipped with a gun should be treated as a ship of war, regardless of whether the guns are intended for defensive or offensive purposes and that any warlike activity of an armed merchant ship is contrary to international law. Germany further took the view that neutral ports should impose the same restrictions on armed merchant ships as on naval ships of belligerent powers. Some of the neutral powers, including the USA, accepted the position of the British government, although others were less tolerant. While the Navy provided the guns, ammunition and trained gunners for the selected merchant ships, it was the practice that those gunners would not wear their naval uniforms in neutral ports, thus propagating the idea that the merchant ship was not a naval vessel.

A memorandum of the German government from von Tirpitz, dated 10 February 1916 entitled 'Treatment of Armed Merchantmen', claimed that armed British merchant ships had indeed initiated attacks against their U-boats, often flying the flags of other states. As a consequence of this, the memorandum stated,

> *It is thus made plain that the armed merchantmen have official instructions to attack the German submarine. England's rules of maritime warfare are adopted by her allies without question, the proof must be taken as demonstrated in respect of the armed merchantmen of other countries also. In the circumstances set forth above, enemy merchantmen with guns no longer have any right to be considered as peaceable vessels of commerce.*

Admiral von Tirpitz also felt this state of affairs should be brought to the attention of neutral powers to warn them against continuing '… *to entrust their persons or property to armed merchantmen of the powers at war with Germany*'.

Leading on from this, in a further memorandum of 13 February 1916 von Tirpitz wrote, in response to his own question, 'Can England be forced to sue for peace by means of a U-boat war?':

> *The most important and surest means which can be adopted to bring England to her knees is the use of our U-boats at the present time. We shall not be able to defeat England by a war on land alone. The unrestricted carrying out of the U-boat war, supported by our other naval craft and by our air fleet — all under a unified and determined leadership — is of the most decisive importance in obtaining the desired result. England will be cut to the heart by the destruction by the U-boats of every ship which approaches the English coast. The ocean's commerce is the very elixir of life for England, its interruption for any length of time a deadly danger, its permanent interruption absolutely fatal within a short time. Every attack upon England's transoceanic communication is therefore a blow in the termination of the war. The more the losses take place with merciless regularity at the very gates of the island kingdom, the more powerful will be the material and moral effect on the English people. In spite of its former resources, England will not be able to make a successful defence against the attacks of submarines directed against its transoceanic commerce, provide they are well planned. That is precisely why a timely U-boat war is*

the most dangerous and, if vigorously carried on, the form of warfare which will unconditionally decide the war to England's disadvantage.

The prerequisites of a successful carrying out of an unrestricted U-boat war are military and economic. In both respects they are noticeably more favourable than in February 1915.

Admiral von Holtzendorff, who had been brought back from retirement to serve as the head of the German Navy General Staff supported von Tirpitz's view regarding the benefits of unrestricted warfare. They appeared together at a council of war on 4 March 1916 in support of the Chancellor, with leading military and political personnel, when the matter of unrestricted submarine warfare was brought before the Kaiser for a decision. Admiral von Capelle argued that there were not enough submarines to ensure success and that their numbers had, in any event, been overestimated. The conclusion of that council was that unrestricted warfare should be postponed, a consequence of which was that von Tirpitz resigned and was replaced by von Capelle. The news of that decision was greeted with surprise in Germany and abroad and viewed as a victory for the more moderate elements in the war council, but von Holtzendorff continued his argument. In December of that year he claimed that the British could be starved into submission within five months before any American intervention could be effective, regarding the Americans as '*disorganised and undisciplined*' and assuring the Kaiser with '*I give your Majesty my word, as an officer, that not one American will land on the Continent.*'

However, by 24 March 1916 the conclusion of the council of war three weeks earlier had, seemingly, not been passed on to *Oberleutnant zur See* Herbert Pustkuchen on UB-29. On that day, the French passenger ferry *SUSSEX*, under the command of Captain Henri Mouffet, was about halfway across the English Channel, having sailed from Folkestone at 13:25 and bound for Dieppe. The captain had just completed threading his way through the buoyed-off mine barriers that protected the Kentish ports when, to his surprise, he observed a torpedo trace heading towards his ship, without any sight or warning of an enemy submarine. He attempted to manoeuvre away from the track but it was too late and the torpedo struck the forepart of the ferry, causing considerable damage to the extent of blowing off the forepart of the ship and injuring Captain Mouffet. The ensuing chaos resulted in panic-driven attempts to launch lifeboats, with women and children reportedly being pushed out of the way by male passengers, and with some mothers trying to throw their children into the boats. Two of the boats overturned through overloading, adding to the fatalities following the torpedo explosion. A Norwich town councillor on board, Mr W.O. Snelling, urged a young English nurse who was assisting wounded passengers to leave them and go with the other women into a boat. She refused, saying that her place should be given to a married man with children as she was single, and continued with her work on board. Her name is not known.

The passenger list included many nationalities, including Mr H. Albeck, a Dane who claimed his medical knowledge was limited to that gained solely from listening to discussions among his medical student friends. The *SUSSEX* had no doctor on board, thus it fell to Mr Albeck to render what medical assistance he could, with considerable success. His successes continued later when rescued by HMS *ALFRIDI* where he carried out two amputations on injured survivors.

Another passenger, an American journalist for the *New York Sun*, Mr Edward Marshall, gave his account of the torpedoing which appeared in *The Times* of 27 March:

> *The boat which capsized was from the starboard davits, about opposite the smoking-room, where I was standing. The boat seemed to make a great deal of water, which must have been due to its condition, as I saw no sea break into it. It was very low in the water as there were so many people in it, and there seemed to be a good deal of excitement and people constantly changing places. The boat suddenly went over, throwing everybody into the sea. I shall never forget the moan which came from those people as they realised the boat was capsizing. I have been in various disasters, but I have never heard so painful a sound before. I should like to pay tribute to an American lady, Mrs. Hilton, the daughter-in-law of a celebrated American judge. Although it was feared that her own daughter had been washed out of one of the boats, as she probably was, Mrs Hilton devoted herself to the injured with a sympathetic energy which was not less than marvellous. I was told that twelve of the crew were killed in the explosion, and I tried to get down to the wrecked parts of the ship, but could not do so, for it was very difficult and I am hampered owing to having lost my leg in the Spanish War.*

So far as I could see, the boat which capsized was not in charge of an officer. There ware certainly no men in uniform in the boat. Various liferafts the width of a door and longer had been thrown into the sea to the drowning people and some of the people from the capsized boat tried to cling to these, with the result that in most cases I saw the rafts overturned. Fifty per cent of those who jumped in the sea were not wearing lifebelts, although I saw plenty of lifebelts on the ship. I saw plenty of men and more women who appropriated two lifebelts, while others lost their heads and did not get one. A lifeboat was sent off to a sailing ship that did not look far off, but the sailing ship turned away.

It would be difficult to exaggerate the indignation which was expressed by the American survivors. The fact that the ship was absolutely unarmed – she did not even carry a signal gun – that she carried no munitions, nor was any part of her cargo designed to give comfort to the fighting forces of the Allies, combined with the fact that she was known to be a boat on which women and children would sail of necessity in making the Channel passage, made the act of those who struck at her particularly inexcusable. To an American who looked about upon the company of white-faced shivering women during the long hours of gloom and peril before the rescue ships appeared, and who listened to the wail of babies vainly wrapped against the chilling cold, sometimes by strangers' hands because their mothers' hands were still forever, a growing feeling of hot anger was inevitable.[94]

It was of course not only the American passengers who felt indignation and anger at the murderous attack which accounted, as a conservative estimate, for the loss of 50 lives, out of a ship's complement of 325 passengers and 53 crew. This callous attack had come only weeks after the German declaration that unrestricted warfare would be postponed, ignoring also the earlier German promises that passenger ships would not be attacked without warning.

Captain Mouffet, who survived despite his injuries, lamented that if the passengers had not panicked and rushed to the boats, the loss of life would have been limited to those killed by the explosion. In fact Captain Mouffet was able to keep his ship afloat and the SUSSEX, or what was left of her, was later towed into Boulogne – the launching of the boats had proved to

---

[94] Bridgland, *Outrage at Sea*, pp.83–84.

be unnecessary but in the panic it did not prove possible to prevent the passengers from doing so.

The French were quick to condemn the attack on the *SUSSEX*, issuing the following press statement:

> *As regards the Sussex, there is no shadow of doubt as to the fact that she was torpedoed without warning. Mr. John Harley, the American correspondent of the United Press of New York, states that on Friday, at 3 o'clock in the afternoon, whilst a dozen Americans were on the deck watching the evolutions of an aeroplane, a loud explosion took place in the fore part of the vessel. No warning was given, and the course of the torpedo was seen by three Americans, Mr. Baldwin (professor), his wife, and his daughter, Miss Elizabeth Baldwin, who have disappeared.*

Although no American lives were believed lost on the SUSSEX, the action posed a dilemma for President Wilson who was still espousing the policy of *'peace with honour'* and resisting calls for US action against Germany. On 19 April however, before Congress concerning the *SUSSEX* attack he announced:

> *... I have deemed it my duty, therefore, to say to the Imperial German Government, that if it is still its duty to prosecute relentless and indiscriminate warfare against vessels of commerce by the use of submarines, not withstanding the now demonstrated impossibility of conducting that warfare in accordance with what the Government of the United States must consider the sacred and indisputable rules of international law and the universal dictates of humanity, the Government of the United States is at last forced to the conclusion that there is but one course it can pursue; and that unless the Imperial German Government should now immediately declare and effect an abandonment of its present methods of warfare against passenger and freight carrying vessels this Government can have no choice but to sever diplomatic relations with the Government of the German Empire altogether.*
>
> *This decision I have arrived at with the keenest regret; the possibility of the action contemplated I am sure all thoughtful Americans will look forward to with unaffected reluctance. But we cannot forget that we are in some sort and by the force of circumstances the responsible spokesmen of the rights of*

humanity, and that we cannot remain silent while those rights seem in process of being swept utterly away in the maelstrom of this terrible war. We owe it to a due regard to our own rights as a nation, to our sense of duty as a representative of the rights of neutrals the world over, and to a just conception of the rights of mankind to take this stand now with the utmost solemnity and firmness.

To this very serious ultimatum, Berlin immediately responded expressing regret that

> *... the sentiments of humanity, which the Government of the United States extends with such fervour to the unhappy victims of the submarine campaign, have not extended to the millions of women and children who are being driven to starvation in order that their pangs may force the victorious armies of the Central Empires to dishonourable capitulation ... It would be an act which never could be vindicated in the eyes of humanity or of history to allow, after twenty-one months of war, a controversy to assume a development which could seriously menace peace between the German and American peoples.*

The German response continued to the effect that the commander of UB-29, Pustkuchen, would be punished and all German submarines received the following order: '*In accordance with the general principle of visit, search, and destruction of merchant-vessels recognized by international law, such vessels, both within and without the war zone, shall not be sunk without warning and without saving human lives, unless the ships attempt to escape or offer resistance.*'[95]

That response from Germany, in an attempt to keep the United States out of the war, came to be known as 'The Sussex Pledge', with the agreement to give adequate warning before sinking a merchant ship and having regard to the safety of those on board – in effect agreeing, once again, to abide by the well established Prize Code. This agreement by no means had unanimous support in Germany as many still believed that unrestricted submarine warfare could still bring a swift victory, even if it did bring America into the war. The response by Berlin also underlined the difficulties being faced in Germany due to the success of the Allied blockade of German ports.

---

[95]   Gibson and Prendergast, *The German Submarine War 1914–1918*, pp.88–89.

The Sussex Pledge however no doubt gave some hope, if not solace, to the merchant seafarer that the likelihood of becoming a murder victim might be diminished.

Although the German government had promised that Herbert Pustkuchen, who had claimed the *SUSSEX* was a troop carrier, would be punished for his action, he was nevertheless still active in the English Channel. Just a week after the *SUSSEX* incident he attacked HMS *PENELOPE* and sank the Dutch steamer *BERKESTOOM* on 25 April. He died on 12 June 1917 with all hands, after being depth-charged by HMT *SEA KING* off Land's End, with a record of having sunk 82 merchant ships and three warships.

After the quiet winter months of 1916 in terms of submarine activities in UK home waters, the *TEUTONIAN*, a tanker of 4,824 tons, loaded with refined oil bound for Avonmouth on 4 March and under the command of Captain R.D. Collins was to be the victim of a resumption of U-boat aggression. Although the widely promulgated orders from the German government stated that submarines would not attack merchant ships without due warning, when a U-boat surfaced nearby, Captain Collins nevertheless ordered full speed to increase his distance from the potential threat. The submarine responded by increasing its speed, eventually overtaking the slower merchant ship and firing warning shots, at which point Captain Collins stopped his ship and ordered the crew to take to the boats. The submarine, later identified as U-32 under the command of the spectacularly named *Kapitänleutnant* Baron Spiegel von und zu Peckelsheim, took up a position on the port beam of his victim, submerged and fired a torpedo, striking the *TEUTONIAN* on the port bow. On surfacing, U-32 fired shells into the tanker, causing it to burst into flames after which it eventually sank. Baron Spiegel did nothing to assist the survivors who were fortunate to be picked up by a patrol craft which landed them at Berehaven, none the worse for wear other than the cessation of their wages and the loss of all their belongings. The following day, the Baron repeated his action, sinking the British steamer *ROTHESAY*, bound for Troon with a cargo of iron ore, again without any casualties but again without any attempt to assist the survivors.

Allied merchant ships were not to be spared either from this resumption of U-boat activity. On 19 March, while at anchor off the Kentish Knock, the 1,744-ton Canadian steamer *PORT DALHOUSIE* was struck by a torpedo just after midnight. An account of this event was given by the ship's chief officer, Mr W.F. Spur:

> The PORT DALHOUSIE *was lying to her anchor, the sea watch being continued, when a loud hissing was heard by me and I looked to see what it was caused by. Almost immediately the ship was struck by, I believe, a torpedo amidships on the port side. She sank within one minute. Only myself, three seamen, and two firemen were saved by jumping into the water or being washed off the deck as the ship submerged and then seizing floating hatches. We were in the water one and three-quarter hours, and were rescued by the steamer Jessie and transferred to a patrol-boat and landed at Ramsgate at 11 p.m. yesterday.*[96]

The sinking of *PORT DALHOUSIE* resulted in the loss of 19 lives, victims this time of *Oberleutnant* Reinhold Saltzwedel in UB-10, adding to the resumption by individual U-boat commanders of attacking merchant ships without warning, regardless of The Sussex Pledge.

Other commanders who had resumed their attacks on merchant ships included von Forstner, of the *AGUILA* and *FALABA* atrocities, who sank the Norwegian steamer *NORNE* on 26 March, the British steamer *RIO TIETE* on 28 March and the British ore carrier *TREWYN* on 30 March. While there were no casualties from the sinking of the *NORNE* or *RIO TIETE*, the fate of the *TREWYN* was less certain. *TREWYN* was on a voyage from Algiers to Middlesborough and was observed passing Gibraltar on 25 March, which turned out to be her last known sighting. On 3 April the steamer *GOVERNOR* reported that a life-buoy showing *TREWYN*'s name and port of registry was seen in the sea off Ushant. Von Forstner however claimed that he had sunk *TREWYN* off Ushant, on 30 March, although the circumstances of that attack are uncertain. What is clear is there were no survivors from the *TREWYN*'s crew of 23, who were all pronounced 'presumed dead'. Their names are engraved on the Merchant Navy Memorial at Tower Hill in London.

Submarine attacks were not limited to steamers, as the British four-masted barque *BENGAIRN*, built in 1890 in Port Glasgow, discovered to her cost. On 1 April 1916, bound from Seattle to Queenstown with a cargo of wheat on

---

[96] Hurd, *The Merchant Navy*, Vol. 2, pp.297–298.

her 112th day at sea and under full sail, her master, Captain Learmont, watched as a submarine slowly surfaced close on the starboard bow. He saw a wisp of smoke from a gun on the submarine's deck, closely followed by a fountain of water erupting under his bow. Captain Learmont knew immediately there was nothing he could do to avoid being captured and ordered the sails to be backed. The ship, having been running under full sail, took a while to stop and the submarine, growing impatient, fired another warning shot.

Captain Learmont and his crew took to their boats, leaving their ship still in the water with sails fluttering and watched helplessly as the submarine circled the ship, firing a series of shots into the unprotected hull. An account of her last moments was recorded by one of the survivors:

Now she began to heel to port; slowly, as if loath to die, and then faster, as, with a roar, all her furniture and moveables broke adrift and rushed to lee'ard. We could see the whole length of her deck now, and the galley range as it burst through the doors and side of the midship house. Not until the masts lay parallel did one of them carry away; then, with tear of splintering wood, the fore topgallant mast suddenly went ... Then the screaming of the rats became a sound that was almost human as, with a sudden plunge, the ship slid under, stern first, and down ... There was only an empty space where, such a little while before, Bengairn had floated in all her beauty. Only the breaking of the waves alongside the boats, and the screeching of the circling gulls broke the silence as we lay on our oars, stunned by what had happened. In the stern sheets the little Captain, who had lost his ship, his Command, and his home, sat gazing at the patch of oily water ... Already the submarine was creeping down towards us, a wisp of white exhaust smoke from its stern. From its foredeck ... bearded men watched our all too apparent helplessness with smiles of satisfaction, a few of them covering us with their automatic pistols ... [The U-boat] edged the mate's boat aside like a feather. There was a guttural command from the conning tower, and the water around us was beaten into a froth as the Commander took the way off his vessel ... The Commander's greeting came down to us ... in excellent English. 'I'm sorry, Captain, you made a good passage. We were not expecting you for another week at least. From Seattle are you not?'[97]

---

[97] Woodman, *More Days, More Dollars*, p.281.

The submarine was in fact U-28 with von Forstner again. He asked Captain Learmont for his papers and some tobacco seen in the bottom of a lifeboat, after which he would be detained no longer. Captain Learmont objected, protesting that the deprivation of a caddy of tobacco was not worthy of '*a seaman and a gentleman*'. Von Forstner replied with, '*It is the action of one who is victorious. You English have had your day. I'll give you sixty seconds longer, Herr Kapitan.*' Captain Learmont gave up his supply of tobacco and U-28 moved away without making any provision for the safety of *BENGAIRN*'s survivors, firing departing shots over their heads. They were picked up three days later by HMS *ANTRIM*.

Clearly von Forstner believed he could act entirely on his own initiative while the dispute over the resumption of unrestricted submarine warfare continued within German circles. At a conference on just this matter, held at Pless Castle on 31 August 1916, Admiral von Holtzendorff argued strongly for such resumption, stating,

> ...*it is within our power to break England's determination to carry on the war to the end of the year; to put off commencing the U-boat war would put off the results in question; in this connection the question must be well considered as to whether our allies will be able to hold out any longer, if we renounce the use of the U-boat weapon we may have reason to believe that this means 'finis Germaniae'.*

The German Secretary of State of the Foreign Office, von Jagow, argued that unrestricted submarine warfare would inevitably lead to the loss of more American lives which would most certainly result in the USA declaring war on Germany. Further, if the USA, as the last neutral world power, were to raise arms against Germany then it was more than likely that the remaining neutral states would be obliged to do the same. As von Jagow summarised, '*Germany will be in such case looked upon as a mad dog against whom the hand of every man will be raised for the purpose of finally bringing about peace.*'

The conclusion of that conference at Pless Castle, as summarised by the German Imperial Chancellor, was that for unrestricted warfare to be successful, some 4 million tons of British shipping would need to be destroyed in a period of about four to six months; a target which was unlikely to be achieved with the naval forces available, particularly with the limited effectiveness of U-boat attacks during hours of darkness. He also expressed uncertainty of the support of Germany's own allies, but agreed that such action would be sure to draw the USA into the war against them.

On 27 November the Ellerman City passenger liner *CITY OF BIRMINGHAM*, on passage from Liverpool to Karachi with 317 souls on board, including 170 passengers, was torpedoed without warning although no submarine was seen. The Ellerman liner's Captain, W.J. Haughton had, despite the declared German government intention not to attack merchant ships without warning, taken every precaution in case such an attack might take place. Passengers had all been instructed in boat drills and had to wear lifebelts at all times. Zigzag courses at 18 knots were being maintained, lookouts posted and the 4.7-inch gun fitted at the stern was kept in constant readiness.

The ship took an immediate list after the torpedo explosion and it was soon apparent that little time remained to launch the lifeboats. The ship was stopped, wireless signals transmitted and all but one of the boats, where the falls were fouled, were clear of the sinking ship within ten minutes. Having assured himself that all personnel were off the ship, Captain Haughton stayed with his ship until it became abundantly clear that nothing further could be done and he slid down the side of the hull into the sea, to be picked up by one of his boats. As he was pulled into the boat he was heartened to hear the sound of some of the women passengers singing '*a heartening hymn*'. They were fortunately soon rescued by the hospital ship *LETITIA*, where Captain Haughton called for a muster when he learned that four lives had been lost in the evacuation of the ship. He had been particularly impressed by the behaviour of the women in abandoning ship and in his later report wrote '*... the women especially showed a good example by the way in which they took their places in the boats, as calmly as if they were going down to their meals, and when in the boats they began singing*'.[98]

The culprit responsible for the attack on the *CITY OF BIRMINGHAM* was Kurt Hartwig in U-32, again ignoring The Sussex Pledge and showing no consideration for the victims of his attacks.

Further atrocities were committed against merchant seafarers, an example of which was the murder of the captain of the Italian passenger steamer

---

[98]   Hurd, *The Merchant Navy*, Vol. 2, p.360.

PALERMO, on passage from New York to Genoa with a cargo of horses, ammunition and general cargo. An account of PALERMO's misfortune on 2 December was given by a survivor to Captain Bone:[99]

> We were unarmed, a slow ship. The submarine hit us with a shot on the bow and then ran up the signal to take to the lifeboats. We did so, and several shots were fired at the Palermo. They did not take effect, however, and a torpedo was sent into her side. She sank within a few minutes. Whether the fact that he had to use a torpedo to send our vessel to the bottom angered the commander I do not know, but the submarine came directly alongside of our lifeboats. The commander was on deck, and yelled, 'Where is the captain of that ship?' The captain stood up and made his way to the side where the German was standing. The German held his revolver close to our captain's head. 'You will never bring another ship across this ocean,' he said, using several oaths, then he pulled the trigger. Our captain fell dead, and we were permitted to continue.

The submarine responsible was the U–72, with the primary role as a mine-layer, whose commander at that time was *Kapitänleutnant* Ernst Krafft. Krafft was appointed to U–72 in January 1916 as his first submarine command and survived the war, having sunk a total of 38 British and Allied merchant ships. He died in July 1954 in the Soviet Vladimir prison camp.

Those in the German government supporting the unrestricted use of submarines had no doubt taken close note of actions of the likes of Baron Spiegel, von Forstner and Hartwig. They had also no doubt taken account of the large numbers of British and Allied merchant ships that were nevertheless still carrying goods to British ports unmolested and the enhanced shipbuilding activities in Britain to replace the lost ships. Further pressure was to be put on the Kaiser to put the U–boats to greater use and to accelerate the building of more submarines.

By the end of 1916 the loss of ships carrying food supplies was reaching a critical stage. At the start of the war, Britain was producing only 35 per cent of her food requirements and thus the need to increase food production to reduce the dependence on imports, mainly from America and Canada, was

---

[99] Bone, *Merchantmen-at arms: the British merchants' service in the war*, p.62.

crucial. The number of farmhands still working the farms was significantly reduced as many had joined up for military service, and the situation was worsened by a harvest failure in 1917.

To counter the dependence on imported food and to replace the male farmworkers, the Board of Agriculture formed the Women's Land Army in 1915 to replace the male workforce with women and by 1917 over a quarter of a million women had volunteered. Many farmers and remaining farm hands resented the imposition of women, in some individual cases because it removed the convenient excuse for a man not to be called for military service, and in others because of a belief that women were simply not capable of undertaking the labouring work of the men. This was found to be untrue, with women soon showing their ability to replace the men. Although there was still resistance throughout the war to the employment of women on the farms, there was some benefit to the farmer as women were paid significantly less than the men. Male farm labourers would earn about £2–10s a week, compared £1–15s a week for women, which was less than could be earned in the munitions factories where many more women were employed.

The government was however concerned that women may become coarsened by their exposure to land work and that they needed to be reminded of their femininity and the standards expected of them, with the caution that: '*You are doing a man's work and so you are dressed rather like a man; but remember that because you wear a smock and trousers you should take care to behave like an English girl who expects chivalry and respect from everyone she meets.*'

CHAPTER 11

THERE WAS TOO MUCH SEA TO SAIL

At the end of 1916 the German leaders were becoming increasingly concerned that despite localised victories against Allied forces it was clear that the war could not be won on land alone. Internal pressures demanded that additional measures needed to be taken to achieve positive progress. The German government, believing their position to be strong enough to force peace on their terms, set out what they considered to be the victories and successes of the Central Powers and approached the Allies, through neutral governments, with a view to entering peace negotiations. On 12 December 1916 that approach was made on the basis that if the Allies were not prepared to negotiate peace terms on the basis of the Central Powers' 'triumphant position', then Germany was prepared '*to continue the struggle to a victorious end*'[100] The Allies rejected the German offer, stating that peace was not possible until and unless the German Central Powers provided full reparation '*... for the rights and liberties of nations violated by Germany since the outbreak of war*'.

There had been high hopes in Berlin that peace could then have been achieved and great disappointment when this was not found to be the case. It was regarded as a lost opportunity to end the war in Germany's favour and thus it was determined that the German government must take whatever steps were needed, regardless of the views of neutral powers, and utilise fully any means to secure victory over the Allied forces.

Germany recognised that the Allied blockades of German and neutral ports had reduced the population to a state of near starvation and that drastic measures would have to be taken. On 31 January 1917 the German

---

[100]   Koerver, (ed.) *German Submarine Warfare 1914–1918 in the Eyes of British Intelligence*, pp.188–189.

Chancellor finally agreed that the submarines should be unfettered in their actions and the Kaiser proclaimed, '*I order the unrestricted U-boat campaign to begin on 1st February with the utmost energy.*'

Great concern was expressed in the Admiralty about this resumption, with Admiral Jellicoe, tasked with specific instructions to defeat the U-boat menace, writing that there was

> *... a serious danger that our losses in merchant ships, combined with the losses in neutral merchant ships, may by the early summer of 1917, have such a serious effect upon the import of food and other necessaries into the allied countries, as to force us into peace terms which the military position on the Continent would not justify, and which would fall far short of our desires.*[101]

Earlier in January, Admiral Jellicoe in his first public statement as First Sea Lord called for an increase in shipbuilding to replace the vessels lost,

> *... to keep up the strength of our mercantile marine, and to provide those gallant fellows, who have gone through innumerable dangers and hardships when their ships have been sunk, with new vessels to carry on the transport of the necessary supplies of food and material for the manhood and the industries of the country. No one recognises more than I do how great has been the output of the shipyards up to the present time. I would only say now, let there be no question of strikes, no bad time-keeping, no slacking; and let masters and men remember how great is their responsibility, not only towards the Navy and the nation, but also towards our Allies.*
>
> *Before I leave this subject, may I presume to remind the big shipping companies of the privilege which is theirs to see that some provision is made out of the war profits for the wives and children of those gallant fellows who have given their lives for their country, when their ships have been sunk, as truly as those who have lost their lives in the battle line? It is not for me to make suggestions, but I venture to say that the hearts of the officers and men would be lightened in the continued presence of danger and the recurring possibilities of disaster if they knew that those they may leave behind them would be cared for and educated.*

---

[101] The National Archives, ADM 116/3421, p.281.

These sentiments were much welcomed as the call by Admiral Jellicoe had put a spotlight on one of the major domestic concerns facing the seafarer. Provision for repatriation should the seafarer survive and provision for dependants remained unchanged since the start of the war, other than a limited insurance provision for loss of personal effects.

The year 1917 was to be a critical period with the lifting of restrictions on the unrestricted U-boat attacks and with little or no regard to the now 'old fashioned' concepts of the Prize Code. The chances of British and Allied merchant seafarers being murdered on the high seas were to increase significantly as the merchant ship, invariably on its own when attacked, still had little with which to defend itself, other than alertness and skill of the crews, the occasional stern gun, and luck. The dilemma facing a ship when challenged was still whether to run, make a fight of it or surrender, with the first two options providing a high risk of death. Without any warning of attack however, even that choice was denied.

The U-boats were quick off the mark with the killing spree accelerating in the first week of February with the sinkings of 84 Allied ships, of which 46 were British, accounting for the loss of 176 lives from the British steamers.

A particularly brutal attack was made on the British steamer *EAVESTONE* off Fastnet on 3 February. She was a Furness Withy transport, of 1,858 tons which left Barry Docks on 1 February on her way to Gibraltar and had the misfortune to encounter U-45, which opened fire at 3,000 yards, soon finding the range and repeatedly hitting the steamer, even as the boats were being lowered. Once the boats had cleared and dropped astern of the ship, the submarine turned her guns on to the boats, firing three shrapnel shells, the last of which killed the master, the steward John Kolm and a donkeyman, also wounding the second officer and two seamen. In total five lives were lost. The first officer was taken on board the submarine and interrogated after which the boats were left, with their dead on board, to make their way the best they could. They were fortunately picked up that night by a Norwegian barque, *REGINA*, but the action of U-45 was a clear indication of the manner in which the submarines were to conduct their campaign without any recourse to the Prize Code, or indeed any consideration of the plight of their victims, or of humanity. U-45 was commanded by Erich Sittenfeld, who was to be responsible for the destruction of five Allied merchant vessels in the first week of February, but was killed later that year, on 12 September in the Irish Sea.

The collier *DAUNTLESS* had been approaching the mouth of the Gironde, from Newcastle, on 4 February when she was attacked by gunfire from UB-39, commanded by Heinrich Küstner. The ship's engines were stopped and both lifeboats lowered, with the occupants of one boat ordered on board the submarine. German seamen took that lifeboat back to the *DAUNTLESS* and took what provisions they could find before placing explosives on board. The surviving crew of the collier were then ordered back to their boats after which the submarine disappeared. The survivors rowed through the freezing night, with the steward dying in the hours of darkness. Land could be sighted briefly the next day, but it soon became obscured by a snowstorm and it was not until the following day that they reached the beach, when the boat was overturned by a large breaker, killing the second engineer and a fireman. Fifteen men lost their lives.

The steamer *WARTENFELS*, originally built for the prestigious German Hansa Line but captured by the British in 1914, was torpedoed without warning on 5 February when 120 miles off Fastnet. Within 40 minutes the master, Captain Edward Webb, found himself a prisoner on board U-81, commanded by *Kapitänleutnant* Raimund Weisbach (who had been the torpedo officer on U-20 when sinking the *LUSITANIA*). Two of the *WARTENFEL*'s crew had been killed and Captain Webb was about to endure the humiliations and deprivations imposed by the German disregard for the lives of the merchant seafarer. His experience was to be regrettably similar to that of Captain H.J.Brooks of the *MASHOBRA*, described earlier. Hurd provides a detailed account of the treatment of Captain Webb, as given below.[102]

> ... *Captain Webb found himself a prisoner on board the U-boat. His ship had been sunk in the early morning, but it was not until seven o'clock in the evening that he was provided with any food, and, although there was plenty on board, he was only given a small piece of bread, besides a pannikin of water. In the meantime, a junior officer, who had served with the Hansa Line before the war, closely questioned him without result. Having spent the night*

---

[102]   Hurd, *The Merchant Navy*, Volume 3, pp. 345–346.

in the quartermaster's quarters, Captain Webb was roused at one o'clock and again questioned, and on his refusal to answer was told that he would be shot on reaching port, or before that if he caused any trouble. He was charged with acting as a decoy, it being suggested his ship was heavily armed. He passed eleven days on board the submarine and was then landed at Helgoland and lodged in a cell. Three days later he was placed on board a small steamer bound for Bremerhaven. The weather was cold and he had no overcoat, nor was any food provided. Owing to fog and ice, the journey occupied twenty-six hours. He was then marched to the town jail, searched and locked in a cell. It was bitterly cold, very little light entered the cell, and the sanitary arrangements were of the crudest character. His bed consisted of a plank; the food was inadequate in quantity and poor in quality.

Three and a half days were spent under these conditions, and early on the morning of the fourth day Captain Webb, in a famishing and weakened condition, was marched with about forty others, mostly fishermen, to the railway station, and entrained for Dülmen. When taken prisoner he had £5 upon him. The Germans deducted one mark for every day he had been kept in prison on the excuse that he ought to pay for his maintenance. Dülmen was reached at six the same evening, and then Captain Webb and his companions, weary mentally as well as physically and badly in need of nourishing food, were taken to a kind of outhouse and stripped, their clothes searched, and they themselves fumigated and given a bath. Though the cold was intense, Captain Webb was kept without a particle of clothing for three hours, and it was while still naked that he was handed an iron basin containing weak oatmeal. His clothing, so wet as to retard his normal circulation, was eventually returned to him. The party were then shepherded into a barrack. The weather was frosty and it was snowing. There was no fire in the barrack, and only a few more fortunate prisoners were given blankets, which were in a filthy condition. On the following day Captain Webb was put into a compound where the conditions were more bearable, but the food remained uneatable and there was very little of it.

Two days after Captain Webb was captured and his ship sunk, U-85 under the command of *Kapitänleutnant* Willy Petz attacked the Anchor Line passenger ship *CALIFORNIA* on her return voyage from New York to Glasgow on 7 February, when about 38 miles off Fastnet. Her captain, John Henderson, was well aware that America had just broken off diplomatic relations with Germany, following the U-boat sinking of the American steamer *HOUSATONIC*[103] and as such was particularly alert to the risk of a U-boat attack. *CALIFORNIA* was of 8,668 tons with a speed of 16 knots and had 31 passengers and 184 crew on board. Approaching the end of her voyage on a fine, clear morning although with a heavy swell running, at about 09:30 Captain Henderson and two watchkeeping officers saw a torpedo streaking towards them. There was not enough time for the evasive manoeuvre immediately ordered by Captain Henderson to take effect and the torpedo struck on the port quarter, the explosion killing five people immediately and the engine room rapidly flooding. With the ship beginning to sink very quickly there was little opportunity to take the way off the ship to enable the boats to be lowered safely and the lifeboats were almost afloat before they could be lowered. One boat overturned, flinging its passengers into the sea and another boat had to be cut loose as the ship sank. Remarkably, 10 boats got away within nine minutes of the torpedo explosion, which must be a great tribute to all on board in such dreadful circumstances.

Captain Henderson went down with his ship, but fate decreed that he should resurface and was in fact picked up by one of his own boats after about half an hour immersed in the freezing waters. A total of 43 lives were lost at the hands of Willy Petz either directly as the result of the explosion or by drowning. The survivors were fortunate to be rescued by a patrol craft which had picked up the distress signal sent by the ship as she was sinking.

The last ship to be sunk by Willy Petz in U-85 was the 6,330-ton Furness Withy steamer *VEDAMORE* which he torpedoed without warning when about 20 miles west of Fastnet later that same day. *VEDAMORE* was on her way to Liverpool with passengers and general cargo from Baltimore and sank in five minutes, leaving little time for the lifeboats to be cleared away and lowered. An 18-year-old apprentice, James Fell, was immediately ordered into a lifeboat by the captain, but refused and went to help the third officer to lower another boat. He was said to have been carrying a spare lifebelt, which he gave to the fourth engineer who had just come out of the engine room. He was later said to have given his own lifebelt to another crew member

---

[103]   The first American ship to be sunk by a U- boat and, coincidentally, the same name as the first ship ever to be sunk by a submarine, in the American Civil War.

who could not swim, but he did not survive the sinking. All passengers were saved but two further crew members died as a consequence of immersion in the freezing sea, despite having been pulled into a lifeboat. Altogether 23 crew members lost their lives on that freezing February day.

The career of Willy Petz was short. His total tally was the sinking of four merchant ships and damaging another, but his last encounter, one month later on 7 March was with the British 'Q' ship HMS *PRIVET*, posing as an unarmed merchant ship. The 'Q' ship had lured U–85 to the surface having suffered considerable damage herself from an unprovoked attack and had even feigned abandoning ship to further deceive Petz. At the appropriate moment, HMS *PRIVET* revealed her own guns and destroyed U–85, which sank with the loss of Willy Petz and his crew of 37. Petz had been responsible, with the sinking of *VEDAMORE* and *CALIFORNIA*, for the loss of 66 British lives.

All these sinkings had of course occurred when the victims were isolated, without there being any possibility of immediate aid – the submarines were certainly not going to give any. The merchant seafarer was only too aware that he was on his own when under attack, even if in home waters and even if there was help in the near vicinity, as became all too evident when the *SAINT NINIAN* attempted to come to the aid of the *CORSICAN PRINCE* on the morning of 7 February.

The *CORSICAN PRINCE*, a steamer of 2,776 tons commanded by Captain G.O. Jones and owned by the Prince Line, had left Dundee the previous day bound for Dunkirk with a cargo of timber and was steaming within the buoyed 'war lane' channel. When about thee miles off Whitby and without seeing any sign of a submarine or having any warning, a torpedo struck her on the starboard side, breaching the engine room bulkhead. A despairing SOS was sounded on her whistle as her crew of 31 had little time to take to the boats and one fireman lost his life during the evacuation. The SOS was however noted by the British *SAINT NINIAN*, a short distance away, under the command of Captain John Barham who decided, in keeping with his instincts to help fellow mariners, to go to the aid of the stricken Prince Line steamer to pick up her survivors. He launched a rescue boat as the U-boat had seemingly disappeared but, unknown to the *SAINT NINIAN*, the U-boat re-surfaced about 200 yards from her with a periscope clearly visible to the survivors of the *CORSICAN PRINCE* who waved and called the alarm to *SAINT NINIAN*. At such a short range, *SAINT NINIAN* was a sitting target and sure enough a torpedo was fired, sinking her within about five minutes and killing 15 of her crew of 28, including the loss of Captain Barham. The submarine again disappeared without offering any assistance and the survivors of both ships were fortunate in being picked up by the HM minesweeper *RECEPTO*. The submarine responsible for both sinkings had been UB-34, one of the smaller coastal U-boats under the command of *Oberleutnant zur See* Theodor Schultz, who was later lost with all hands when his UB-34 struck a mine off the coast of Holland in November 1917.

The day after the sinkings of the *CALIFORNIA*, *VEDAMORE*, *SAINT NINIAN* and *CORSICAN PRINCE* gave rise to one of the more extraordinary events emanating from an encounter between a British merchant ship and a U-boat, where the captured master of a British steamer surrendered a U-boat to the Royal Navy.

At about 23:20 on 8 February, the 1,311 ton British collier *HANNA LARSEN* was off Spurn Point on her way to load a cargo of coal on the Tyne when four shells were fired at her from an unseen submarine. Her master, Captain Thomas Reid, stopped his ship and had the lifeboats readied for lowering. After a period of about 15 minutes, during which time there had been no further action and no sighting of a submarine, Captain Reid decided to get underway again. After a few minutes another shot was fired and this time Captain Reid decided to abandon ship, but the shooting continued as the boats were being lowered and the *HANNA LARSEN* was hit several times, during which one crew member was killed and four others wounded. The submarine then made its appearance, calling Captain Reid and his chief engineer on board and sending a German boarding party to the damaged collier, placing bombs on board to sink the vessel. The submarine was the UC-39, commanded by *Kapitänleutnant* Ehrentraut and, taking the captured captain and chief engineer below, he left the dead and injured crew in their boats to fend for themselves.

Having sunk the Norwegian steamer *HANS KLINCK* the previous day, Ehrentrant attacked another Norwegian steamer, the *IDA*, in the morning following his sinking of the *HANNAH LARSEN*, which Captain Reid was able to observe. UC-39 fired more than 25 rounds into the defenceless Norwegian, continuing his fire even after the ship had stopped with the crew desperately trying to get clear of their ship in the lifeboats. Ehrentraut sent a boarding party over, which found the chief officer and a steward dead on the deck, and placed the bombs to finish the ship. No attempt was made to assist the survivors in the boats and UC-39 submerged and left the scene.

Later that day Ehrentraut sighted another steamer and surfaced, intending to sink her by gunfire, but was dismayed to find that he had run into the path of a destroyer, HMS *THRASHER*. The submarine made an emergency dive, but could not evade the depth charges of the destroyer, suffering considerable damage with the sea pouring through the conning tower. Ehrentrant had little option but to surface and immediately came under fire from the destroyer. He climbed out of the conning tower, presumably with the intention of surrendering, but was immediately shot dead. An engineer who showed himself was also shot and wounded. Captain Reid realised that all on the submarine would soon be killed so, rapidly fashioning a white flag, he decided he would climb up the conning tower and show his white flag, shouting to the destroyer to stop firing as he was a British prisoner. Fortunately the destroyer heeded his call and stopped firing, and their crew watched in some surprise as the surviving U-boat crew climbed on deck with their hands raised while Captain Reid directed operations from the conning tower. Captain Reid, his chief engineer and 17 German survivors were taken on board *THRASHER* and landed later at Immingham, from where it was reported that the Germans seemed pleased to accept the safer status of prisoners rather than to continue to face the hazards inherent in their own pursuance of the directive to resume unrestricted warfare.

Even if survivors from a U-boat attack escaped the emergency evacuation, the shelling and the torpedo explosion, the chances of survival in an open boat, without a near landfall and in anything other than calm and clement weather were slim, as were the chances of an early rescue. One of the most harrowing but comprehensive descriptions of survival at sea in a lifeboat was however given by Captain B. C. Chave of the *ALNWICK CASTLE* to his owners, the Union Castle Line, written from the safety of his eventual rescuer, the French steamer *VENEZIA*:

SS VENEZIA, at Sea, 28th March 1917.

With deep regret I have to report the loss of your steamer ALNWICK CASTLE, which was torpedoed without warning at 6:10 a.m. on Monday,

19th March, in a position about 320 miles from the Scilly Isles.

At the time of the disaster there were on board, besides 100 members of my own crew and 14 passengers, the Captain and 24 of the crew of the collier transport TREVOSE, whom I had rescued from their boats at 5:30 p.m. the previous day, their ship having been torpedoed at 11 a.m. the previous day, two Arab firemen being killed by the explosion, which wrecked the engine room. I reported this rescue by W.T. after dark. The Captain of the TREVOSE reported having seen another steamer blown up while in his boat, probably by the same submarine.

I was being served with morning coffee at about 6:10 a.m. when the explosion occurred, blowing up the hatches and beams from No. 2, and sending up a high column of water and debris, which fell back on the bridge. The Chief Officer put the engines full astern, and I directed him to get the boats away. All our six boats were safely launched and left the ship, which was rapidly sinking by the head. I destroyed by sinking the two bags of Admiralty mail which were ready in my cabin; also the secret code books and sailing orders.

The submarine lay between the boats, but whether she spoke to any of them I do not know. She proceeded NE after a steamer which was homeward bound, about four miles away, and soon after we saw a tall column of water, etc., and knew that she had found another victim. I got in touch with all the boats and, from the number of occupants, I was satisfied that every one was safely in them. The one lady passenger and her baby of three months old were with the stewardess in the Chief Officer's boat. I directed the Third Officer to transfer four of his men to the Second Officer's boat, to equalise the number, and told them all to steer between east and east-northeast for the Channel. We all made sail before a light westerly wind, which freshened before sunset, when we reefed down. After dark I saw no more of the other boats. That was Monday, 19 March.

I found only three men who could help me to steer, and one of these subsequently became delirious, leaving only three of us. At daylight we found our sea anchor and the rudder had both gone. There was too much sea to sail. We manoeuvred with oars, while I lashed two oars together and made another sea anchor. We spent the whole of Tuesday fighting the sea, struggling with oars to assist the sea anchor to head the boat up to the waves, constantly soaked with cold spray and pierced by the bitter wind, which was now from *the north. I served out water twice daily, one dipper between two men, which made a portion about equal to one-third of a condensed milk tin. Fortunately I had made a practice of keeping in the boats a case of condensed milk, a case of beef, two tins of biscuits, and a skein of amberline and some twine and needle, besides the regulation equipment; also I had provided a bundle of blankets for each boat. We divided a tin of milk between four men once a day, and a tin of beef (6lbs) was more than sufficient to provide a portion for each person (twenty-nine) once a day.*

During the night of Wednesday-Thursday the wind dropped for a couple of hours and several showers of hail fell. The hailstones were eagerly scraped from our clothing and swallowed. I ordered the sail to be spread out in the hope of catching water from a rain shower, but we were disappointed in this, for the rain was too light. Several of the men were getting light-headed, and I found that they had been drinking salt water, in spite of my earnest and vehement order.

At 4 a.m. the wind came away again from north-west, and we made sail, but unfortunately it freshened again, and we were constantly soaked with spray, and had to be always bailing. Our water was now very low, and we decided to mix condensed milk with it. Most of the men were now helpless, and several were raving in delirium. The foreman cattleman, W. Kitcher, [of ALNWICK Castle] died and was buried. Several of the men collapsed, and others temporarily lost their reason, and one of those became pugnacious and climbed about the boat uttering complaints and threats. The horror of that night, together with the physical suffering, are beyond my power of description.

When daylight came, the appeals for water were so angry and insistent that I deemed it best to make an issue at once. After that had gone round, amid much cursing and snatching, we could see that only one issue remained. One fireman, Thomas, was dead; another was nearly gone. My steward, Buckley, was almost gone. We tried to pour some milk and water down his throat, but he could not swallow. No one could now eat biscuits. It was impossible to swallow anything solid. Our throats were afire, our lips furred, our limbs numbed, our hands were white and bloodless. During the forenoon of Friday, the 23rd, another fireman, named Tribe, died, and my steward, Buckley, died; also a cattleman, whose only name I could get as Peter, collapsed, and died about noon.

To our unspeakable relief we were rescued about 1:30 p.m. on Friday the 23rd by the French steamer VENEZIA, of the Fabre Line, for New York for horses. The French captain, M. Paul Boniface, handled his empty vessel with great skill, and brought her alongside us, sending out a lifebuoy on a line for each of us to seize. We were unable to climb the ladders, so they hoisted us one by one in ropes until the twenty-four live men were aboard. The four dead bodies were left in the boat, and she was fired at by the gunners of the VENEZIA in order to destroy her, but the shots did not take affect.

I cannot speak with sufficient gratitude of the extreme kindness and solicitation which were shown us by all on board.

'The position of our rescue was in 46° 19' N, 9° 13' W, about 160 miles from the nearest land, which was the northern coast of Spain. We had sailed about 200 miles in a south-easterly direction. I doubt if we should have survived another night after our last issue of water. I gave the main facts of the situation to the captain, and he sent out a radio message announcing our rescue in such a manner as to appraise all ships in the vicinity of the possibility of finding some of the other five boats. Captain Boniface also left his course that afternoon and proceeded to the north-west in the hope of seeing some of the other boats.

I conclude my report with an expression of sincere and deep gratitude to Captain Boniface and the officers and crew of the VENEZIA, to whose most generous kindness we owe a speedy recovery from the effects of our exposure. The doctor is an aged gentleman of seventy-five years, who most nobly exemplifies the gallant spirit of French self-sacrifice. He, too, has done his utmost on our behalf.

Captain Chave's account is remarkable for its clarity and detail, giving a most vivid description of the horrors of attempting to survive in an open boat in winter in the North Atlantic, yet gives no complaint about his own condition or of succumbing to despair, other perhaps than his poignant comment that 'there was too much sea to sail'. His experience of the five days adrift is an example to all of his steadfastness and resolve to overcome the most dreadful of situations, plus his superb seamanship and personal authority.

Chief Officer Blackman, with 31 souls in his boat, including the female passenger with her baby, was found by Spanish fishermen off Cape Ortegal, five days after the rescue of Captain Chave with only 21 still alive and all near the point of insanity due to lack of water. Chief Officer Blackman's later report stated:

> *Although we had occasional showers of rain everything was so saturated with salt that the little we did catch was undrinkable. We even tried licking the woodwork (oars, tiller, seats, etc.) to gather up the rain spots and so moisten our mouths, but the continual spray coming over rendered this of little use. In fact we actually broke up the water beaker in order to lick the inside of the staves, which we found saturated with moisture, and to us delicious.*[104]

The baby, amazingly, survived the ordeal of the lifeboat, but died shortly after being rescued and landed in Spain, after having been adrift for nine days and sailed a distance of 380 miles.

Of the six boats successfully launched, two were never seen again and one can only surmise the fate of those on board in the cold, inhospitable waters of the North Atlantic Ocean in winter. Apart from the boats of the captain and the chief officer, one other boat was found with 27 still alive and another with 20 living and five dead. Out of the total of 139 souls on board, 40 had lost their lives as the result of the torpedo attack.

After a short period of convalescence Captain Chave returned to sea and was knighted in 1921 for his services to the Merchant Navy, retiring in 1932 as Commodore of the Union Castle Line. After the outbreak of World War II he volunteered to return to sea, joining the RNR as a lowly lieutenant in the sea transport branch until 1943. He later became the Chairman of the Sub-Commissioners of Pilotage for Southampton and the Isle of Wight, retiring from that position in 1951, aged 80.

The submarine responsible was the U–81, commanded by *Kapitänleutnant* Raimund Weisbach, responsible also for the earlier sinking of the *WARTENFELS* and the capture of Captain Webb. Weisbach had shown no compunction about attacking without warning and had the previous day also sunk the *TREVOSE* with the loss of two lives. Weisbach's actions against merchant shipping came to an end a few weeks later, when on 1 May U–81 was himself torpedoed by a British submarine, E54 and spent the rest of

---

[104]   Edwards, *War Uunder the Red Ensign 1914–1918*, p.164.

the war as a prisoner. On his return to Germany he was hailed as a much decorated 'war hero', dying in 1970.

The month of February, as the first month of the new period of unrestricted submarine warfare, brought about the highest monthly total of ship losses since the start of the war. A total of 114 British merchant ships were lost to U-boats and 14 to mines, with a total loss of 425 lives.[105] During that month, four U-boats were lost, all around the UK coastline, three of which were sunk by Royal Naval ships and one was blown up by her own mines.[106] It was clear where the balance of power lay.

The month of March proved to be even worse, with 146 British merchant ships sunk and 702 lives lost, to set against the destruction of four more U-boats. One particularly poignant incident was the loss of the small wooden three-masted sailing ship, *REWARD*, built in 1878. She was shelled and sunk by U-72, under the command of Ernst Voight on 13 March, while on passage between Falmouth and Guernsey with a cargo of coal. All the crew of five were lost, including the master, Captain John Cawsey and his 13-year-old son Sidney who had been at sea for some time with his father and was employed as the ship's cook. While boys of such a young age were not common on British merchant ships, there were however several losses of boys under the age of 15, employed usually as a mess boy.

---

[105] Koerver, (ed.) *German Submarine Warfare 1914–1918 in the Eyes of British Intelligence*, p.694.

[106] Gibson and Prendergast, *The German Submarine War 1914–1918*, p.372.

CHAPTER 12

THE DEAD ARE LEFT TO THE SEA

After the dreadful losses in the first two months of the reinvigorated submarine campaign, the United States was also finding the situation intolerable with the increasing loss of American lives. On 3 April 1917 President Wilson felt forced to make a speech to Congress when he said, in effect as a prelude to a declaration of war against Germany;

> *Civilisation itself seems in the balance, but right is more precious than peace, and we shall fight for the thing which we carry nearest to our hearts, for democracy, for the right of those who submit to authority to have a voice in their own government, for the rights and liberties of small nations, for the universal domination of right, for such a concert of free peoples as will bring peace and safety to all nations and make the world itself at last free. To such tasks we dedicate our lives, our fortunes, and everything we have, with the pride of those who know the day has come when America is privileged to spend her blood and might for the principle that gave her birth, happiness and peace. God helping her, she can do no other.*

Two days later, on 5 April, the United States declared war on Germany, thereby fulfilling the prophesy of many in the German government that the reintroduction of unrestricted submarine warfare could drag America into the war against them. The gamble had therefore been taken by Germany that the action against all Allied shipping would starve Britain into submission before America could really bring her considerable resources effectively into action.

The declaration of war had been a difficult move for President Wilson, as the United States and Germany had been major trading partners, with

American policy very much against becoming involved in a European war. There had been considerable internal political pressure to remain uninvolved and to act only as a peacemaker to broker an end to the struggle. There was also significant resentment of the British blockades of German and neutral ports and the 'board and search' policy which had been carried out by the Royal Navy, much to the detriment of American commerce. In practice, the United States regarded its involvement not so much as an ally of Britain but as an 'Associated Power', or an independent belligerent, to be in a position to ensure that Germany would be defeated and that America could dictate the eventual peace treaty.[107]

Prior to the US declaration of war, Admiral W.S. Sims of the US Navy (the same US naval officer who had drawn international attention to the inadequacy of open lifeboats following the *TITANIC* tragedy), had been despatched to Britain for a meeting with the British First Sea Lord, Sir John Jellicoe, when Jellicoe reputedly stated '*The German submarines are winning the war*'.[108] Sims learned that about 1 million tons of merchant shipping was lost every month – a loss which could not be sustained in terms of continuing to provide civilian and military populations with the provisions and equipment needed. The rate of shipbuilding could not replace those lost and there was a great shortage of merchant seafarers to crew the ships. Old ships, often in a poor condition, were being sent back to sea, including the requisitioning of old wooden sailing ships, and neutral countries were keeping their ships in port to avoid the high loss rate. Walter Page, the US Ambassador in London declared '*What we are witnessing is the defeat of England*'.[109] The Admiralty estimated that unless the loss rate could be significantly reduced then the war could be lost by November of that year, in keeping with the German estimates.

The merchant seafarer continued in much the same way as at the start of the war, watching the escalation of action against merchant ships with little change either in the support or protection available. The month of April 1917 saw an even further escalation of merchant ship losses as well as an increase in the levels of barbarity exercised by some U-boat commanders,

---

[107]   Gibson and Prendergast, *The German Submarine War 1914–1918*, p.158.

[108]   Ibid., p.159.

[109]   Ibid., p.159.

with The Sussex Pledge soon forgotten. Of these April losses the murder of the crews of the British steamers *TORRINGTON* and *TORO* stand out as among the most inhumane acts perpetrated by any commander of a U-boat.

On 8 April the *TORRINGTON*, a steamer of 5,597 tons under the command of Captain Anthony Starkey was homeward bound from Savona to Barry in ballast, about 150 miles off the Scilly Isles with a typically multinational crew of 37 men from Britain, Greece, Sweden, Sierra Leone and India. At about 11:30 a lifeboat was sighted in the distance and Captain Starkey ordered the helmsman to steer towards it, at which time he noticed a torpedo heading straight towards him. His attempt to manoeuvre away from the torpedo's track was unsuccessful and the torpedo struck forward of the bridge, with a tremendous explosion which threw debris and water high above the ship and Nos 2 and 3 holds began to fill rapidly.

TORRINGTON was equipped with a four-inch gun on the poop, but with the ship sinking by the bow and with the stern high in the air, the gun was not able to bear on the submarine. The ship soon stopped in the water and the submarine surfaced and began shelling the sinking ship. Captain Starkey felt he had no option but to take to the boats, still under fire, and managed to get both boats safely away without any casualties. He took charge of the starboard boat and his chief officer, Charles Cleves, took charge of the port boat. The submarine then came between the boats and fired on Mr Cleves' boat, presumably killing them all and destroying the boat, as there was to be no further sighting of those men or of their boat. Captain Starkey and the 16 remaining crew were taken on board the submarine with Starkey immediately taken below and subjected to a particularly hostile and insulting interrogation, with his remaining crew kept on deck. He was initially accused of lying about his name when the U-boat commander produced an out-of-date Lloyds List, showing the name of Captain Starkey's predecessor and accused of lying again when, after stating his ship was armed with a stern gun, he had not been able to bring it to bear on the submarine due to the stern being lifted high out of the water. When asked why his gunners were not in uniform, Captain Starkey replied that they had not had time to change into their best uniforms.

While Captain Starkey was being interrogated, the survivors from the starboard boat were kept on the deck of the submarine while the lifeboat's provisions were being brought aboard the submarine and the lifeboat then wrecked. What had happened to the port lifeboat was not clear, but Captain Starkey later noted that some provisions from that boat had been brought aboard the submarine. He was told by the U-boat commander that he would be shot as a pirate and, as for his crew, '*let them swim*'.[110] The threat to '*let them swim*' became all too clear when the submarine moved away from the *TORRINGTON* and then submerged for about 20 minutes, resurfacing by the sinking ship from where the boarding party sent by the U-boat was returning with looted supplies. There was no sign of the survivors who had been on the U-boat's deck, thus it must have been that the submerging of the submarine had been for the specific purpose of washing those men off the deck – a calculated act of murder. Captain Starkey had not seen what happened to his men or to the starboard boat and had assumed that his men had been put back into their boat and left to fend for themselves. It was only later that the radio operator of the submarine told him what had happened.

Captain Starkey was kept a prisoner on the U-boat, in company with Captain Ashfield of the *PETRIDGE* and Captain Draper of the *UMVOTTI*, plus a gunner of each of those ships. It was probably the boats of one of these ships, both of which had been sunk that morning by the same U-boat, which Captain Starkey had first seen. He was taken to Germany to be a prisoner for the rest of the war and it was only after his release that the *TORRINGTON* murders became known.

The U-boat responsible was the modern and well equipped U-55 under the command of *Kapitänleutnant* Wilhelm Werner who, a few days later, committed much the same atrocity when he came across the 3,066-ton steamer *TORO*, under the command of Captain George Hopley. The Ellerman Wilson steamer had been homeward bound with general cargo from Alexandria to Hull on 12 April, about 200 miles off Ushant, when Werner, again without warning and while still submerged, struck the *TORO* with a single torpedo causing the steamer to sink rapidly. Two boats cleared the sinking ship, the one with Captain Hopley on board being brought alongside the U-55 when he, plus a gunner, were brought onto the U-boat and subjected to much the same treatment as had been meted out to Captain Starkey. Fourteen survivors of the *TORO*'s crew were left on deck, having first had all their lifejackets removed and their boat taken by the U-55 crew

---

[110]   Bridgland, *Outrage at Sea*, p.160.

to board *TORO* and take what provisions they could. The submarine then moved away and later submerged, following which none of *TORO*'s survivors could be seen. U-55 returned to the site of *TORO*'s sinking to recover her own boarding party and Captain Starkey was invited by Werner to view the final shelling and sinking of his ship from the conning tower. Once again, Werner had committed an atrocious act of barbarity with the calculated murder of 14 more merchant seafarers, including two brothers, James and Joseph Hardy, both firemen. Werner's further activities are recorded later.

The chief officer, who was in charge of the second boat from *TORO*, with 16 others on board were believed to have been rescued on 15 April by the *BELLAGIO*.

The practicalities of lowering lifeboats in any other than benign weather conditions and with the ship stopped and upright had always been a particular point of concern of seafarers, as was the lack of shelter in the boats from the weather. On the afternoon of 13 April the Ellerman Wilson steamer *ZARA*, of 1,331 tons was bound from Shetland to Norway when she was torpedoed without warning by U-30 and sank within three minutes of the torpedo explosion. Remarkably, in that limited time the crew managed to lower two boats, with the chief officer, Mr William Golightly, taking the starboard boat, and the master, Captain G. Nicoll and the second officer taking the port boat. Captain Nicoll reported that 11 crew and 11 passengers perished at that time, either from drowning or from the initial explosion. The boats hoisted sails and were in the sea for 50 hours before they managed to reach an island off the Norwegian coast, where they were rescued by local fishermen. During those 50 hours four firemen and the chief cook died from exposure, with the remainder suffering from exhaustion and exposure. Altogether 27 lives were lost, including that of the chief officer. U-30 had been commanded by *Kapitänleutnant* Franz Grünert, who survived the war.

That same afternoon ordeal by lifeboat followed for the crew of *KARIBA*, on passage from Dakar to Falmouth when, in a position about 250 miles off Ushant, she was struck without any warning by a torpedo fired by U-27. With only a few minutes to escape and a starboard boat smashed by the explosion, the crew managed to launch two lifeboats which were able to keep together for two hours before losing sight of each other. Survivors were picked up by a French trawler after nine days adrift in open boats, with 11 men having died from exposure in the boat, with a further two succumbing later in hospital.[111] The U-boat responsible was commanded by *Kapitänleutnant* Gerhard Schulz whose next victim, two days later, was the British steamer *GRETASTON*, torpedoed off the Iberian coast with the loss of all hands – a total of 29 lives. In two days Schulz had killed 42 British merchant seafarers, without, it would seem, making any effort to secure their safety. He, however, survived the war.

The trials and privations of the merchant seafarer continued, as was seen in the sinking of the converted Anchor Line passenger ship *CAMERONIA*. At 10,968 tons, twin-screwed, with a maximum speed of 19 knots and capable of carrying 2,650 troops, she was well suited for her wartime role. On passage carrying troops from Marseille to Alexandria, in an area well tainted by U-boats but with two destroyers as escorts, she was performing the standard zigzag manoeuvres with additional lookouts and military signallers posted in readiness for communication with the escorting destroyers. Boats were already swung outboard with a guard party by each boat. *CAMERONIA* was taking as many precautionary measures as could reasonably be expected when, in a position about 150 miles east of Malta, she was struck without warning by a torpedo.

The account of this event is best reported in the words of her master, Captain David W. Bone, providing a level of detail now rare in the remaining annals of the Mercantile Marine in World War I. It also relates the suddenness of the unexpected attack, disrupting the routine of a large ship at sea already in a state of alert:[112]

An alarmed cry from aloft – a half uttered order to the steersman – an explosion, low down in the bowels of the ship, that sets her reeling from her stride. The upthrow comes swiftly on the moment of impact. Hatches, coal, shattered debris, a huge column of solid water go skyward in a hurtling mass to fall in torrent on the bridge. Part of a human body strikes the awning spars and hangs – watch-keepers are borne to the deck by the weight of water – the steersman falls limply over the wheel with blood pouring from a gash in his forehead. Then silence for a stunned half minute, with only the thrust of the engines marking the heart-beat of the stricken ship.

---

111 Hurd, *The Merchant Navy*, Vol. 3, pp.21–22.

112 Bone, *Merchantmen-at-arms: the British merchants' service in the war*, pp.96–99.

Uproar! Most of our men are young recruits: they have been but two days on the sea. The torpedo has gone hard home at the very weakest hour of our calculated drill. The troops are at their evening meal when the blow comes, the explosion killing many outright. We had counted on a proportion of the troops being on deck, a steadying number to balance that sudden rush from below that we foresaw in emergency. Hurrying from the mess decks as enjoined, the quick movement gathers way and intensity: the decks become jammed by the pressure, the gangways and passages are blocked in the struggle. There is the making of a panic – tuned by their outcry, 'God! O God! O Christ!' The swelling murmur is neither excited nor agonised – rather the dull, hopeless expression of despair.

Captain Bone continues to describe the unexpected action of a small, young bridge boy who, seeing the turmoil on the decks below and the impossibility of the troops' officers exercising any control over their men in the noise and pandemonium, picked up a bridge megaphone and shouted in his broad Glasgow accent, '*Hey! Steady up you men doon therr, ye'll no' dae ony guid fur yersels croodin th' ladders.*' This unexpected call from the bridge boy had the desired effect, immediately bringing the flows of movement of men to a halt, with order on deck being restored.

By this time the engines had stopped and sufficient way was off the ship to allow the lifeboats to be lowered. The bow was sinking rapidly with little time left to clear the sinking ship and, with nearly 3,000 people on board there were boats for just over half that number, but with ample raft capacity for the remainder. Captain Bone continued his narrative describing the lowering of the boats:

Our drill, that provided for lowering the boats with only half-complements in them, will not serve. We pass orders to lower away in any condition, however overcrowded. The way is off the ship, and it is with some apprehension we watch the packed boats that drop away from the davit heads. The shrill ring of the block-sheaves indicates a tension that is not far from breaking point. Many of the lifeboats reach the water safely with their heavy burdens, but the strain on their tackles – far beyond their working load – is too great for all to stand to it. Two boats go down by the run. The men in them are thrown violently to the water, where they float in the wash and shattered planking. A third dangles from the after fall, having shot her manning out at the parting of the forward tackle. Lowered by the stern, she rights, disengages, and drifts aft with the men clinging to the life-lines. Their life-belts are sufficient to keep them afloat: the ship is going down rapidly by the head, and there remains the second line of boats to be hoisted and swung over. The Chief Officer, pausing in his quick work, looks to the bridge inquiringly, as though to ask, 'How long?' The fingers of two hands suffice to mark our estimate.

The decks are now angled to the deepening pitch of the bows. Pumps are utterly inadequate to make the impression on the swift inflow. The Chief Engineer comes to the bridge with a hopeless report. It is only a question of time. How long? Already the water is lapping at a level of the foredeck. Troops massed there and on the forecastle head are apprehensive; it is indeed a wonder that their officers have held them for so long. The commanding officer sets example by a cool nonchalance that we envy. Posted with us on the bridge, his quick eyes note the flood surging in the pent 'tween decks below, from which his men have removed the few wounded. The dead are left to the sea.

Captain Bone continued to describe the frantic efforts of the escorting destroyers to find and attack the submarine and then the superb seamanship demonstrated by both destroyers in picking up the survivors from the sea and directly off the crippled *CAMERONIA*. The first run to go alongside the stricken troopship was HMS *NEMESIS*, enabling troops to jump from the sloping deck of the troopship directly on to her deck, the noise of which was described by Captain Bone as '… *the thud and clatter of the troops jumping to her deck sets up a continuous drone of deliverance*'. Finally, listing heavily with the weight of the troops on her decks, *NEMESIS* swung away and replaced HMS *RIFLEMAN* who had been keeping a watchful eye on the possibility of the submarine making a second attack.

This time *RIFLEMAN* came alongside, but in a stern–first manoeuvre in case the *CAMERONIA* should go down in a rush taking with her the smaller vessel and also enabling her to make a rapid departure from the side of the sinking ship if necessary. The contact between the two ships was made '*with a resounding impact that makes her living deckload to stagger*'. Captain Bone's narrative continued:

We lose no time. Scrambling down the life-ropes, our small company endeavours to get foothold on her decks. The destroyer widens off at the rebound, but by clutch of friendly hands the men are dragged aboard. One fails to reach safety. A soldier loses grip and goes to the water. The Chief Officer follows him. Tired and unstrung as he must be by the labours of the last half-hour, he is in no condition to effect a rescue. A sudden deep rumbling from within the sinking ship warns the destroyer captain to go ahead. We are given no choice to aid our shipmates: the propellers tear the water in a furious race that sweeps them away, and we draw off swiftly from the side of the ship.

CAMERONIA then plunged beneath the waves, some 40 minutes after the torpedo explosion.

The chief officer had played a major role in the evacuation of the ship, losing his life in the last moments when rescue was at hand. It seems clear from Captain Bone's account that his crew had put the rescue of the passengers, in this case the troops, ahead of their own safety. Accounts of the total loss of life vary considerably, but there is some consensus that 129 troops and 11 crew members lost their lives.[113], [114]

Captain David Bone returned to sea, becoming the Commodore Captain of the Anchor Line and later seeing action in World War II. He was awarded the CBE and knighted for his services to the Merchant Navy, retiring in 1946 after 57 years at sea. He was also a prolific author of books regarding many aspects of seafaring.

The CAMERONIA had been sunk by U–33, under the command of *Kapitänleutnant* Gustav Sieb, who had earlier claimed responsibility in 1916 for the sinking, by mines he had laid, of the BRITANNIC (sister ship of TITANIC). He survived the war.

The destruction, primarily of British merchant shipping, had continued unabated throughout the month of April. On 24 April 1917, a day when 26 Allied and neutral merchant ships were lost, the Elder Dempster passenger liner ABOSSO, bound from Lagos to Liverpool and about 180 miles off Fastnet was struck by a single torpedo, fired without warning from U–43. Built in 1912 and of 7,782 tons, with her sister ships APPAM and APAPA,

---

[113]   Gibson and Prendergast, *The German Submarine War 1914–1918*, p.244.

[114]   Tennent, *British Merchant Ships Sunk by U-Boats in World War One*, p.12.

she was one of the largest classes of ships in the Elder Dempster fleet and was armed for her own protection. In the dark evening at about 21:05 a torpedo struck in the after part of the engine room; her master, Captain James T. Toft, ordered stop engines and for the distress signal immediately to be broadcast along with firing distress flares. Acting contrary to the procedures of the rehearsed lifeboat drills, four boats were immediately launched without orders from any of the officers, suffering the inevitable fate of launching while the ship was still underway. The three boats between them had 41 passengers and 23 crew members on board and all were lost as the boats hit the water and were swamped. Fortunately, as *ABOSSO* initially began to settle on an even keel Captain Toft took the opportunity to lower the other boats, even though the ship still had some way on. As the ship continued to settle in the water, she took a sudden list to starboard, making the final abandonment even more difficult. Captain Toft remained on the bridge and he, with several members of his crew, was sucked down as the ship sank beneath the waves, but he resurfaced and was picked up by one of his own boats. All survivors were rescued by a British destroyer and all were landed the next evening. Although *ABOSSO* could carry up to 400 passengers, there were only 127 on board at the time, with a crew of 133, but a total of 65 lives were lost, 39 being passengers and 26 crew members, nearly all of whom were stewards.

Captain Toft returned to sea, as did so many following the trauma of a sinking, often as soon as they could. Thus some months later, on 28 November, he was in command of *APAPA*, the sister ship of *ABOSSO* and again bound for Liverpool from West Africa. His escorting destroyers had departed as he was approaching Liverpool and considered to be within protected waters. There were 119 passengers and 132 crew on board. Late in the evening, when about three miles off Point Lynas, often a location used for the embarkation of the Liverpool pilot, *APAPA* was hit by a tremendous explosion as a torpedo struck aft on the starboard side, causing the ship immediately to settle in the water, but on an even keel. Captain Toft took the way off the ship and proceeded to lower the boats amidst the alarm and cries of many children on board. Although the seas were choppy, all boats were safely lowered to the surface of the sea and were preparing to cast off when a second torpedo struck, again on the starboard side, wrecking the boats close by the point of explosion and killing the occupants. The second torpedo caused *APAPA* to heel suddenly to starboard, to the extent that the stays supporting the single funnel gave way and the funnel crashed into one of the boats containing 30 people, which was immediately sunk. Other debris, including the wireless aerials and rigging became entangled with the boat falls. Had it not been for the second torpedo it is likely that all boats would have cleared the ship without loss of life. As it turned out, 77 lives were lost: 38 passengers and 39 crew.

Captain Toft, as before on the *ABOSSO*, remained on his bridge, finally being washed off as the ship sank, some 10 minutes after the first torpedo struck. He surfaced and was found clinging to the wrecked remains of one of his boats. He again returned to sea, retiring in 1932.

APAPA had been sunk by U-96 under the command of Heinrich Jeb, who later argued that he only fired the second torpedo because he had not appreciated the damage done by the first as the steamer had remained upright. He further stated he could not afford to wait to see the outcome of the first torpedo strike as there could be British warships in the vicinity. Jeb was listed as a war criminal by the British government for his action against *APAPA*, in addition to his actions against other merchant ships later in the war.

While both *ABOSSO* and *APAPA* carried guns, they had not had the opportunity to deploy them, due to the secretive attacks made by the U-boats hidden beneath the waves. When the rare opportunity presented itself to British shipmasters to engage in combat to protect their ships however, that opportunity would be seized. One such example of this was the spirited and courageous defence made by Captain W. Fordsham in command of the 4,309-ton Lamport & Holt steamer *TERENCE*, also on 28 April – the same day as the attack on *ABOSSO*.

Although some 200 miles off the Irish coast and bound for Liverpool from Buenos Aires, Captain Fordsham had posted lookouts on the forecastle, the crow's nest and aft, while at the same time the gunners were at the ready, aft by their gun. The gun was a standard fitment of a 12-pounder by then fitted on an increasing number of British merchant ships, although the shortage of such armament necessitated guns being taken off steamers as they cleared a danger zone, to be placed on another ship about to enter the zone. The ship's four lifeboats were swung out in readiness should an emergency evacuation be necessary.

At 13:20 with the second officer on the bridge with Captain Fordsham, an object, described in the Master's Statement as having '*the appearance of a large caterpillar, apparently moving through the water. It was a whitish colour with two specks at about one fifth from each end of the object*'.[115] The object of course was a hitherto unseen submarine about one and a half to two miles away, approaching from four points on the port bow. The helm was immediately put over to bring the object astern and all hands were called to their stations. Some 17 rounds were fired at the submarine without effect and the submarine, or object, disappeared in the haze allowing Captain Fordsham to resume his course with the standard zigzag manoeuvres. Later that afternoon at 16:55 the wake of a torpedo was seen approaching from the starboard quarter, which *TERENCE* was able to avoid, but the submarine then surfaced and a gun battle ensued without any hits on either vessel until about 19:00 when the submarine began firing shrapnel shells. By this time *TERENCE* had fired 74 rounds with only 16 remaining and Captain Fordsham ordered these to be kept in reserve in the event of a submarine surfacing close enough to improve the chances of a hit. Shortly after this, with the submarine still shelling the steamer, another submarine appeared on the port bow, firing two torpedoes which missed. Eventually this submarine surfaced, abreast of the other and joined in the shelling, although this ceased around 20:00 due to darkness. The *TERENCE* continued zigzagging, but at 23:05 finally a torpedo struck. By this time the crew of the *TERENCE* had endured enough after the near 10-hour battle and took to the boats which got away in a very few minutes, but with the loss of one man who had jumped from the ship.

Captain Fordham remained alone on the bridge in the dark, but was soon joined by his chief officer and together they searched the ship to ensure none was left on board. The second officer had been aware that Captain Fordsham was still on his ship and rowed the lifeboat back to pick him up, but it was only due to the persuasion of the chief officer that Fordsham agreed to get into the second officer's boat, declaring he would rather be killed than be taken as a prisoner to Germany. The boats' sails were hoisted and, 61 hours later, they made it safely to the Irish coast, landing at Killard Point where they received '*a real hospitable welcome*'.

---

[115]   The National Archives, ADM 137/3987.

The courage and tenacity of Captain Fordsham and his crew must surely be one of the most remarkable stories of a merchant ship refusing to surrender until all hope was lost, requiring two U-boats and four torpedoes to bring the matter to a close. It is perhaps an insight into the toughness and determination of the man that his formal report makes no mention of the hardships of 61 hours spent in an open lifeboat in the North Atlantic. He was later awarded the DSC for his action.

U-81 under the command of *Kapitänleutnant* Raimund Weisbach claimed to have fired the torpedo which struck *TERENCE*. Earlier that same day Weisbach had sunk the British steamer *JOSE DE LARRINAGA* with the loss of 12 lives, including that of her master, Captain D.H. Parry. Weisbach's career included being a watch officer on U-20 when it sank the *LUSITANIA*, but it came to an end on 1 May 1917 when U-81 was in turn torpedoed by the British submarine E-54. Weisbach was one of the few survivors and spent the rest of the war as a prisoner in Britain.

The alarm about the successes of the U-boats was such that the Admiralty informed the government in April 1917: '*In a single fortnight 122 ocean going vessels were lost. The rate of British loss in ocean-going tonnage during this fortnight was equivalent to an average round-voyage loss of 25 per cent — one out of every four ships leaving the United Kingdom for an overseas voyage was lost before its return*'.[116]

By the end of April, merchant ship casualties peaked with a total loss in that month of British, Allied and neutral ships variously reported as between 444 and 474, or an average of 15 to 16 a day being sunk with their valuable cargoes. Nearly all these casualties had been due to U-boat action. Of these, 155 British merchant ships alone had been sunk during April, including 14 accounted for by mines, with the loss of 1,125 lives.[117] The situation was so dire that it was estimated that unless the tide of disastrous losses could be turned, Britain had less than six weeks of food supplies remaining.

The carnage continued throughout the year with continued acts of brutality by the U-boats, as was the case with the defensively armed Elder Dempster 4,397-ton steamer *ADDAH* which was torpedoed without warning on 15 June while on passage from Montreal to Cherbourg. The

---

[116] Koerver, (ed.) *German Submarine Warfare 1914–1918 in the Eyes of British Intelligence*, p.xxxiv.

[117] Gibson and Prendergast, *The German Submarine War 1915–1918*, pp.160–161.

master and crew immediately took to their boats and once clear of the ship U-69 surfaced and placed a boarding party into the chief officer's boat to return to *ADDAH* to plunder any stores they could. They returned to the submarine in the lifeboat after which the lifeboat, with its occupants, was abandoned. The master's boat had its stern blown off by gunfire, killing eight of its occupants, but UC-69 continued firing on the men in the water. Gunfire was then turned on to the chief officer's boat and, in the belief that all survivors had been killed, UC-69 submerged. In total nine men had been murdered and the remaining survivors were fortunate to be picked up the next day by a French steamer. Some time later the body of one of the *ADDAH*'s crew was picked up, showing bullet holes in his head and in his lifejacket; evidence of having been shot while in the water.

UC-69 was commanded at that time by *Kapitänleutnant* Erwin Waßner who sank 80 ships and received numerous commendations for his bravery. He survived the war and was listed as a war criminal by the British authorities for his brutal action against the *ADDAH*.

One of the most horrendous fates to befall a British merchant seafarer was to be the lot of the crew of the *MARISTON*, a steamer of 2,908 tons under the command of Captain John Stubbs. On the morning of 15 July 1917, while on passage from Almeria to her home port of Glasgow with a cargo of copper ore and about 80 miles west of Fastnet, the ship was torpedoed without warning, followed by two explosions which quickly destroyed the ship. Eighteen of her crew were thrown into the sea, the remaining 10 having been either killed by the explosions or drawn down with the ship. The cook, Charles Williams, managed to climb onto a hatch, which he used as a raft until he was rescued some 15 hours later. Before his rescue, he was however to witness the unimaginable horror of seeing all his shipmates being pulled down, one by one, by a school of sharks in a feeding frenzy. He was the only survivor out of the ship's complement of 29.

In the midst of that horror the submarine responsible for the sinking, U-45, surfaced. Seeing the death throes of the shark attack the commander, Erich Sittenfeld, who could certainly have saved at least some of the men, decided he could no longer watch the appalling scene and submerged to leave his fellow seafarers to their dreadful fate. He suffered retribution a few months later when he was killed off the north coast of Ireland, the victim of a single torpedo fired by HM submarine D-7.

The ship's Agreement and Account of Crew for the *MARISTON* showed that the youngest victim of the sinking was 16-year-old John Gilmor Barclay, an apprentice on his first trip to sea. The oldest was Captain John Stubbs, at 63 years of age, who might have been expected to have retired but for the desperate need for masters and crews by 1917. Charles Williams survived this dreadful ordeal only to lose his life on 19 August 1918 when he was serving as the cook on the *PALMELLA*, torpedoed in the Irish Sea with a loss of 28 lives.

While the nature of the deaths of the *MARISTON* crew might not be considered the direct responsibility of the U-boat commander, the deaths of the crew of the *BELGIAN PRINCE* most certainly were. On 31 July 1917 the 4,765-ton steamer was torpedoed off the Atlantic coast of Ireland. There was little time to take to the boats but two boats were cleared away and lowered, with the occupants taken on to the deck of the submarine. The master, Captain Harry Hassan, was taken below, as had been the case with both the *TORRINGTON* and the *TORO*, and the remaining crew left on deck. The German crew then set about systematically throwing the lifeboat oars away and smashing the boats with axes. Lifejackets were seized from the survivors and thrown away, although three men managed to hide their lifejackets under their coats. The submarine then got underway, leaving 42 British seamen on the deck and, as Werner had done before, submerged leaving them helpless in the water. The only three survivors, Chief Engineer Thomas Bowman, Second Cook W. Snell and Able Seaman George Silessi were rescued by a destroyer after 39 men had been murdered and Captain Hassan taken prisoner.

The sinking of the *BELGIAN PRINCE* has been attributed in conflicting sources to Paul Wagenfür, in command of U-44 and to Wilhelm Werner of U-55. While both boats were in the vicinity of the *BELGIAN PRINCE* at the time of the atrocity, the *modus operandi* was very much that of Werner. Wagenfür was killed a few weeks later in the North Sea, but Werner survived the war.

An extraordinary example of 'the biter being bitten' was the case of the torpedoing of the British steamer *OLIVE BRANCH* in the Arctic on 2 September 1917. Struck without warning, as had become so commonplace with the unrestricted attacks, Captain Charles E. Carlen ordered the boats to be lowered and they were safely got away within five minutes, after which the

U-boat began to shell the ship. Unknown to *Kapitänleutnant* Georg Schmidt on U-28 however, the *OLIVE BRANCH* was carrying munitions which were hit by one of the shells, causing a massive explosion. That explosion blasted a truck carried on the deck of the steamer high into the air, falling onto the deck of the U-boat, throwing those on the deck into the freezing sea. The Office of the Admiralty's Chief Censor reported, '*The U-boat sank immediately. The explosion was terrific*'. For about 15 minutes it was quite dark, and when they could see again many of the people in the boat had become quite black on account of the powder, but three of her crew, each swimming with a revolver in his mouth, approached the English lifeboats and asked to be taken in. The captain of the *OLIVE BRANCH* wanted to pick them up, but the crew refused apparently because the Germans carried revolvers with them. The three Germans were left where they were, and had to suffer the same fate as their comrades.[118] In that unfortunate case, it was the German seafarers whose dead were left to the sea.

The *OLIVE BRANCH*'s survivors successfully landed at Helnoc after a 65-hour voyage in their boats. The one loss of the 45-strong crew had been that of the cook, D. McGill, at the time of the torpedo explosion.

An example of the continuing and increasing support in Germany for U-boat attacks without warning on merchant ships and a blatant disregard for the lives of their crews can be seen in a report by a German agent in Holland who declared, '*I am convinced that, if the crews of neutral steamers, which are torpedoed, are saved, or even if the crew of the submarine do their utmost to save them, the effect of the submarine warfare is mostly lost.*'[119]

The Kaiser's hopes that the escalation of the submarine attacks would intimidate the neutral powers to seek an 'arrangement' with Germany had however met with little success, even though concessions were offered to Spanish and Swedish ships. Dutch ships were given 'permission' to carry corn from British ports to Holland and to fish in nominated areas, but these 'concessions' were, perhaps unsurprisingly, ignored by the U-boats resulting in a high casualty rate and a hardening of anti–German attitudes by those neutral states. There is nevertheless little evidence that the merchant seafarers

---

[118]   The National Archives, ADM 137/4000.

[119]   Koerver, (ed.) *German Submarine Warfare 1914–1918 in the Eyes of British Intelligence*, p.215.

of the neutral states or from Britain were intimidated. As Koerver stated, *'British seamen displayed remarkable sangfroid in the face of the submarine menace, and instances could be multiplied of men who continued to serve in the merchant service even after several experiences of the effects of torpedoes or mines.'*[120]

---

[120] Ibid., p.204.

CHAPTER 13

SOMETHING MUST BE DONE

Escalating losses in the early part of 1917 had become unacceptable, making it increasingly obvious that 'something must be done' to reduce the devastation caused to merchant shipping and the rapidly diminishing availability of crews. Apart from the loss of vital goods for the war effort and food for the population, the fatality rate for British merchant seafarers was proportionately higher than that suffered by troops in the trenches. The initial Admiralty view was that surface ships of the Royal Navy would be enough to protect merchant shipping and that the sheer number of British merchant ships plying the seas could suffer some losses without seriously threatening the delivery of essential supplies. It was also believed that the Prize Code would apply; a mistaken view for which the merchant seafarers were paying such a high cost.

As a civilian entity, merchant shipping was still trying to operate as a commercial activity, with profits and losses to take account of as they had in peacetime. Long established trading patterns had their commercial commitments to which the war had of course added an entirely new dimension. British shipping companies still competed with each other and British companies continued to compete with other countries for the carriage of goods. British liner shipping companies continued to publish lists of their sailings to attract cargoes and shipowners reserved the right to send their ships where they chose.

One measure to reduce the rate of ship losses was the adoption of camouflage, in a manner known as 'dazzle painting', to break up the outline of a ship and thus make it less easy to identify. While this was shown to have a very limited effect, if any, on reducing losses, the measure was generally welcomed by the merchant seafarer in that it suggested that the precarious nature of their livelihood was being recognised and that something was being done to help them.

Of considerable effect in the reduction of merchant ship losses had been arming a number of them against surface U-boat attacks, although an initial view by some was that the measure could be counter-productive, as the obvious gun on deck encouraged the U-boat to attack while submerged. By December 1915 some 766 British merchant ships had been provided with guns to protect themselves, but by February 1917 this had increased to nearly 3,000 ships, leading to a significant reduction of sinkings of defensively armed ships compared to those unarmed. For the period 1 January 1916 to 31 January 1917, Thompson provides the following figures:[121]

Defensively armed ships attacked	310
of which escaped	236
Sunk by torpedo without warning	62
Sunk by gun-fire from submarine	12
Unarmed ships attacked	302
of which escaped	67
Sunk by torpedo without warning	30
Sunk by gun-fire, bombs etc.	205

These figures show that 76 per cent of armed merchant ships escaped attack, but only 22 per cent if unarmed. However, the success of the armed steamers and the resumption of the unrestricted U-boat campaign at the beginning of February resulted in fewer U-boats exposing themselves on the surface of the sea, relying on a submerged attack with torpedoes.

Some consideration was given to the possibility of building ships that would be more likely to survive a torpedo attack. Lord Rhondda, a Welsh industrialist who became Minister of Food Control in the latter stages of the war, drew attention to the large amounts of desperately needed food that were being lost as a result of U-boat attacks on merchant ships. He asked '... *whether everything practical is being done to render our new merchant ships capable of resisting torpedo attack*'. Lord Rhondda had some personal experience of torpedo attacks, having been a survivor of the *LUSITANIA* sinking in May 1915.

---

[121]   Thompson, *The War at Sea 1914–1918*, p.197.

The baton was picked up by Mr F. Allen, Vice-chairman of the Khedivial Mail Steamship Company, which had suffered losses of its own from torpedo attacks. He attempted to persuade the Ministry of Shipping, which had set out a programme for building the '*largest amount of tonnage in the shortest time*' to consider the feasibility of constructing stronger ships. Naval architects were consulted and plans drawn up with the idea of enabling a ship struck by a torpedo to remain afloat for a period of time long enough to enable a rescue to be effected which, Mr Allen considered, would be feasible within home waters. The possibility of building such ships was admitted but the idea was dismissed on the grounds that more steel would be required, the ships would take longer to build and the costs would be too high. The First Lord of the Admiralty admitted that such a plan may well prove in the long run to be beneficial and that '... *against the increase in costs in building such ships should be set ... the serious financial loss to the nation incurred every time a ship of the ordinary type was sunk, and the perhaps even more formidable loss of irreplaceable cargoes*'. The plans were shelved and the merchant seafarer could expect to continue to risk his life on '*a ship of the ordinary type*'.

The greatest contribution to the protection of ships and their crews was undoubtedly the introduction of an effective convoy system. The concept of marshalling a group of ships and providing them with an armed escort was by no means a new one. Indeed, from the start of the war, British India ships carrying Indian troops from Bombay to the European theatre had been successfully escorted by warships without encountering any great practical difficulties. While this practice had certainly been given consideration by the Admiralty early on in the war, for a number of reasons it was decided not to adopt the convoy system on a widespread basis, apart from which, until the United States entered the war, there were not enough suitable warships to make it effective.

The commercial implications of compulsory convoy operations were that shipowners were naturally reluctant effectively to lose control of their property and liner schedules would be disrupted. It could take weeks to gather a convoy together with the consequential loss of earnings, with charterers complaining that cargoes arriving at the same destination at the same time would suffer a reduction in value at the marketplace. Further, it was argued that such a system would hand a commercial advantage to neutral countries such that it would be difficult to recover their position at the end of the war. Delays in marshalling a convoy and the slower speeds of the convoy, at least for the liner ships, of course meant that fewer voyages could be completed with the consequent reduction in freight earnings, but with greater proportional expenditure for crew, fuel and maintenance for the amount of cargo carried. When a ship was lost, the owner would claim on his insurance for his ship and the shipper for his cargo, and the financial burden of payment of crew wages would cease. Insurance premiums for ships travelling in a convoy would not be reduced.

There were other objections to compulsory convoy systems from the practical aspects. The Admiralty and many shipmasters believed it would be extremely difficult for merchant ships to maintain convoy positions, especially when undertaking zigzag or other manoeuvres in concert with other ships at close quarters. Practical difficulties were also seen in the event of a merchant ship attempting to take avoiding action from a submarine attack with the consequent risk of a collision with another in the convoy and, as many masters pointed out, the number of available qualified watchkeepers had diminished due to their being taken into the Royal Naval Reserve. A particularly significant objector to convoys was Admiral Jellicoe, who not only believed that merchant ships would be unable to conduct themselves according to convoy requirements, but was uncertain as to what actions were realistically available to escorting warships. He was also of the opinion that there were insufficient warships of the appropriate type to undertake convoy escort duties even if they were to be deemed of use in reducing the merchant ship losses. The Prime Minister, Lloyd-George, had little time for Jellicoe, regarding him as out of touch, and held him responsible for not finding a method of reducing merchant ship losses. Lloyd-George was supported in this stance by Admiral Sims, who had been appointed as commander of all US naval forces now engaged in the war. Jellico was relieved of his position in a very controversial decision and replaced by Admiral Beatty, after which the Admiralty was instructed to commence the widespread adoption of escorted convoys. Convoys were quickly introduced and became commonplace by the end of that year.

With the warship escort for the convoys, the choices available to a U-boat commander to make his attack and flee with little chance of retribution were more limited. The more frequent method of attack, particularly if the merchant ship was believed to be unarmed or lightly armed had been to surface and attack by gunfire. By so doing however the submarine immediately revealed its position to the armed escort and became exposed to a counter-attack. To dive, the submarine relied on gaining forward speed to enable the vanes to take it underwater, combined with emergency filling of ballast tanks; an event which would take several minutes while exposed on the surface. Attacking a merchant ship in a convoy would therefore generally mean a torpedo attack with less chance of hitting the victim, while making a rapid departure before the naval escorts could find the submarine. The development of improved new depth charges and techniques in deploying them proved to be a considerable disincentive to the submarine's activity and existence. As Admiral Tirpitz later commented in his memoirs, the convoy system heralded the defeat and destruction of the U-boats.

The success of convoys in reducing ship losses was incontrovertible. The first convoy through U-boat waters from Gibraltar arrived in England without any losses on 20 May. By August 1917 all homeward-bound ships from Gibraltar, the United States and the South Atlantic were convoyed safely. By October, no fewer than 1,502 steamers in 99 convoys had been brought into port with the loss of 24 vessels, of which 10 had been sunk in convoy, with the remainder either lost after separating or, it was claimed, through the disobedience of their masters.[122] The loss of 24 steamers out of 1,502 represents a loss rate of less than 2 per cent, which compares with a rate earlier in the year of one in four steamers, or 25 per cent, not completing their voyages. The casualty rate of U-boats also increased, with 33 sunk in the last four months of 1917, compared to 22 lost in the whole of 1916.[123]

The merchant ships amply demonstrated their abilities to maintain convoy formations, – a significant feat in achieving the fine adjustments of speed necessary and positioning in conditions of darkness and often heavy seas. This reduction in merchant ship losses was of course of great encouragement to their crews. Not only were the chances of being sunk significantly reduced, but there was significant comfort in that they stood a better chance of being picked up by an escort rather than the consequences of spending periods at sea in an open boat and/or becoming a prisoner of the Germans.

There were nevertheless ships which preferred to travel on their own,

---

[122]   Gibson and Prendergast, *The German Submarine War 1914–1918*, pp.176–177.
[123]   Ibid., p.366.

usually because of their higher speeds and the urgency of their voyage. One such ship was the 14,348-ton Anchor Line passenger liner *TUSCANIA*, converted as a troop carrier. On 5 February 1918 and under the command of Captain P.A. McLean, the ship was carrying over 2,000 American troops and general cargo from Halifax to Liverpool at a speed of 16 knots and armed only with a four-inch naval gun. When north of Rathlin Island, with the Scottish coastline visible on the port side and that of Northern Ireland on the starboard, she was struck by a torpedo amidships, wrecking the superstructure and the lifeboats above the point of impact. The troops quickly went to their allocated boat stations but several survivors later claimed they could not free the davits due to rust and, although they had been given lifeboat drill during the voyage from Halifax, they had little knowledge of how to swing the boats out or to lower them from the davits. In the event, several boats capsized during their launch, with consequent loss of life in the freezing sea. *TUSCANIA* took a list to starboard so that those lowering boats on the port side had to use the oars to keep the side of their boats clear from the rivet heads as they slid down the side of the hull.

Rescue was fortunately at hand with the near presence of the destroyers HMS *MOSQUITO* and HMS *PIGEON*, both of which performed great acts of seamanship in putting themselves alongside the sinking *TUSCANIA* to get the troops off. Others climbed down ropes to get to the destroyers' decks but when the destroyers had taken all the survivors they could they steamed off to let another take their place. One report was of a very large army cook who had climbed down the rope, only to see the rescue destroyer depart, whereupon he surprised both himself and his fellow soldiers by rapidly climbing back up a 60-foot rope to the relative, although temporary, safety of *TUSCANIA*'s deck. It was claimed that when safely back in barracks, he was quite unable to make any progress in an attempt to repeat his remarkable rope-climbing feat. Many troops were still in boats in the heavy weather and in the sea. The attempts by the destroyers to find the submarine and their use of depth charges caused further casualties. In total, 210 lives were lost, including 44 crew,[124] including two brothers, Daniel and Dennis Boyle, both trimmers from Glasgow.

The submarine responsible was UB-77 under the command of

---

[124]   Gibson and Prendergast, *The German Submarine War 1914–1918*, p.288.

Kapitänleutnant Wilhelm Meyer, who had been shadowing *TUSCANIA*, waiting for dawn to break before firing two torpedoes. He left the scene as soon as possible once he was satisfied that at least one torpedo had struck – the other had missed – to get as far away from his victim as he could before any British warships could reach the stricken ship.

On 26 February 1918, in the approaches to the Bristol Channel and displaying all the markings to identify herself clearly as a hospital ship, the *GLENART CASTLE* encountered UC-56 under the command of Wilhelm Keisewetter. Three years previously the same ship, then named the *GALICIAN*, encountered the converted German liner *KAISER WILHELM DER GROSSE* whose commander released the *GALICIAN* on humanitarian grounds. The encounter in her new role as a hospital ship with Keisewetter was to be a very different matter.

Just before 04:00 UC-56 fired one torpedo from a range of about 650 yards, striking the ship on the starboard side with a tremendous explosion, wrecking much of the ship's side, some boats and the wireless room, while plunging the ship into darkness. An account of abandoning the hospital ship was later given by Fourth Officer George Scarlett who was about to go on watch:

> *I went straight up onto the bridge and received orders from the Captain to go and get my boat away at once. I went down to my boat, No. 5 lifeboat, the third boat on the starboard side. I then saw that the ship had been struck just abaft amidships on the starboard side under No. 7 boat, which was wrecked. My boat's crew were standing by and I ordered the boat to be cast adrift at once and had lowered it about four or five feet when the Chief Officer came and shouted 'Every man for himself!' The ship then took a heavy list to starboard; the water swept the boat up against the davit heads and smashed it to pieces before we could do anything to cut it adrift. I saw the other boats' crews on the starboard side trying to get their boats away, but none were cleared away in time.*
>
> *Two or three men jumped overboard. I was waiting for them to get clear of the ship's side but the next minute I was swept overboard as the ship went down. I managed to get hold of a raft and crawled into it. There was another raft close by with three men on it. I saw nothing of anyone else from the ship, but could hear cries from the water for some time afterwards.* [125]

---

[125]   Bridgland, *Outrage At Sea*, p.167.

SOMETHING MUST BE DONE

The experience of the fourth officer was replicated by many of the survivors. Only seven of the boats got away, with many of them in a damaged condition from the explosion and from the sinking ship itself, which went down within seven minutes of the attack. Survivors in the freezing waters, clinging onto whatever wreckage became available to them reported the presence of a U-boat, moving slowly through the carnage, but offering no assistance or acknowledgement of its crime, despite desperate calls for help from people in the water. While there was no report of the U-boat firing on the survivors while abandoning ship, there were reports of the U-boat crew firing on the boats once they were clear of the ship, perhaps in an attempt to remove all witnesses to their brutality. Various newspaper accounts of the atrocity cited the recovery of the body of a junior officer of the ship marked with gunshot wounds. As he was wearing a life jacket it seemed likely he had been shot while in the water.

One of the rescue vessels was the USS *PARKER*, which was based at Queenstown and had been on escort duty, arriving some 15 hours after the sinking, by which time the wind force had increased and a heavy swell was running. The commander of the *PARKER* was reluctant to lower a boat because of the rough seas plus the possibility of the U-boat lurking in the vicinity of their victims to attack any rescue ships. In an extraordinary act of selflessness and bravery two US sailors dived into the freezing and rough seas to swim towards a life raft some 50 yards away to rescue four men – fellow seafarers. They brought all four back, with considerable difficulty, to the safety of the *PARKER* which had remained underway to avoid being a sitting target.[126]

GLENART CASTLE had been on her way to pick up wounded troops from Brest and thus it was fortunate that there were none on board as there could have been a much higher casualty rate. As it was, out of a total of 186 souls on board, 166 lost their lives, including 8 nurses, 7 medical officers and 47 medical orderlies. Also lost was the master, Captain Bernard Burt, who was last seen at his post on the bridge of his ship, supervising the abandonment. Understandably there was outrage at the actions of Keisewetter who, while admitting sinking a large ship at that time in the Bristol Channel denied, despite a weight of evidence to the contrary, that *GLENART CASTLE*

---

[126]   Ibid., p.169.

was identifiable as a hospital ship. He claimed he thought the ship, the only British ship he had sunk, might have been an armed merchant cruiser.

Keiswetter later had to call at Santander due to engine trouble and was immediately interned by the Spanish government. He had been declared a war criminal by the British government and was handed over to Britain after the war, but released on a legal technicality on the grounds that Britain had no right to hold a detainee during the Armistice. Outraged at this release the Director of Naval Intelligence declared, on 28 June 1919, '*To use meticulous legal points to allow such a diabolical scoundrel to escape is really too much.*'[127]

GLENART CASTLE was but one of 12 hospital ships of Britain and her Allies sunk by U-boats. The attacks on hospital ships were clearly in contravention of international law, but the standard response of Germany to such attacks was that they believed the hospital ships were misused in that they would carry troops and/or armaments, or at least war supplies, although this probably could not be discounted on every occasion. Statements by U-boat commanders that troops had been observed on board hospital ships could not be discounted either as indeed wounded troops would be wearing their uniforms. It is however notable that no British or Allied hospital ships were sunk by a surface warship of the German Navy.

The German government was nevertheless convinced that some hospital ships were being misused and, at the end of March, announced that all hospital ships in the English Channel and in the Mediterranean would be sunk. In view of the German announcement, on 26 May 1917 two British hospital ships, the *DOVER CASTLE* and the *KARAPARA* left Malta together, bound for Gibraltar and escorted by two destroyers, HMS *CAMELON* and HMS *NEMESIS*.

DOVER CASTLE had been built as a passenger liner of 8,271 tons for the Union Castle Line in 1904 and requisitioned as a hospital ship. On 26 May she was under the command of Captain T.H. Wilford with 700 patients and staff and a crew of 141[128] when, at around 19:00, she was struck by a torpedo amidships on her starboard side, immediately killing seven stokers. *KARAPARA* escaped under cover of a smoke screen made by *NEMESIS*. *DOVER CASTLE* remained on an even keel and *CAMELON* managed to

---

[127]   Ibid., p.175.

[128]   Gibson and Prendergast *The German Submarine War 1914–1918*, p.249.

take off all the patients, staff and crew safely, apart from Captain Wilford and 16 volunteers from his crew who tried to save the ship. After a while, Captain Wilford considered that as his ship did not seem to be sinking any further, he might try to make port under the ship's own power and *CAMELON* left for Bona.

Very shortly after the destroyer departed, a second torpedo struck *DOVER CASTLE*, this time just under the bridge, and the ship sank within three minutes. Fortunately there was no further loss of life and Captain Wilford and his volunteer crew were rescued some six hours later. A subsequent inquiry brought into question the effectiveness of the destroyer escorts and escort procedures were duly amended. The question no doubt also arose as to how the submarine had remained undetected for over an hour in the vicinity, enabling it to fire the second, fatal torpedo.

The submarine responsible was UC-67 under the command of *Oberleutnant zur See* Karl Neumann, who had been shadowing the small convoy for some hours before he felt he could get himself into the best position to fire his torpedo. Unlike Keiswetter with the *GLANART CASTLE*, Neumann acknowledged that he was fully aware of the status of the hospital ships and was acting in compliance with orders from the German government. Neumann was listed as a war criminal for his attack on the hospital ship and survived the war, becoming one of the most successful U-boat commanders with a record of having sunk 67 enemy ships.

While the *DOVER CASTLE* suffered a relatively small loss of life, the potential for a very heavy loss of life from a hospital ship was tragically realised with the loss of 234 lives when the hospital ship *LLANDOVERY CASTLE* was sunk by U-86 under the command of *Kapitänleutnant* Helmut Patzig on 27 June 1918.

LLANDOVERY CASTLE was a Union Castle passenger liner converted to serve as a hospital ship for the Canadian government and, on 27 June under the command of Captain R.A. Sylvester, the ship was on her way from Halifax to Liverpool. She carried 80 officers and men of the Canadian Medical Corps and 14 nurses to transport wounded and sick Canadian forces back to Canada under their commanding officer, Lt. Colonel Thomas MacDonald. With her crew of 148, there were 258 souls on board.

At about 21:30 on a calm evening, in a position some 116 miles off Fastnet the unarmed ship was struck by a torpedo amidships on the port side and so severely damaged that she sank within 10 minutes. It was later established, despite German claims to the contrary, that there were no munitions or combatants on board.

By all accounts there was remarkably little panic and while many of the 19 lifeboats on board had been severely damaged by the torpedo explosion, many were safely lowered to the water, although some were only to be capsized and wrecked as the *LLANDOVERY CASTLE* sank. Many people in the water were killed or wounded as debris from the sinking ship shot up to the surface.

Many remarkable testimonies of bravery were given, including the following great tribute to the courage and steadfastness of the young Canadian nurses by Sergeant Arthur Knight, who was in charge of No. 5 lifeboat:

Our boat was quickly loaded and lowered to the surface of the water. Then the crew of eight men and myself faced the difficulty of getting free from the ropes holding us to the ship's side. To save the boat we tried to keep ourselves away by using the oars, and very soon every one was broken. We were carried towards the stern of the ship, when suddenly the Poop deck seemed to break away and sink. The suction drew us into the vacuum, the boat tipped over sideways, and every occupant went under.

Unflinchingly and calmly, as steady and collected as if on parade, without complaint or a single sign of emotion, our fourteen devoted nurses faced the terrible ordeal of certain death — only a matter of minutes — as our lifeboat neared that mad whirlpool of water where all human power was helpless. I estimate we were together in the boat about eight minutes. In that whole time I did not hear a complaint or murmur from one of the sisters. There was not a cry for help or any outward evidence of fear. In the entire time I overheard only one remark when the matron, Nursing Matron Margaret Marjory Fraser, turned to me as we drifted helplessly towards the ship and asked: 'Sergeant, do you think there is any hope for us?' I replied, 'No', seeing myself our helplessness without oars and the sinking condition of the stern of the ship. A few seconds later we were drawn into the whirlpool of the submerged afterdeck, and the last I saw of the nursing sisters were as they were thrown over the side of the boat. All were wearing lifebelts, and of the fourteen two were in their nightdress, the others in uniform. It was doubtful if any of them came to the surface again, although I myself sank and came up three times, finally clinging to a piece of wreckage and eventually being picked up by the Captain's boat.[129]

The second officer, Mr Chapman, later gave evidence that he had seen five boats lowered from the starboard side, although two had capsized, with two boats clearing the ship on the port side, one of which had Captain Sylvester on board; in the circumstances a remarkable feat bearing in mind the extent of damage to the ship and the rapidity of the sinking. The five surviving boats then began trying to pick people out of the water when U–86 surfaced and began moving among the boats and people in the water. The captain's boat was ordered alongside but Captain Sylvester initially refused, stating he was engaged in picking two men out of the sea at that time. The U-boat commander, Patzig, again ordered the lifeboat to come alongside immediately or be shelled, accusing the captain of sheltering American aviators on board, which was denied. Patzig then ordered two of his men to haul one officer out of the boat, so roughly that he sustained a broken leg. That officer identified himself as Major T. Lyon, a doctor in the Canadian Medical Corps, and was put back into the lifeboat. U–86 then moved away from Captain Sylvester's boat to further inspect the scene of carnage.

Major Lyon later reported that they had only moved a short distance away from the submarine when they again asked for him. The U-boat then took the second and fourth officers out of the lifeboats to question them, before returning them to the lifeboat. The lifeboat then hoisted its sails and began to get underway, at which time, in Major Lyon's account, '*Suddenly we saw the submarine coming at us at full speed. There was no doubt of their intention to ram us. She missed us by less than two feet. Had we been stationary we certainly would have been submerged.*'

Sergeant Knight, after being separated from the nurses, had found himself swimming towards what he believed to be No. 19 lifeboat, when he saw it being shelled and sunk by the submarine. He clambered on to a piece of wreckage and was later picked up by the captain's boat. In a moment of confusion, when the submarine came alongside the captain's boat, he

---

[129]   'The Sinking of the Llandovery Castle', the Great War Primary Documents Archive.

mistook it for a British rescue vessel and dived out of the lifeboat, grabbing a line from the U-boat. The U-boat crew threw him back into the lifeboat.

Another victim of U–86 was Private G.R. Hickman who had abandoned ship in No. 7 lifeboat, which was seen by the U-boat about an hour and a half after the sinking. He was taken on board the submarine for questioning as to whether there were any American airmen on board, which he denied. He was then transferred to the captain's boat.

Along with Captain Sylvester, the second officer and others, Knight and Hickman confirmed that the U-boat began ramming the lifeboats and rafts at speed, firing on people in the water. It was clear that Patzig had no intention of leaving survivors who could give any evidence of his barbaric actions, but omitted to kill the 24 people in the captain's boat. It can only be assumed that Patzig believed he had sunk the captain's boat, which had by then drifted away in the darkness. They were the only survivors out of the 258 souls who had been on board the *LLANDOVERY CASTLE* and who had witnessed Patzig's brutality. They were rescued some 36 hours later by HMS *LYSANDER*.

Shortly afterwards a harrowing experience awaited Midshipman Kenneth Cummins RNR on the armed merchant cruiser HMS *MOREA* on his first trip to sea. (He was later to become Captain Cummins in the Merchant Navy). He recounted:

> *We were in the Bristol Channel, quite well out to sea, and suddenly we began going through corpses. The Germans had sunk a British Hospital ship, the* Llandovery Castle, *and we were sailing through floating bodies. We were not allowed to stop – we just had to go straight through. It was quite horrific, and my reaction was to vomit over the edge. It was something we could never have imagined .... particularly the nurses; seeing these bodies of women and nurses, floating in the ocean, having been there some time. Huge aprons and skirts in billows, which looked almost like sails because they dried in the hot sun.*[130]

Major Lyon, in his later testimony said: '*I can emphatically state that the submarine made no attempt to rescue anyone, but on the contrary did everything in its power to*

---

[130] 'Obituary. Kenneth Cummins', the *Independent*, 18 December 2006.

destroy every trace of the ship and its personnel and crew', and, paradoxically, '*All I can say on behalf of the submarine crew is that they were coolly polite in their questions to us.*'

Kapitänleutnant Helmut Patzig and his crew were cited as war criminals and taken before the Court of Supreme Justice in Leipzig. By the time the Court hearing could take place, Captain Sylvester had died and Patzig had disappeared, but two officers who had participated in the killings were found, Ludwig Dithmar and John Boltd, to face the Court. The outcome of that is discussed in a later chapter.

Despite the losses of the many ships still travelling alone, the introduction of the convoy system had brought about a huge, if long delayed, response to the call that 'something must be done'. The April 1917 losses had been of the order of 474 Allied ships, whereas in August of the same year that total had dropped to 219 ships – a significant tribute to the effectiveness of the convoy system, although mines continued to claim, on average, about 10 British merchant ships a month.

Losses of U-boats and their crews, with a consequential reluctance of men to serve on them, became a major source of concern for the Germans, with younger and inexperienced crews being exposed to the rapidly increasing effectiveness of the convoy escorts in tracking them down. Submarines were being sunk as fast as they could be built. Another valuable response to the 'Something must be done' call was the development of effective depth charges which began to take a serious toll on the U-boats, as earlier depth charges were notorious for being small and ineffective and of little concern to a submarine commander.

While the protection of convoy escorts and the improvement of anti-submarine measures were welcomed, the merchant seafarer still faced a very high probability of being killed. Some larger and faster merchant ships continued to take their chances away from the protection of the convoys, with many yet to pay a heavy price in the remaining months of the war.

CHAPTER 14

RMS *AUSONIA*

Very few detailed personal accounts now remain of survivors of a World War I U-boat attack and their subsequent battle for survival. This chapter is therefore devoted solely to the story of the sinking of RMS *AUSONIA* and the journey of the survivors, as recounted by the master, Captain Robert Capper, DSC, RD, RNR and by a stewardess, Mrs Theresa Edgar. This account is taken from documents held at the Merseyside Maritime Museum of Liverpool and reproduced here with the museum's kind permission.[131] The story is a record of their ordeal over eight days and nine nights in an open lifeboat in the freezing conditions and heavy weather in the North Atlantic. It includes a vivid description of the damage done by the torpedo explosion and the experiences of some of the crew in abandoning ship, as well as the captain's log entries during the lifeboat journey. It gives also some of the subsequent correspondence on their return to England and the words of a remarkable interview given much later by Mrs Edgar to an American newspaper.

The Cunarder RMS *AUSONIA* was a passenger vessel of 7,907 tons with a capacity for 90 second-class and 1,000 third-class passengers. The ship was built in 1911 for the Thompson Line before she was bought by the Cunard Steamship Company to start the company's service to Canada.

On the evening of 14 April 1918, bound from Avonmouth to New York, *AUSONIA* was fortunate to escape from a submarine attack. In Captain Capper's report to his owners and to his marine superintendent, Captain D. Lyon, he stated that a submarine was sighted breaking surface about 50 to 70 yards away on the port quarter, following in the ship's wake as she undertook normal 20 and 40 degree zigzag procedures every 10 minutes. On getting the

---

[131] Archive ref: DX/186/30–37.

report of the sighting, Captain Capper ordered course to be altered to bring the submarine astern and for all possible speed, and again altered course '*to bring a very black patch of clouds ahead*' to make it a little more difficult for the submarine to see him, while firing two rounds from the six-inch gun at the U-boat. Continuing to take evasive action, more rounds were fired and the ship worked up to just over 13 knots. Nothing more was seen of the submarine. However, about two hours later the aft lookout '*saw a torpedo cross the ship's wake, almost at right angles, from port to starboard, about 10 to 12 yards off the rudder*'. The ship's course was altered and again nothing further was seen, leading Captain Capper to conjecture that more than one submarine had been operating and possibly in communication with each other '*as the ship had made about 30 miles on the set course and possibly 33 to 34 miles through the water, between the time of sighting the submarine and the torpedo missing the rudder*'. *AUSONIA* continued on an otherwise uneventful passage to New York and in conclusion to his report on the event to Cunard, Captain Capper wrote, '*I wish to state that the behaviour of the passengers and crew during the experience was all that could be desired, great credit is due to the Engineers for the way they worked up the ship's speed, also to the Officials and crews standing by ready for orders to handle or man their respective boats.*'

Despite this experience of being on guard against a U-boat attack and successfully defending his ship against one, or possibly two, submarines, in just over one month's time Captain Capper and the *AUSONIA*, painted in 'dazzle colours', were not to be so fortunate.

On 27 May 1918, *AUSONIA* was anchored in the River Mersey as part of a convoy awaiting the escort of six American destroyers. Heaving up the anchor at 10:30 she made her way to the rendezvous position off the Skerries, picking up the escorts on the way and making good speed through the day and night. During the morning of the 28th, the presence of a submarine was detected and attacked by the escorting destroyers, not to be seen again. In Captain Capper's account he wrote '*At 9:30 p.m. arrived at dispersal point when escort turned back, the ships in convoy dispersed and proceeded independently all well, with fine clear weather, dark night and smooth sea, the ship steaming well all through the night making a good 13 knots.*' *AUSONIA* was bound for New York.

On 30 May, Captain Capper records in some detail:

When I was taking my p.m. observations (P.V.), I had just got to my cabin door when I heard a dull thud as though a big gun had been fired close to the ship. I then saw the track of a torpedo coming from the starboard quarter or about two points abaft the starboard beam. The ship was hit in No. 5 hold, and the explosion smashed up No. 9 boat, buckled the davits, opened her decks, and lifted up rafts, ladders and booby hatches into the air which fell, some on deck but mostly overboard. At this time, possibly half a minute after the hit and the explosion of the torpedo, I was back on the bridge. I put the Engine Room telegraph to Stop and Full Astern but no reply bell sounded. I tried to sound off Boat Stations on the ship's whistle but nothing happened when I pulled on the lanyard. The electric current was off as the dynamo was then under water. During this time a yellowish smoke was coming out of No. 5 hold which had a sickly and nauseating smell. The ship filled up so rapidly aft (the deep tank and engine room after bulkheads, also the starboard tunnel were all torn, twisted and burst in) that she did not keep her headway very long, so we very soon had ten boats in the water with a slight mishap to only one, No. 2. After putting chronometers, sextants and navigation books into a boat, I made a round of the decks, excepting the port side of after deck which was jambed up with wreckage. It was then I went to the engine room which I saw was filling rapidly, as I could not see the cylinder tops and on the surface of the water in the engine room and No. 5 hold was a thick layer of cork shavings. The Marconi Operator had sent out the ship's position, 48.00N 24.00W, torpedoed and sinking, about twelve times on the auxiliary apparatus (the main current cut off) before he made for the boats. The ship was so deep aft by this time that it was only because the upper steerage ports were closed that the water didn't rush into her through them; her deck round the after part of her wheelhouse was only a foot or so from the sea.

During the havoc caused by the explosion two young crew members were engaged in a desperate bid to reach the lifeboats, scrambling among the debris and carnage. The 17-year-old butcher boy Mathew Robinson and 16-year-old pantry boy Maurice Lister, both on their first trips to sea, were in the cooling chambers with no direct line of exit and separated by a gaping hole in the deck. Mathew Robinson had several wounds on his hips and thighs, with both legs broken just above the ankle. Maurice Lister also suffered two broken legs and was trapped by the hole in the deck, but his friend Robinson managed to scramble on his hands and knees and drag a board across the gaping hole enabling Lister to crawl across. Both boys then managed to climb up two sets of ladders on their hands and knees to reach the boat deck, where they were then helped into the boats by other crew members.

Altogether, 10 boats were lowered, although one was badly damaged by it having been lowered before way was off the ship and was abandoned. Captain Capper made a tour of the decks but could not get into the port side of the after deck on account of the wreckage and, as he wrote '… *Not seeing anyone on deck and it seemed useless to attempt the store rooms as I thought it possible another torpedo might be let off at us, I got my greatcoat and left the ship by stepping off the gunwhale into the Second Officer Noel's boat, on the starboard side aft of the saloon deck ladder'*. From the time the ship was hit until the boats were cleared away, some 12 to 15 minutes elapsed and, as Captain Capper stated, '*There was no panic and the crew, including the stewardess, behaved magnificently.*'

The end of *AUSONIA* was described thus by Captain Capper:

After half an hour after the vessel was torpedoed and when we were in the boats, a submarine's periscope was sighted on the port bow – some 500 yards away. The submarine came to the surface on the starboard bow. He opened fire on the ship with his for'head gun, which I think was a four or five inch gun. He continued to shell the ship and I estimate some forty shells were fired. These shells were fired from different angles and several fell among the boats, dangerously near to two – a shell dropping about fifty yards from one and possibly some eighty yards from the other. Finally the vessel settled down aft. The submarine steamed slowly along the starboard side of the ship, pumping shell after shell into the engine room and smashing up the after bridge and gun platform. She worked along until she got into a fore and aft line with the ship, and after firing several shots from this direction, the poor old AUSONIA's stern went under until she seemed to stand on end for about half a minute before she sank, stern first, in a perpendicular position.

After the vessel had disappeared, the submarine came round the boats. I had taken the precaution to remove my coat. I was at the oars when he spoke to us. With revolver in his right hand and megaphone in his left, the interrogating officer yelled out 'Come alongside'. I counted about fifteen hands on deck who were jeering and laughing at us. The Officer asked 'What ship; where from; where to, cargo, owners and when we left'. He visited all the boats and I understand asked similar questions excepting the boat containing the stewardess – he did not interrogate this boat. The submarine gave us the direction to steer North East. The crew of the submarine were all big strapping men, oily and filthy, and they looked as though they had not seen water for a considerable time. The submarine herself was a vessel about 250 to 300 feet long and I could see on her port quarter the number 44 in figures about a foot long. They had been riveted to her side. I cannot say whether she was of the latest type or not. The man I took to be the Captain had a pointed reddish beard and the Chief or Interrogatory Officer had a moustache. Both were well made. After the submarine had been round all the boats we could see him putting up his wireless which I am given to understand is the usual method, when circumstances permit, of notifying their bases that they have had another victim. The submarine then steered away on the surface on a northerly direction where he was lost from view of the boats.

Captain Capper mustered the boats and had a headcount of his 149 crew members which revealed eight hands missing, who turned out to be stewards who, at the time of the explosion, were having their tea just above the point where the torpedo struck. With eight boats partly full, he decided that in view of the likely difficulties to be encountered in keeping the boats together it would be preferable to reduce to seven boats which, with 20 per boat, would not be overcrowded. The identity of the submarine was uncertain, as some crew members noted the number 42 was riveted to the starboard quarter of the submarine, conflicting with the number 44 seen on the port quarter. After transferring water and stores from the unwanted boats, Captain Capper placed the individual boats in the charge of Chief Officer Murdoch, First Officer Neale, Second Officer Noel, Third Officer E. Canby, Fourth Officer Legg, Bosun Harry Bartholemew and then himself, securing all on board the boats before nightfall.

The account continues,

By this time we had our sails up and were proceeding in a North Easterly direction. Before night set in I gave instructions to the officers in charge of the other boats that they were to keep together, my intention being to go to the nor'ard as fast as possible and get into the track of convoys and failing a convoy to steer on an easterly course to make the land. During all this time the weather was fine with smooth sea light southerly wind (force two to three) visibility full.

There was nothing in Captain Capper's account to suggest that he had anything but a positive view of the outcome of his situation. He calculated that the boats were some 590 nautical miles from the nearest land, which was the Irish coast, with the entirely pragmatic view that they had to make the best of the situation. The boats started off in fine weather, keeping together during the night and making about two knots.

The following are extracts from Captain Capper's detailed account.

May 31st (Friday)

... about 2:30 a.m. I saw and hailed Neale who answered and saying he and his crew were all right. At daylight, about 4.00 a.m. these two boats, 1st Officer Neale and Bosun, were not in company and could not be seen. As it was such fine weather I concluded that they had sailed closer to the wind and were to windward of us and that we would see them during the day. This day Friday was fine with light southerly wind and not much weigh on the boats, still we did all we could to help each other by keeping the tow ropes out of the water. Noon observations placed us 48 miles from where the ship was lost. During the day the Doctor was kept busy attending to Mr. Robinson who had both legs broken. In the evening I put him into the 2nd Officer's boat to attend to Mr. Lister, both legs broken and the Junior Marconi Operator with smashed finger. Got the Doctor back in our boat before dark and had a good night throughout.

June 1st 1918 (Saturday)

Fine day with little wind. Did some pulling at different times to keep boats along, also for exercise, but it made us very thirsty and having little water had to reduce ration to ½ wine glass per man per meal. Noon observations placed us 50 miles from last observations. Had to reduce the bread ration to 1½ biscuits per day per man as we had a long sail ahead of us at this rate of progress.

June 2nd 1918

Set in dull and rainy, wind changeable, all hands in the boats wet to the skin, which made us very despondent as some had very little clothes and there was no shelter. The weather continued bad all day, the tow ropes parted and having no others decided to cast off and sail on our own but all to keep close together so as not to lose sight of each other. The other four boats to take their course from me. Made several attempts to catch rainwater but without any result so we took turns at lapping up the water collected on compass glass. This saved us considerable water. Towards night the wind freshened from west and we had a bad night.

June 3rd 1918 (Monday)

The weather cleared but there was a lumpy sea and a fresh breeze, the boats making good headway which tended to keep the hands in good spirits. Observations at Noon showed we had made 101 miles since Saturday's observations making an average of about 50 miles a day since we had been in the boats. During the day the weather became bad, strong WNW wind. Had to reef sail for the night and watch her very carefully. The steersmen were very weary from want of sleep and rest.

June 4th (Tuesday)

Dawn with very bad weather, the sky at sunrise was wicked looking (and what we took, in our boat as an omen for what?) there being a very marked large cross formed by the clouds. By about 8.00 a.m. it was blowing a gale with a dangerously high sea, hard squalls and heavy rain. The boat was taking so much water over that we were continually baling. My observations at Noon, after much difficulty, showed we had made 124 miles for the day which made us more cheerful. The gale continued all day and through the night.

June 5th 1918 (Wednesday)

At daylight I hove to so as to let the other four boats catch up to me as they were two or three miles apart. When we got together again about 8.00 a.m. I set a course and we kept the boats running for all we could but owing to the reefed sail and bad weather my Noon observations showed only 72 miles for the day's run. The wind increased again during the afternoon, and the rough sea gave us an anxious night.

June 6th 1918 (Thursday)

Dawned with fresh gale, boats running with reefed sails and shipping much water. My Noon observations showed 125 miles from our last observations which was 'some' sailing, considering the weather and reefed sails. The gale let up towards night but during this day 2nd Officer Noel became separated from us during the bad weather through steering too far to the southward, but the other three boats kept well together. We shook out the reef before night and let her go for all she could as things were looking somewhat serious, hands becoming more or less demented, our water was getting low and only a couple of day's bread remained.

June 7th 1918 (Friday)

I could not see any of the other three boats but I knew if they had steered the course I had set for them they would make the land if their food and water held out. It was now very apparent that the long exposure, wet through, short rations, want of sleep and rest, and exercise, was telling on the boat's crew. The Assistant Purser (Hodgkinson), Robinson, and a couple of the engine room hands were very much off their head, so much so that I had to severely talk to them in endeavours to humour them. During the forenoon the wind was falling but there was a very dangerous sea which caused us much concern about our mast and sail and the boat was shipping a great deal of water. My Noon observations taken under much difficulty gave the satisfactory result of 112½ miles for the day and only 20 miles from the Fastnet Rock. During the afternoon it fell to a dead flat calm SW swell, but about half past twelve in the afternoon, A. Hassett, A.B. made out land on our port bow which was something to put life into us if anything would. We tried to pull on the oars but the hands were so emaciated and weary that we could not pull, that's all. We now had visions of a submarine coming along and putting us out of our misery as we knew he had [sunk] many fishing boats off the Irish coast. At dusk we saw a light on a rock which I took to be the Fastnet, but eventually turned out to be Bull Rock. We did all we could to pull the boat towards that light, the sail hanging like a rag but the current or tide were too much for us. In spite of it all we kept all available hands at the oars all night until about 4.00 a.m. on.

June 8th 1918 (Saturday)

We saw a vessel astern of us to whom we signalled by burning the red flares. She saw and answered them OK. It turned out to be HMS ZENNIA who picked us out of the boats after being 16 hours in sight of land. After a wash and something to eat we landed at Berehaven about 8.00 a.m. and learned from the CO that that Chief Officer Murdoch, 3rd Officer Canby and 4th Officer Legge had been picked up at 8.00 p.m. on Friday and landed at Valentin. We got a few clothes. I made my report to the Admiralty officials, telling them what Hassett, Turner, Caldecott and Gibson had repeatedly spoken about in the boat: viz. that Robinson had saved Lister's life. I then sent off wires to the Company and home. At 2.00 p.m. we left for Cork. At 8.00 p.m. left Cork for Kingston the Chief Officer and his party joining us at Limerick, all of us travelling home to Birkenhead arriving there at 6.30 p.m. Sunday 9th June. 2nd Officer Noel was picked up on Saturday June 8th, but 1st Officer Neale and Bosun Bartholomew with their boats and crews were lost making a total of 44 casualties out of a crew of 149.

Regrettably Mathew Robinson later succumbed to his injuries in hospital raising the total to 45 casualties. The survival of Captain Capper, after nine nights and eight days with three boats was a remarkable feat of navigation, seamanship and leadership as well as courage and determination. In a later account of the event he recalled,

The gale, although making things most uncomfortable – in the boat water had to be continually baled out – proved our salvation, the wind and sea driving us to our desired object. On making land, the wind suddenly fell and we were in sight of this land for 15 hours before being picked up. In the meantime the men did their utmost at the oars to get further inshore, but owing to their emaciated condition the boat scarcely moved in the water ... During the whole of this time, great credit is due to the manner in which the crew behaved themselves, accepting the conditions as only British Sailors would. Particular praise is due to the stewardess – the only woman on board the vessel, and who was in my boat. She had a terrible experience. For the first three days she was violently sick, and I thought she would collapse. On recovering she found it almost impossible to eat the hard biscuits but by sheer determination, courage and pluck she stuck it out and I am pleased to know that on landing she showed wonderful spirits, and was able to travel along with other members of the crew to Liverpool.

The only time Captain Capper seemed to have revealed any inkling of despair or pessimism was when in sight of land and unable to reach the shoreline because of lack of wind, with his reference to his fears that a submarine might appear and 'put them out of their misery' so close to their destination. He knew that had been the fate of several fishing boats off the Irish coast. He was also aware of warnings given to shipmasters that German submarines sometimes disguised themselves by raising sails and giving the impression of a vessel in distress to lure potential rescues ships and thus his plight might well be ignored even if found. He also drew attention to regret the lack of any shelter obtainable in the boat and to the inaccuracy of the compasses, as he put it, '*The greatest anxiety to me was the boat compasses, as I found these to be some three, four or five points out. I made special efforts to compare the boat compasses with mine at the time of P.V. night and morning, also at noon whenever the sun was visible.*'

The arrival of *AUSONIA*'s survivors in Liverpool was of course a matter of some celebration and many commendations were made regarding their courage and achievement. On 11 June 1918, just three days after their return, the Liverpool and London War Risks Insurance Association wrote to Captain Capper to notify him of a resolution which stated:

That the thanks of the Association be accorded to Captain Robert Capper of the s.s. 'Ausonia' for the seamanlike skill and courage shewn by him in sailing his lifeboat to land after his vessel had been sunk by enemy action on 30th May, 1918, and for the precautions taken by him to secure the safety of the other lifeboats, and that the sum of one hundred guineas be voted to him out of the funds of the Association as a mark of their appreciation.

One call to Cunard for a bravery award singled out Third Officer Canby who, for some while, had to steer his boat unaided for lack of a competent seaman to assist him. Captain Capper put pen to paper on 25 June 1918, writing:

I note with the greatest of pleasure and satisfaction that someone has shown some interest and made mention of Mr. E. Canby, Third Officer, but as far as

I am aware, not of the other Officers, namely Mr. Murdoch, Chief Officer, Mr. Noel, 2nd Officer and Mr. Legg, 4th Officer who each had charge of a boat.

Mr. Canby I am pleased and proud to say showed very remarkable and cool courage, seamanship, ability, patience and dogged determination during the awful experience he was compelled, like his brother officers, to face and endure. Mr. Canby was unfortunate in having to steer his boat practically himself for some considerable time after being cast adrift owing to the seamen in his boat not being competent, and until I was able to arrange for another seaman to be transferred from one of the other boats to his so that he could get some rest. I eventually arranged this transfer and so relieved him of the strain he had been under. Mr. Canby also had a mishap to the rudder of his boat caused by the tow-rope to the boat astern of his, and he had to steer his boat with an oar in which he was successful until the rudder was repaired, for which he deserves great credit.

Mr. Canby deserves the highest recognition and appreciation for the very capable manner in which he managed to sail his boat safely through the very heavy weather encountered.

The same high mark of appreciation and praise is due to the other officers before mentioned, who had the same trials and privations in a more or less degree to go through, particularly as regards the management of their crews, several of whom became partially demented through exposure and mental strain.

In conclusion I may say that the surviving officers are each deserving of the highest praise and recognition for the very capable manner in which my orders and instructions (as to the course they were to steer with the compasses they had) were carried out. I can conscientiously say that it is owing to the courage, bravery and determination of all the officers in the face of such a difficult situation, knowing that they were about 590 miles away from the nearest land and the very poor prospects of being picked up by a passing vessel, and finally making the land, that the lives of 105 of the 'Ausonia's' crew were saved from the fate of the two boats which were unfortunately parted from us on the night the ship was torpedoed and sunk.

I sincerely hope and trust that full recognition and appreciation will be given to all the officers for their co-operation.

I am, Sir, your obedient Servant.

Captain Capper, who was 45 years of age, also held the rank of Commander RNR and was awarded the Distinguished Service Cross for his very considerable achievement. He already had a reputation as a fine seaman after rescuing 103 passengers from the burning Spanish passenger ship SS *BALMES* in November 1913 when master of the Cunard liner *PANNONIA*.

The stewardess referred to by Captain Capper was a Mrs Theresa Edgar, who recounted her experiences in the lifeboat to an American journalist, Helen Hoffman, in 1919, when she had clearly resumed her seafaring career after recovering from the *AUSONIA* ordeal. Mrs Edgar was described as a young widow of a seafaring man with already considerable experience of Atlantic crossings who had been at sea on the RMS *MAURETANIA* when war was declared and had served on the *LUSITANIA* and *LACONIA* before they suffered at German hands. Her appearance was described as '... *an attractive little person, with the fresh colouring of the English woman, and a pretty oval face framed in a tousling mop of auburn hair*'.

Mrs Edgar described her ordeal as follows:

Late Thursday afternoon, being very tired and having nothing to do, I lay down in my cabin and was soon fast asleep. A terrible explosion awakened me a little later. It was about 5 o'clock. Thinking that the danger had passed when I lay down, I took off my dress and slipped on a kimono. I had my shoes on. Merely curious, I walked down the alleyway when the Chief Steward came rushing down the stairs. 'For God's sake,' he called to me, 'get on your lifebelt. The boat is sinking.' I hurried on deck and saw that the stern was dipping down into the sea.

As the journalist noted, Mrs Edgar revealed a certain aspect of femininity,

I had just bought a new spring hat in London. It was a pretty shade of pink. I liked it better than any other hat I had ever had. I rushed back to go and get the hat. That is the only thing I saved. I put it on and wore it for one day when the waves did their worst. I lost all my personal belongings.

The boats had been quickly lowered and as we carried no passengers the whole crew, with the exception of one boat load, including the Chief Officer, physician and about twenty others, was rowing away from the sinking ship when I climbed down the rope ladder into a boat. At the same time, on the

213

*port side, Captain Robert Capper, the last to leave, was jumping into a boat
to save his life, when it was seen the ship was past saving. There were seven
lifeboats in all.*

*The submarine when it saw our men could not operate our ship's
guns came to the surface and, running between us fired about forty rounds
into* AUSONIA. *The ship seemed fairly to lift out of the sea, stood for a
fleeting moment on her nose, as it were, and dropped into the water. With the
Germans standing at their guns, the captain of the submarine whipped out a
revolver and pointing it at the men in different lifeboats ordered them to come
alongside. Covering with the revolver, as one after another drew up before
him, he ordered them to throw up their hands, while he questioned them as to
the name, destination and mission of the boat. When he spied my pink hat,
he seemed surprised, and remarked in perfect English to his comrades, 'Why,
there is a lady in the boat.' Finally, after having questioned the last boatful,
to their satisfaction, the crew smiled at us − or rather, it was a sarcastic sneer I
should say − and turned and left us to our fate.*

*I believe it was Captain Capper's foresight that saved us, for with his
wonderful optimism he reminded us we were in the wake of steamers with a
good chance of being rescued, but he said it may be longer than we think, so
we at once will go on rations. If we hadn't done that we probably would have
starved to death, as we have reason to believe the men in other boats did. In
order to divide the rations so they would last until we were picked up, we had
three tablespoonfuls of water three times a day, a half of a biscuit three times a
day, and a slice of bully beef once a day. I didn't eat the beef because I suffered
so from thirst, which the beef seemed to increase, and while the men urged
upon me their share of water, I did not want to accept any undue favours, so
that they would regard me as a nuisance.*

*The weather at the time we were torpedoed was fine, but during the
night the breeze freshened and at daybreak two of the boats were not seen.
They never came to shore. We stretched a rope from boat to boat so that we
could all keep together, but after the sixth day a terrific gale set in, and fearful
that the boats would collide, we had to cut them loose. With sails up, the gales
helped us to speed towards land. Waves sprayed us and rains drenched us. I
don't know how we managed it, but we all felt somehow we would be saved
and we never gave up hope. During the night my sensations were sad, I can
assure you. The Captain had thrown a bag into his boat and this contained a*

white flannel shirt, which he gave me. I think I would have perished without it. This, with one of the blankets with which the lifeboats were supplied, kept me from freezing. We battled with heavy seas at times, and often during a night when it was as black as pitch, our chances of seeing home again seemed very small indeed.

On Friday, eight days after we had been torpedoed, the gale that had helped us speed to the shore died down. This was when the weary sailor men began to show signs of the effects of exposure and lack of food. They had no strength left to pull the oars. For several hours they remained in this plight, and I think the thought pierced everyone's mind sometime during that day, that unless help came very soon we couldn't stick it out much longer. But still hoping for the best, the Chief Officer stirred us all by declaring that he was sure he had sighted land.

The chief officer was in a different boat which had become separated from Captain Capper. Captain Capper in fact recorded an A.B., Mr. Hassett as having first sighted land.

Then at last real hope did come. There was a light we saw in the distance on Friday night, presumably a lighthouse and Captain Capper sent up some flares. Never shall I forget that tiny ray of hope in the east, with death staring us all in the face. That lighthouse was our salvation. It signalled a rescuing British war vessel, and on the Saturday this ship bore down upon the most grateful group of people the Atlantic had ever looked upon. We were a terrible looking lot; the men unshaven and wet to their skins; my hair, which had not been combed for nine days, blowing every which way; and bedraggled and half dead we were pulled aboard the warm, cosy compartments of the warship. None of us will ever forget that wonderful breakfast, which we devoured like hungry wolves, after which we made such toilettes as the accommodation afforded.

After landing at Berehaven, the survivors were taken to Holyhead for the crossing to Liverpool. Mrs Edgar expressed her fears for that crossing in the light of her recent ordeal, but would seem to have overcome them sufficiently to resume her career at sea.

At the end of her account of her survival, Mrs Edgar stated that apart from suffering from rheumatism in her feet, which she blamed on them being wet all the time in the boat, she had suffered no lasting ill effects and,

> *I love the sea. I am happier on it than on land. After my husband died I had to earn my living and I prefer this to anything else. I try not to think of the experience in the lifeboat. Perhaps if I should dwell on it I should go crazy. I do not deny it was terrifying. Crouched in the bottom of a boat, drenched for days, not knowing what moment would be our last, was not an experience to be forgotten in a hurry. But why dwell on the past when there is so much worth living for the future?*

The fortitude shown by Mrs Edgar, who returned to sea with Cunard, must be one of the most remarkable displays of character and resolve in such testing circumstances. Her concern as the ship was sinking to return to her cabin to recover her hat is an interesting insight into the psychology of someone faced with disaster and her concern regarding her appearance when being rescued shows she still, justifiably, had pride in herself and thoughts of how she might be perceived by others. It is clear she suffered along with other survivors and made no attempt to seek preferential treatment due to her femininity, even though others offered her their shares of water and food.

As she and many other women who sailed on the merchant ships said at the time, 'Our men are in the trenches braving death, should we not be taking equal chances with them?' A truly remarkable and courageous lady.

The conduct of Captain Capper was outstanding and in the finest tradition of the British Mercantile Marine. That those in the boats survived must surely be a tribute to Captain Capper's leadership to inspire their confidence in his judgement and competence. His feat as a navigator must have few equals in the conditions the boats experienced. The simple act of taking an accurate sextant angle, exposed in a heaving open boat itself must have been extremely difficult, apart from which he clearly managed, in extraordinarily difficult circumstances, to maintain his navigation tables and record the daily events in the boats. An outstanding, brave and resourceful man, Captain Capper died in Liverpool in 1947, aged 95.[132]

RMS *AUSONIA* was in fact sunk by U-62, under the command of

---

[132] National Archives, ADM 340/23/55.

Kapitänleutnant Ernst Hashagen, who stated that he was on his way to the Azores as U-boats were forced to seek their targets far from land, out of the range of the convoy escorts, and he came across *AUSONIA* quite by chance. He survived the war, surrendering to the British on 22 November 1918. He also died in 1947.

CHAPTER 15

KNOW YOUR ENEMY

At the outset of the war the British and Allied merchant seafarers could anticipate being treated in an honourable and humane manner by any German warships they might encounter, bearing in mind the German Prize Code statement that '*All acts shall be done in such a manner – even against the enemy – as to be compatible with the honour of the German Empire.*' Bearing in mind also that the submarine was not believed to have sufficient capability to cause a significant danger, there seemed little to fear in addition to the normal perils of the sea. They soon learned that their greatest peril came from beneath the waves once the U-boat commanders used their initiative to demonstrate that they had a powerful weapon to curtail Britain's trade.

The conduct of the commanders of the German commerce raiders was almost without exception fair and courteous, displaying many acts of chivalry within the applicable limits of the rules of warfare; the Prize Code. Von Muller of the *EMDEN* and Fritz von Lüdecke of the sister ship *DRESDEN*, for example, had shown great concern for the safety and well-being of their victims.

The converted cargo steamers *MÖEWE* under the command of Nikolas zu Dohna-Schlodien and *WOLF*, commanded by Karl Nerger, and the three-masted sailing ship *SEEADLER* under the command of Felix von Luckner were all regarded in high esteem by their victims and were lauded by many neutral states as romantic buccaneers of days gone by. They captured and sank very many British and Allied merchant ships by appearing to be ordinary cargo steamers flying neutral flags, until near enough to their unsuspecting victims to reveal their true colours and their armament.

The differences between the behaviour of the German naval officers of the surface ships and of those on the submarines is difficult to explain, bearing in mind they were all recruited from the same pool of manpower and trained to the same professional and operational standards. The ethics of chivalry and honour had been high initially, encompassing mutual respect for the seafaring fraternity, with many German and British officers having socialised before the war; indeed many German officers and ratings had served on British merchant ships.

The Submarine Service of the German Navy was, as with the British equivalent, a new arm of the Navy which had to be subject to training specific to the vagaries of the submersible and had to develop its own traditions and reputation. Officers and crews were normally drafted into the Submarine Service following a stringent selection process which took particular account of the tasks they were to carry out and the restricted conditions in which they would have to work. They would have to be medically fit and those with any serious offences in their backgrounds would be rejected. Volunteers were occasionally accepted, although their requests for transfer from general service were usually looked upon rather sceptically as being driven by a desire for the higher wages paid in submarines.

Officers to command the submarines were normally drawn from destroyer flotillas, and underwent initial rigorous and selective training courses and exercises for about three to six months, with the duration of courses shortening as later submarine losses took their toll. On completion of their training, they would be destined either for the large U-type submarines or for the smaller UC or UB types and within these categories a selection would be made as to which officers should take command immediately, and which would first have to carry out duties as officer of the watch before being given command.[133] After specialists and seamen had completed their training they would be retained in a reserve pool and often placed on board a submarine cruise for training purposes, providing a ready and available supply of manpower to replace crew members.

To ensure the supply of navigating and watch-keeping officers, men from their merchant service with a master's or first mate's certificate were transferred to the Submarine Service and, after following a selective training course, were used primarily as navigating warrant officers. They were

---

[133] Koerver,(ed.) *German Submarine Warfare 1914–1918 in the Eyes of British Intelligence*, pp.20, 21.

sometimes promoted and commissioned as officers of the reserve and used as watch officers. Later in the war, some of these reserve officers were given command.

The on-board conditions were, as with any submarines of that era, extremely basic and lacking in comfort, with little if any facility for personal space or privacy. Lack of ventilation while submerged, lack of water for the crew to wash themselves or their clothes, combined with the smells of cooking and the engine room, not to mention often unreliable toilets, made for a distinctly malodorous climate on board. Ventilation of the U-boat was a major concern in determining the length of time a boat could remain submerged, defined by von Forstner as '*The length of time that a U-boat can remain under water depends ... on the atmospheric conditions at the moment of plunging, and on the amount of oxygen and chemicals taken on board. We can stay submerged for several days, and a longer period will probably never be necessary.*'[134] The need for self-discipline and a tolerant attitude towards shipmates was paramount to develop the bond of comradeship.

It soon however became apparent that the U-boat officers and crews were looked upon with some disdain by the remainder of the German Navy and, in common with submariners of most nations, many U-boat crews considered themselves to be a little separate and a little 'special'. Stealth was important for the survival of a submarine and as far as the German Submarine Service was concerned, the operations of the U-boats were treated with a considerable amount of secrecy even from the rest of their Navy.

Certainly the U-boat commanders exercised a greater independence of action than their contemporaries on the surface and they often took initiatives that, while not always condoned by their superior officers ashore, were not necessarily disapproved of. A very early example of this was the first sinking of British merchant ship, the *GLITRA*, which demonstrated the enormous potential to disrupt Allied trade with little risk to the submarine. Even those U-boat commanders who had committed atrocities against unarmed merchant seafarers ran little risk of rebuke.

Throughout the course of the war, some 473 men commanded the German and Austrian U-boats. Of these, 20 were regarded as 'U-boat aces',

---

[134]   *The Journal of Submarine Commander von Forstner. U-boat War 1914–1918,*
          Vol. 2., p.31.

defined as those who sank more than 100,000 tons of shipping, with 18 listed as war criminals by Great Britain.[135] There were other U-boat commanders who may well have been pursued as war criminals had they not lost their lives during the war.

Heading the list of 'aces' was *Kapitänleutnant* Lothar von Arnauld de la Perière, who completed 10 cruises in the Mediterranean, where he sank a total of 194 ships amounting to 450,000 tons. He was a Prussian aristocrat who commanded two U-boats throughout the war, U–35 and U–139 and adhered to the Prize Code, although he was listed as a war criminal by Italy for the sinking of Italian ships. He survived World War I and was active in World War II reaching the rank of vice admiral before being killed in an air crash in Paris in 1941.

Some U-boat commanders were regarded by the general public in both Britain and America with a certain amount of admiration for their skill and bravery. An example of such a commander was *Kapiatänleutnant* Otto Weddigen who had made a name for himself on his first submarine command, U–9, by sinking three British battle cruisers in one attack on 22 September 1914, namely HMS *ABOUKIR*, *CRESSY* and *HOGUE*. This proved a very early and salutary lesson in the effectiveness of submarine warfare. Weddigen later claimed HMS *HAWKE* as another victim on 15 October of that year, bringing his total of British naval loss of life to 1,990 souls. He transferred to U–29 in February 1915, sinking or damaging five British and one French merchant ship without any loss of life. He was referred to as a 'gentleman pirate' in recognition of the courtesy and consideration shown to his merchant seafarer victims, in sharp contrast to other U-boats.

An article of the *Morning Post* of 15 March entitled '*U-29 as Gentlemen Pirates*' stated: '*The captains, officers and crew – 95 in all of the three steamers which were attacked by a German submarine off the Scilly Isles on Friday morning were landed at Penzance on Saturday afternoon. The three steamers were the* Indian City ... *the* Headlands ... *and the* Andalusian ... *No lives were lost*'.

As referred to in an earlier chapter, Weddigen lost his own life on 18 March 1915 off the Pentland Firth, when U–29 was lost with all hands after being rammed by HMS *DREADNOUGHT*.

---

[135] Gibson and Prendergast, *The German Submarine War 1914–1918*, pp.378, 379.

The references to 'gentleman pirates' were however very few, with the press in Britain and in the USA frequently carrying articles and letters regarding the perceived atrocities of the U-boats, labelling some U-boat commanders as 'pirates'. An article under the heading of '*The Pirate U-8*' reported an announcement by the Secretary of State for the Admiralty in April 1915 regarding special restrictions to be enforced on captured U-boat crews:

> *Since the war began his Majesty's ships have on every occasion done their utmost to rescue from the sea German officers and men whose vessels have been sunk, and more than 1,000 have been saved, often in circumstances of difficulty and danger , although no such treatment has ever yet been shown to British sailors in similar distress.*
>
> *The officers and men thus taken prisoners have received the treatment appropriate to their rank and such courtesies as the Service allows; and in the case of the* EMDEN *were accorded the honours of war.*
>
> *The Board of Admiralty do not, however, feel justified in extending honourable treatment to the twenty-nine officers and men rescued from submarine U-8. This vessel has been operating in the Straits of Dover and the English Channel during the last few weeks, and there is a strong probability that she has been guilty of attacking and sinking unarmed merchantmen and firing torpedoes at ships carrying non-combatants, neutrals and women.*
>
> *In particular the steamship* ORIOLE *is missing, and there is grave reason to fear she was sunk at the beginning of February with all hands – twenty.*

Following that announcement there were articles and letters in the British press with demands that the captured commander and crew of U-8 should be tried at the Old Bailey for piracy and murder.

On 6 March 1915, Commander P.V. Oliver, the captain in charge of the detention quarters wrote to the Admiralty:

> *Sir. I have the honour to submit herewith a list of 29 German Prisoners from Submarine U-8 received in these Quarters yesterday. They have no effects, other than the clothes they were wearing on leaving their Boat. I have caused*

to be issued to each prisoner One Towel with Soap. Whilst they are here, may three additional Petty Officers be lent to the Quarters?[136]

The naming of the commander of U–8, *Kapiatänleutnant* Alfred Stoß, as a 'pirate' in view of his sinking of five British merchant ships without making any attempt to assist the survivors would seem entirely justified. Unsurprisingly, Stoß took a different view of his actions and complained about his treatment at British hands. His letter of 9 March to Commander Oliver stated:

> *The officers and crew of His Majesty's German Submarine U-8 have been lodged here since the 5th March. The accommodation is felt to be dishonourable by the officers and crew because:*
>
> 1. *They live in a building, in which only English sailors 'under detention' live.*
> 2. *In this building the German Officers and men are treated as regards being watched, care, living, cleanliness and routine in the same manner as the 'first stage men under detention'.*
> 3. *Because absolutely no difference in the living and the treatment of the officers, warrant officers and crew is made.*
> 4. *Because the officers and men are forbidden any kind of correspondence communication with their nearest relatives.*
>
> *It does not appear to me evident why this accommodation, derogatory to our honour, has been ordered. It is not in accordance with international customs.*
>
> *The crew of U-8 fought in honourable battle up to the end in accordance with the order of His Majesty, the German Kaiser. When the boat began to sink the crew became prisoners of His Majesty the King of Great Britain and Ireland.*
>
> *It is found especially dishonouring by the crew that this form of accommodation should be ordered for them, without declaration of any apparent reason or preliminary form of trial.*
>
> *I beg in the name of the officers, warrant officers and petty officers and*

---

[136]   The National Archives, ADM 116/1418.

crew that an immediate change and amelioration in the present treatment may be made.

I beg especially for:

1. *Separate treatment of Warrant Officers and crew.*
2. *For Officers and Warrant Officers the possibility of mutual intercourse, better food and the attendance of a servant for keeping the rooms clean.*
3. *Opportunity to sleep in beds or hammocks for everybody.*
4. *Permission to correspond with one's near relatives.*[137]

It is of interest to note Stoß's reference to honour in the light of his own actions against unarmed merchant ships, whereby the five British steamers he sank in the English Channel on 23 and 24 February were all torpedoed without warning, including the *HERPALION* with loss of three lives. His cause for complaint was somewhat different from that of British officers and crews described earlier, in particular the murder of Captain Fryatt of the steamer *BRUSSELS* and the brutal treatment of Captain Edward Webb and the crew of the steamer *WARTENFELS*, among others.

The Admiralty concern for the fate of the British steamer *ORIOLE* was justified as she had indeed been sunk on 30 January 1915 with the loss of all hands, not by U-8 but by Walther Schweiger in U-20. This act was recorded as the first sinking of a merchant ship by torpedo with the loss of all hands. Schweiger later went on to distinguish himself as one of the more notorious 'aces', including his sinking of *LUSITANIA* and the sinking or damaging of 49 merchant ships before losing his own life in the North Sea on 5 September 1917.

Max Valentiner was another U-boat commander who could certainly not be regarded as a 'gentleman pirate'. He ranked third on the list of U-boat 'aces', and was acknowledged as a particularly skilful commander who was awarded many military honours for his development of techniques to sink shipping without being sighted, contrary to the Prize Code, with minimal risk to his boat and its crew. When in command of U-38 and later of U-157 he was active in the North Sea, the Atlantic, the Mediterranean and the

---

[137] Koerver, (ed.) *German Submarine Warfare 1914-1918 in the Eyes of British Intelligence*, p.247.

Black Sea. His record included the sinking of 143 merchant ships and one warship (the 'Q' ship HMS *REMEMBRANCE*). He was responsible for at least 1,480 known casualties, including the torpedoing of the French troop transport *LE CALVADOS* off the coast of Algeria on 4 November 1915, with the loss of 740 lives, leaving only 55 survivors. On 30 December he then sank the British liner, the *PERSIA*, which was a gruesome example of the callous torpedoing of a ship without any warning and a total disregard for the safety of the survivors. He was listed as a war criminal and was charged with 15 alleged breaches of the Laws of War but never brought to trial. He served in World War II as a training officer for the U-Boot-Waffe and died in Denmark, aged 65, in 1949.[138]

On the rare occasions that merchant seafarer captives were held on the U-boats they generally received good treatment by the U-boat crews. One such account is that of Captain Davis Evans of the steamer *PENNISTONE*, torpedoed on 11 August 1918 when about 140 miles off Nantucket. Captain Evans stated his ship had been about three miles astern of a convoy of 18 ships, with the escorting cruiser at the head of the formation when hit by U-156. The submarine came alongside the stricken ship, taking Captain Evans, who had lost an engineer and a fireman in the explosion, with his surviving crew in two small boats on board the submarine. They were quartered with the crew of the submarine with about 40 men in one space, sleeping on wooden lockers.

Captain Evans remarked that there seemed to be lax discipline within the submarine crew, with frequent arguments between the officers and ratings, although otherwise the Germans seemed fairly contented and he noted the very foul air on board. Several of the crew spoke English and some had served on German merchant ships, but the war was never mentioned, the sinking of ships never discussed and Captain Evans was never questioned for information. He and his crew received the same rations as the submarine crew but there was little contact with the submarine commander and there was no insulting or abusing the British prisoners. Captain Evans considered he and his crew were well treated, given the limitations of life on board a submarine. After some six days the Norwegian steamer *SAN JOSE* had been sighted and Captain Evans, who had been allowed to spend much of the time on deck, was sent below as the submarine attacked. The Norwegians

---

[138]   Bridgland, *Outrage at Sea*, p.135.

abandoned their ship and their lifeboats were lying alongside the submarine when Captain Evans was allowed back on the deck of the U-boat. He was given the option of staying on the submarine or joining the Norwegians in their boats and he elected to join the Norwegians. They were given provisions for three or four days and told they were 84 miles from Cape Sable but were later picked up by the *DERBYSHIRE* after 25 hours in the boats.[139]

Captain Evans never knew the name of the commander of U-156 and British sources believed it was probably Lothar von Arnauld de la Perière, but German sources state it was *Kapitänleutnant* Richard Feldt[140] who, after a career of sinking 35 British and Allied merchant ships and one warship, died with all hands just over a month later on 25 September in the North Channel.

In overall terms, most U-boat commanders considered they had fulfilled their duty once they had captured or sunk a merchant ship, with little conscious attempt to kill their civilian victims, with some even taking risks to their own boats by towing the lifeboats closer to land and providing them with rations and medical equipment. Some even sent radio messages to advise any other ships in the area of the position of the survivors to aid their rescue, although not all merchant ships were equipped to receive this information. Clearly, a submarine on the surface presented a very exposed target and the commanders believed their priority was to safeguard their crew and their boat. Taking the survivors on board, as was sometimes done, presented obvious difficulties in accommodation and would reduce the operational effectiveness of the boat.

The reputation of the U-boat commanders was however compromised to such an extent by the brutality of many that they were described thus:

As regards the stigma of inhumanity which rests with the Submarine Service as a whole, it is possible to acquit the greater number of officers of any worse fault than that of a somewhat blind acceptance of their government's policy, and, in view of the orders received, it is not to be wondered at if certain of the more brutal commanders followed them to a logical conclusion.[141]

---

[139] Koerver, (ed.) *German Submarine Warfare 1914–1918 in the Eyes of British Intelligence*, pp.629–632.

[140] www.uboat.net.com, wwi.

[141] Koerver, (ed.) *German Submarine Warfare 1914–1918 in the Eyes of British Intelligence*, p.215.

The 'stigma of inhumanity', unfortunately for British Allied and neutral ships, was to apply to many of the U-boat commanders with the deliberate murder of crews as they tried to abandon ship, even to the extent of firing on survivors in the water and in their boats, with some instances already described in this book. There were also clear attempts to ensure there were no survivors and thus no evidence of the identity of the U-boat and its commander.

There were many acts of extreme brutality and inhumanity, but among the most callous were certainly those of Wilhelm Werner with U-55. Born in 1888, Werner joined the German Navy in 1908 and was appointed to his first U-boat command, UB-9 in 1915, with a promotion to *Kapitänleutnant* and the command of U-55. It was from U-55 that he committed the known atrocities against the British steamers *TORRINGTON*, *TORO* and, probably, *BELGIAN PRINCE*. These were instances where the survivors of the initial attacks were brought on to the deck of U-55 and their lifeboats deliberately wrecked, following which U-55 submerged, thus drowning them as described earlier. Those actions alone were responsible for the murder of 88 merchant seafarers. Additionally, the British steamers *YOLA* and *VINE BRANCH* were sunk with all hands by Werner in February and April 1917 respectively, with the further loss of 77 merchant seafarers. In total, Werner sank 63 British and Allied merchant ships with a total loss of life of 343 souls.

Werner was listed as a war criminal by the British government but fled to Brazil after the war, working on a coffee plantation but returning to Germany in 1925. By that time his charge as a war criminal had been reduced to that of the murder of *TORRINGTON*'s crew, but he never stood trial. He joined the German SS, becoming a member of the staff of Heinrich Himmler and acted as a liaison officer for the Sudetenland. In 1933 he became a member of the Nazi Reichstag, dying aged 57 in 1945 as Germany surrendered in World War II.

Kapiatänleutnant Georg-Günther von Forstner, as commander of U-28, gained notoriety mainly for his brutal action against the *FALABA*, when 104 lives were lost. In total he sank, damaged or captured 27 British and Allied merchant ships, causing a total of 158 lives to be lost, all of which happened to be from British registered ships. He was not listed as a war criminal and survived the war, giving his account of his time in a U-boat entitled *The Journal of Submarine Commander von Forstner*, published along with Paul

König's *The Voyage of the Deutschland,* and von Spiegel's *The Adventures of the U-202.* In his journal, first published in 1916, he provided some descriptions of actions against merchant shipping, but refrained from naming the ships.

Unsurprisingly, von Forstner makes no mention of the loss of life he inflicted but does claim, in several instances, that many of his victims thanked him for his humanity and for rescuing them from the sea, but again no names are given. He is very disparaging of the attempts by merchant ships to resist his attacks and particularly disdainful of the attempts to ram, writing:

> *The English authorities even went so far as to inaugurate a sharp-shooting system at sea by offering a reward to any captain who rammed or destroyed a German submarine, although the latter could only obey this command at the risk of their lives; but what cared the rulers in England for the existence of men belonging to the lower classes of the Nation? They offered tempting rewards for these exploits in the shape of gold watches, and bribed the captains of the merchant marine with the promise of being raised to the rank of officers in the Reserve.*[142]

Von Forstner also goes on to describe a skirmish involving a small British steamer which claimed it had rammed and sunk a U-boat (not U-28) to much acclaim in England, only for the U-boat to survive without damage and later having the pleasure of finding the blade of a propeller embedded in the wall of the submarine's turret, that blade later to grace the German submarine museum.[143] The story almost fits the description, given earlier, of Captain Bell's encounter between an unidentified U-boat and his ship the *THORDIS*, on 28 February 1915, and his belief that he had rammed and sunk a U-boat. Indeed Captain Bell had been rewarded with a gold watch inscribed with the words '... *for sinking the first German submarine in the great European War 1914–1915'.* He was also commissioned as a lieutenant in the RNR, awarded a DSC, a substantial financial reward for him and his crew and a celebratory dinner at the Mansion House in London. Von Forstner's observation on '*the existence of men belonging to the lower classes*' underlines a view among some, or even many, that the lives of merchant seafarers were of little consequence.

---

[142] Von Forstner, *The Journal of Submarine Commander von Forstner,* p.45.

[143] Ibid.,p.46

An unusual event was described by von Forstner immediately following his sinking of the British steamer *IBERIAN* on 30 April 1918 with the loss of seven lives. Subsequent to the rapid sinking of the ship, von Forstner reported a great explosion, shooting large pieces of debris high into the air, amongst which was what he described as a gigantic aquatic animal of approximately 60 feet in length. He claimed that he, with six others in the conning tower, had seen a large creature which they could not identify, with four limbs, having large webbed feet, a long pointed tail and head which tapered to a point. There had been insufficient time to take a photograph as the creature sank within a few seconds and there was no further report or evidence to support that unusual sighting.

U-boat crews also suffered their own hardships and horrors at the hands of their enemies, due to their own particular difficulties in escaping from a doomed boat. *Kapitänleutnant* Baron Freiherr Spiegel von und zu Peckelsheim, commander of U-93, recounted his own experiences after attacking what seemed to him a small, insignificant, black three-masted schooner on the evening of 30 April 1917.

He was on his way back to base after completing the maiden cruise of U-93, but on sighting the schooner decided to attack to bolster his tonnage figures. Giving little thought to his prey he closed to about three miles and opened fire, at which the schooner initially seemed to take little note, but shortly hove to and began to lower her boat. The submarine approached from the stern of the schooner, assuming little possibility of it being armed. As he got closer, von Spiegel could see that his shots had inflicted damage to the schooner and he assumed that she had been abandoned and accordingly ceased fire until he could get closer. He was nevertheless very cautious in his approach to the apparently deserted vessel, and came up on the schooner's port beam at a distance of about 75 yards, preparing to sink her by gunfire. At this point the schooner raised her white ensign and a moveable gun platform appeared which immediately engaged the submarine. The ensuing battle resulted in serious damage to the schooner, but U-93 suffered the loss of the forward gun and the gun crew, and another shell stopped the submarine's main engines and it thus began drifting at the mercy of the schooner. Von Spiegel ran down the deck towards the after gun to supervise the action but the gun was hit, the gun layer standing next to him had his head blown off and von Spiegel and the two survivors on the after deck were thrown backwards. Von Spiegel recalled:

> *Then I felt a cold sensation about my legs. We were up to our knees in water.*
> *A moment later we were swimming in the Atlantic and the U-93 had sunk*
> *beneath us. A dreadful pang of anguish shot through me at the thought of my*
> *fine new boat and my crew going down to their last port on the cold silent*
> *bottom of the sea, and a touch of ironic pity for those five British captains*
> *who, skippers of prosaic freighters, had never signed articles about making a*
> *last voyage in an iron coffin.*
>
> *I couldn't forget my crew, my friends going down out there, drowned like*
> *rats in a trap, with some perhaps left to die of slow suffocation. I could imagine*
> *how some might even now be alive in the strong torpedo compartments,*
> *lying in darkness, hopeless, waiting for the air to thicken and finally smother*
> *them.*[144]

The schooner that von Spiegel had so unwisely attacked was a Royal Naval 'Q' ship, HMS *PRIZE*, which had suffered considerable damage during the close quarters gunfire exchange. The *PRIZE*, commanded by Lieutenant W. E. Sanders, nevertheless managed to pick up the three survivors from U-93, but she was now damaged and without power. By a stroke of fortune, although the ailing schooner's engineers were unable to restore power the U-93's machinist's mate had been one of the survivors and managed to repair and restart the main engine, enabling the *PRIZE* to reach safety at Pembroke Dock. Lieutenant Sanders was awarded the Victoria Cross for his brave actions; Baron von Spiegel spent the rest of the war in a prisoner of war camp at Donnington Castle. (While a POW it was discovered that von Spiegel was the author of a book describing the activities of a fictional 'U-202', claiming many successful actions against Allied shipping. It turned out, as von Spiegel later admitted, that the actions he described as his own experiences had indeed been added to from the experiences of other U-boats as well as his own.)[145]

The fate of U-93 however had not been sealed. The second-in-command, Wilhelm Ziegner, had witnessed the action at the after gun and

---

[144]   Gray. *The U-boat War 1914–1918*, pp.185, 186.

[145]   Von Spiegel, *The Adventures of the U-202. U-Boat War 1914–1918*, Vol. 2.

ingge ENEMY

saw the decapitated body of the gun layer, but no sign of von Spiegel or the two others and assumed they must also have been killed. Although on his first operational patrol Ziegner, with remarkable presence of mind in the circumstances, made a rapid assessment of his boat's condition while still under continuing fire from PRIZE and considered that if he should submerge the boat it was unlikely to surface again. He was able to make use of the swirling snow squalls to escape the further attentions of the PRIZE, whose commander believed that the submarine could not have withstood the amount of damage inflicted on her and still survive. U-93 had lost much of its fuel and fresh water, the remainder of which had to be severely rationed, plus there were several seriously wounded men on board. Ziegner faced the dichotomy of needing to select a course to avoid enemy warships yet having enough fuel to return to port. He selected a course to take his submarine high into the Arctic Circle, east of Iceland, where he ran into appalling weather conditions. On two occasions he sighted Allied warships but was saved from further engagement by reduced visibility and snowstorms, with the advantage that the damaged submarine now sat very low in the water offering a much reduced silhouette. On one occasion, in the belief that the U-boat was to be subject to a further attack Ziegner had the boat prepared for scuttling. The weather was such that watchkeepers had to be lashed to the conning tower rails but, after managing to navigate a minefield close to home, U-93 made it back to her home port. Ziegner's nine-day voyage *deserves to rank as one of the epics of submarine history.*[146] He returned to the submarine service but died in 1919 at the age of 28.

In the small hours of 22 April 1918 UB-55, under the command of 27-year-old *Kapitänleutnant* Rudolph Wenninger, was bound from Zeebrugge to the English Channel. Having completed her trimming trials the boat continued on the surface for a few hours before submerging to a depth of 12 metres. After a short while a grating sound was heard, followed by a heavy explosion causing considerable damage as water rapidly entered the boat from the stern torpedo compartment and the engine room. The boat began to sink rapidly as the consequence of her encounter with a mine, touching the seabed at a depth of 25.3 metres. It was clear to all on board that the submarine could not be saved.

---

[146]   Gray, *The U-boat War 1914–1918*, p.192.

The following account is recorded by Koerver:[147]

The water now began to penetrate from aft into the control room …and the batteries began to gas. The admission of water aft gradually increased the pressure in the boat until breathing became very difficult and, to prevent a further increase of air pressure, the men in the bow compartment shut the door leading to the warrant officers' quarters. Several unsuccessful attempts were made to open the fore torpedo room to enable the men there to escape … As the water continued to rise in the torpedo room, the men gave up every hope to escape, and to prevent slow death by suffocation some committed suicide by putting wadding in the nose and mouth and throwing themselves into the water in the boat. Others tried to shoot themselves, but the pistols had become wet and did not fire.

Finally the water rose to a height of 3 feet, and then only was it possible to force open the forward and conning tower hatches. The Commanding Officer and the Engineer Sub-Lieutenant affected their escape through the conning tower hatch, and about 20 of the crew escaped through the foremost hatch. The air pressure in the men's' lungs was so great that they were unable to keep their mouth closed while rising to the surface, and continually exhaled large volumes of air.

Of those who came to the surface only six were rescued by a passing trawler, the MATE. *In the case of several men the sudden change of pressure caused their lungs to burst, and they sank again, screaming with agony. Nearly all the survivors had lost consciousness by the time they were rescued; and some days after their capture they were still expectorating blood and complaining of deafness.*

Of the crew of 35 men, only six survived, including the commanding officer, Ralph Wenninger and the engineer, Friedrich Dietrich.

Perils of war awaited survivors in the water, regardless of their nationality. In the case of the merchant seafarers the cause of death was usually given as death from drowning and, while no doubt drowning was the final cause of death, the proximate cause of death was often by gunfire and the enormous impact on the human body from shells, depth charges or explosions from a sinking ship, which could cause loss of consciousness resulting in drowning.

---

[147] Koerver,(ed.) *German Submarine Warfare 1914–1918 in the Eyes of British Intelligence*, pp.491–493.

Often survivors were found to have vomited blood and to have evacuated their bowels due to internal injuries.[148] They were also often struck by debris from their sinking ship and invariably suffered from shock and hypothermia.

Other perils included the spying on the sailing schedules of shipping from a number of ports including Queenstown, where so many survivors had been landed or, as Captain James William Holmes put it, '*Queenstown itself was an "unsafe port" to leave, for the submarines operating outside had friends in the harbour who kept them informed of all ships' sailing dates, so it became expedient to leave on another date than that announced.*'[149]

* * *

As already mentioned, the wartime dangers did not of course exclude the normal perils of the sea which continued to claim its victims. One such victim was the four-masted barque *ARCHIBALD RUSSELL*, the last commercial sailing vessel built for a British owner, which sailed on 2 December 1914 from Tocopilla with a cargo of nitrates, bound for Queenstown. The barque was under the command of Captain Robert Montgomery who had his wife and infant son on board. He had sailed without being able to complete replenishment of stores in the hope and expectation that he would encounter another vessel on the long voyage to top up. [150] In the event the vessel began to run out of food and all on board suffered from the ravages of scurvy and starvation. No other ship was encountered on that long and lonely voyage until 1 March, when the Spanish steamer *OPU-MENDI* shared what little she had on board with Captain Montgomery and his crew. By that time the captain and his wife had watched their infant son die from starvation and were overcome with grief. On 10 March the British steamer *LAPLAND* provided the barque with two weeks' rations and the voyage ended, after 123 days at sea, on 4 April. '*It was one of the epics of the sea. It passed unnoticed in the general tragedy of war.*'[151]

---

[148] Brigland, *Outrage at Sea*, p.58.
[149] Holmes, *Voyaging*, p.177.
[150] Ibid., p.176.
[151] Hope, *Poor Jack*, p.301

CHAPTER 16

THE RECKONING

Little enough mention has been made of the role of women on British merchant ships, but their courage and steadfastness was a match for that of their male colleagues. Women were employed almost exclusively as stewardesses, waitresses, nurses and laundry staff, with little experience of the ways of seamanship that helped so many men to escape and survive a sinking ship. As the account of Mrs Edgar of the *AUSONIA*, and many other women, showed gender was no reason to seek special treatment when abandoning ship or in surviving lifeboat voyages. Another extraordinary, but very different, experience was that of Violet Jessup, a stewardess who had the distinction of surviving a collision when on board the RMS *OLYMPIC* and the sinkings of the sister ships *TITANIC* and *BRITANNIC*. When serving on *BRITANNIC* the ship struck a mine and Violet had to abandon ship, nearly losing her life when she jumped out of her lifeboat to avoid the turning propellers of the stricken ship. She was still pulled under the water, striking her head on the ship. As Mrs Edgar had insisted on finding her new hat before abandoning ship, Violet also showed her femininity by complaining she had not rescued her toothbrush.

The decrease in the number of merchant seafarers available to maintain the supply lines to Britain was almost immediate at the outbreak of war, but there was little encouragement for women to replace the men at sea, in contrast to many other civilian occupations. Within 48 hours of the declaration of hostilities some 8,000 officers and men from the merchant fleets voluntarily joined the armed services and, while most of those enlisted in the Royal Naval Reserve, some joined the Army and served in the trenches. Others were purloined by the Royal Navy to join the Royal Naval Division, almost along the lines of the 'shanghaiing' of generations ago. Some seafarers had deserted to serve on American ships for better pay and conditions. Ships that had long been out of service, including old wooden clippers, had been recommissioned with retired merchant seafarers brought back to support the depleted crew numbers in a final effort to maintain the supply lines to Britain.

Losses of merchant seafarers, men and women, from enemy action created significant problems in crewing the ships, but the losses had not just been from the transfers to the armed services or due to enemy action, as

> ... although 14,428 seafarers lost their lives in British ships from this cause [enemy action], another 3,348 were lost through the ordinary risks of the sea and over 3,000 died from illness and disease. Of deaths from diseases in twelve months, in 1914, of 224,663 men serving in the Army 672 died [0.3per cent]; of 126,830 serving in the Royal Navy 412 died [0.3per cent]; but of 170,349 Britishers serving in the Merchant Service, 1,328 died [0.8per cent].[152]

That disproportionate loss of life of the British merchant seafarers was no doubt some reflection of their working conditions and lack of access to medical care.

The loss of ships and lives by U-boat attacks nevertheless continued into the last month of the war in the Mediterranean with a lone wolf in the guise of *Oberleutnant zur See* Hans Schuler in command of UC-74. On 2 November 1918 he sank two British steamers off the coast of Egypt, the *SURADA* and the *MURCIA* with one casualty. The *MURCIA* has the dubious distinction of being the last steamer to be sunk by a U-boat attack, following which UC-74 made it to Barcelona having run out of fuel, surrendered to France and was interned on 21 November.

The U-boats had been recalled from the recognised sea lanes to the German North Sea operations and were charged with the task of attempting to achieve what they had attempted to achieve at the start of the war, namely a successful attack on the British Grand Fleet at its war anchorage. The aim, as a last ditch attempt to turn the tide of the war, was to attack the British fleet with the German High Seas Fleet. U-boats of the Flanders Submarine Flotilla were to make an initial foray into Scapa Flow prior to the German

---

[152] Course, *The Merchant Navy*, p.276.

fleet's assault, with newly built smaller ocean-going UB-116 given the task of leading the submarine attack. On 25 October the U-boat sailed from Helgoland on this last courageous and desperate bid, with a crew reputedly composed entirely of volunteer officers under the command of 26-year-old *Oberleutnant zur See* Hans Joachim Emsmann.[153], [154] On the evening of 28 October, UB-116 was seen by the shore defences at Stanger Head on her approach to Scapa Flow. Turning away, the U-boat submerged and then headed directly for the boom defences of Hoxa Sound and was picked up by the hydrophones of the shore defences. The inevitable occurred and UB-116 was struck by the simultaneous explosion of a row of mines. The following morning debris and oil were seen on the surface and patrol craft were despatched to drop depth charges to bring the abortive attack to an end. UB-116 was lost with all hands, 36 men, but earned her place in history as the first U-boat to be sunk by a shore-controlled minefield and the last U-boat to be sunk in action. The futility of her operation was underlined by the fact that the Grand Fleet was not at Scapa Flow but in the Firth of Forth.

On the same day as the abortive attack at Scapa Flow the German battleships *THÜRINGEN* and *OSTFRIESLAND*, which had been languishing in the Schilling Roads due to the effective Allied blockade, were ordered to sea in a last desperate gesture but their crews refused to sail as they believed they would face certain death. The crews sabotaged the ships' capstans so they could not weigh anchor and the stokers drew the fires from the boilers.[155] It is ironic that a German submarine, U-135, was then ordered to the scene to await orders should the mutiny continue. The intention no doubt was to sink the battleships if ordered to, but in the event boarding parties were sent to the battleships and the mutiny was quelled on 31 October, although not before considerable threat and counter-threat. The Flanders Flotilla of submarines, torpedo-craft and patrol craft remained loyal to the Kaiser and the Imperial Navy[156] but the battleships did not proceed to sea and all hostilities ceased on 11 November 1918.

---

[153] Koerver, (ed.) *German Submarine Warfare 1914–1918 in the Eyes of British Intelligence*, p.198.

[154] Gibson and Prendergast, *The German Submarine War 1914–1918*, p.327.

[155] Gray, *The U-boat War 1914-1918*, p.259.

[156] Gibson and Prendergast, *The German Submarine War 1914-1918,* pp.329.

Finally, the U-boats which had been transformed from the hunters to the hunted had been defeated, largely due to the combination of the successful convoy system eventually adopted, the minefields laid and the skills of the Royal Navy in its unremitting harassment of the submarines. It was however the men and women of the merchant ships who, with great courage in adversity, maintained the flow of goods to Britain, whose history, as described by the historian G.M. Trevalyan '... *has frequently underlined the unaccountable contrast between their inherent indiscipline and grievances and their steadfastness, resilience and resourcefulness in action; recognised over the centuries and remarked upon in Nelson's days*'.[157]

In much the same vein Hurd states:

> ... *if the officers and men of the Merchant Navy had not exhibited powers of endurance beyond anything known in the history of the sea, defeat would have come to the Allies. Their armies would have been without essential sea-borne reinforcements of personnel and necessary replenishment of munitions, and the civilian populations behind the lines would have been brought to the verge of starvation. Nor could the hastily mobilised armies of the United States have been transported across the Atlantic, mainly in British ships. The British merchant seamen held on with incomparable devotion until at last the plans of the naval authorities began to take effective shape, and then the clouds steadily lifted.*

As a further tribute to the merchant seafarers, Hurd summarises in his final paragraph of his treatise on the Merchant Navy,

> *The men of the Merchant Navy in the ordeal by sea in the years of the Great War created new and lofty traditions of national service, which they have handed on to their successors as a rich heritage. The history of the part which British merchant seamen took in the world-wide struggle of 1914-18 may well be the chart and compass of the men who in future years will be called upon to man British ships in war or in peace.*[158]

---

[157] Trevelyan, *English Social History*, p.499.

[158] Hurd, *The Merchant Navy* Vol.3, p.372

At last the welcome and long sought-after surrender of the U-boats was finally carried out under the naval conditions of the Armistice of 11 November, which included the following clause:

> *To surrender at the ports specified by the Allies and the United States all submarines at present in existence (including all submarine-cruisers and mine-layers, with armament and equipment complete). Those that cannot put to sea shall be deprived of armament and equipment, and shall remain under the supervision of the Allies and the United States. Submarines ready to put to sea shall be prepared to leave German ports immediately on receipt of wireless orders to sail to the port of surrender, the remainder to follow as soon as possible. The conditions of this Article shall be completed within fourteen days of the signing of the Armistice.*

Harwich was chosen as the surrender port, which was the base of the Harwich Force under Commodore, later Rear Admiral, Sir Reginald Trywhitt and 20 November saw the first of the surrendered U-boats approaching in a long line. They had been boarded by British crews who took over from the Germans and raised the white ensign above the German flag. Understandably, the Germans regarded this as a final act of humiliation and many of the commanders refused to participate in the act of surrender, leaving that task to their subordinate officers. Also understandably, the U-boat crews were extremely nervous of the reception they might receive in Harwich and were well aware of British public opinion regarding their treatment of merchant shipping and their crews. They may indeed have also been aware of the many instances of merchant seafarer victims being paraded through German towns and subjected to abuse, contempt and humiliation before being taken to degrading prison camps.

In the event, the practice of the Admiralty was to repatriate the U-boat crews to Germany as swiftly as possible in a bid to avoid the potential for such reciprocal displays. Such was the concern for the protection of the U-boat crews from assault by the British public that the Armistice Committee was obliged to issue the following statement; '*In answer to a direct question, the British Admiral unreservedly guaranteed the absolute safety of the crews of all submarines immediately on their arrival at an English port. There is no danger as regards the crews' personal liberty and safety.*' Nevertheless, the scenes at the surrender of the

U-boats would no doubt have gladdened many a heart among the merchant seafarers as it was the turn of the U-boat crews to face the humiliation of surrender, but few would have been able to bear witness.

Many of the U-boat commanders had wished to scuttle their boats rather than hand them over to the Allies and several were scuttled in Italy, but the Allies threatened permanently to occupy Helgoland if that happened, as a final blow to the U-boat bases and activities. At a meeting held in Rosyth regarding the surrender of the German Navy, the British Admiralty Board made it clear that they would not tolerate any subversive actions by the U-boat crews, stating; '*The Germans, in the lawless state of the submarine crews, are reaping as they have sown. They must expect to be held strictly responsible for any "regrettable incidents" which occur though their inability to control their underwater craft.*'

By the 2 December some 122 U-boats had surrendered at Harwich and, while generally with good discipline shown both by British and German forces, the surrenders did not pass without incident. In at least one incident the German commanding officer refused to con his vessel under the white ensign, so was removed from the con and the vessel safely brought to its berth without his assistance. Other officers showed their unwillingness to sail their vessels under the white ensign so changed out of their uniforms into civilian clothes. Another incident was that where the crew of a surrendered German submarine were being taken ashore in a motor launch when it was noticed that the white ensign had been removed from their U-boat. The crew were taken back to their submarine and their belongings searched. The search revealed the stolen ensign in a bundle, along with other articles and fittings that had been taken. The German crew were '*loud in their indignation against the man who had taken the ensign, some even requesting the British officer to keep the man and "hang him"*'.[159]

The commanding officer of U-90, 27-year-old von Wanganheim also refused to take his boat into the harbour while sailing under the white ensign and told the British officer while inspecting the submarine on its surrender,

I hate you and England ... We have lost the war but I will fight against you in the next war ... I will then a Japanese boat command and fight against

---

[159] Koerver, (ed.) *German Submarine Warfare 1914–1918 in the Eyes of British Intelligence*, p.707.

you and America ... I was second-in-command of U-32 when she torpedoed CORNWALLIS – this was the happiest day of my life – my one regret is that only 30 men went down.[160]

The battleship HMS *CORNWALLIS* was torpedoed on 9 January 1917 with the loss of 15 lives out of her complement of 720.

Other U-boat commanders were loath to surrender their boats, several of which fortuitously sprung a leak and sank while under tow of a British vessel on the way to Harwich. One of these commanders was Otto Hersing, who had been in command of U-21 throughout nearly four years of the war, sinking 40 ships, including British and French warships, with heavy losses of life.

The human side of the surrender is recounted where *Kapitänleutnant* Oelricher surrendered U-98 to Commander Stephen King-Hall and was asked if the Zeiss binoculars hanging around his neck were his own or a government issue. Oelricher 'solemnly' placed the binoculars around King-Hall's neck and offered his hand. Despite the orders that shaking hands with the enemy was not to be permitted, King-Hall could not resist doing so as Oelricher looked so miserable and uttered a 'Thank you' as he left his boat to return to Germany.[161]

While the U-boat had finally been defeated its role had been of great significance on the outcome of the war. The U-boat weapon had so very nearly brought Britain to her knees and, had there been more U-boats deployed there is every reason to believe that Britain would indeed have been starved to surrender, despite the steadfastness of the men and women of the merchant steamers. At the same time, the callousness of many of the U-boat commanders and the lack of control over their activities had played a very large part in bringing America into the war by the sinking of American ships and the murder of America's citizens. By that token it may be said that far from almost bringing Germany victory, they were instrumental in bringing Germany defeat.

The U-boats had undoubtedly been the greatest enemy of the merchant seafarer and the generally held view is that a total of 14,721 lives were lost

---

[160]   Ibid., p.708.
[161]   Gray, *The U-boat War 1914-1918*, p.264.

from British merchant and fishing vessels from enemy action in this dreadful war.[162], [163] Course gives a figure of 14,228, although it is not stated whether this includes the loss of life from British fishing vessels.[164] (What is beyond dispute is that lives were lost mostly due to U-boats acting in contravention of the Prize Code). Other sources suggest slightly differing numbers, for example the Statistics of the Military Effort of the British Empire During the Great War states 14,661 lives lost, but it may reasonably be assumed that the loss of life was in fact greater due to lack of reporting and occasional errors in crew listing. British ship losses amounted to 3,154 vessels, including fishing vessels, out of a world total of 6,374 vessels lost in the war, of which 5,725 were lost to the U-boats.[165] The loss of 210 British merchant ships in the month of April 1917 alone, due to the full force of unrestricted U-boat activity and lack of defence and protection for the merchant ships, was clearly not a situation which could be endured.

The number of U-boats at sea on their 'merchant war' cruises was small compared to the number of their victims. For example, in 1914–1915 during the first period of unrestricted submarine warfare between March and September 1915 the number of boats at sea, from all submarine bases, varied between 6 and 14. This level of activity continued until the latter part of 1916 to 29, increasing from the time the second period of unrestricted warfare was declared to 61 boats at sea, again from all bases. Although these numbers were diminished by the increasingly successful actions against the U-boats, a daily presence of between 20 to 30 boats was maintained until the German surrender.[166]

U-boat losses were high, although different sources provide slightly differing figures with regard to the numbers of U-boats sunk and their crew losses. When making allowances for those boats that were scuttled in the last days of the war and those interned by neutral states, the figure taken is

---

[162]   Hurd, *The Merchant Navy*, Vol. 3, p.379.

[163]   Koerver, (ed.) *German Submarine Warfare 1914–1918 in the Eyes of British Intelligence*, p.694.

[164]   Course, *The Merchant Navy*, p.276.

[165]   Koerver, (ed.) *German Submarine Warfare 1914–1918 in the Eyes of British Intelligence* pp.695–696.

[166]   Gibson and Prendergast, *The German Submarine War 1914–1918*, pp.354, 355.

that 178 U-boats were lost to direct enemy action (of which 133 sank with all hands)[167] with a total loss of 4,780[168] or 5,409[169] lives, depending on the source utilised.

The month by month progression of loss of life throughout the war is shown in Figure 16.1. The data for the merchant and fishing vessel losses illustrates an increase in the middle of 1915, subsiding in the early part of 1916 when in fact U-boat activity was at it lowest, with only one U-boat deployed against merchant shipping in the Atlantic. The imposition of the second period of unrestricted submarine warfare in 1917 shows the dramatic increase in the losses of ships and lives, peaking in the early part of 1917, with 473 Allied merchant ships being sunk,[170] of which 210 were British. This level of loss, clearly unsustainable, finally persuaded the Admiralty to introduce a convoy system. The effectiveness of that system is evident in the reduction of ship losses, although the losses of lives on the merchant ships maintained a high level until just before the end of the war. Also shown is a marked increase in the losses of U-boats and their crews, particularly due to the increased and enhanced effectiveness of Admiralty activity.

The high 'spike' on the graph shown in May 1915 reflects the high loss of life from the *LUSITANIA*, quoted earlier as 1,198 lives lost out of the 1,959 souls on board. The count of total souls on board and lives lost in this most publicised of loss in the war however varies between different reference sources. Hough records a total loss of 1,198 lives, including 128 Americans,[171] while Thompson records the total loss of life as 1,195, of which 140 were American.[172] This example demonstrates the uncertainty in the available data collated and recorded in Figure 16.1 and the difficulty in establishing an accurate total of men and women lost throughout the war. Some sources include the loss of passengers, while others do not, but it is more than likely that a greater number of lives were lost than those recorded in the remaining available data.

---

[167]   www.uboatnet wwi.

[168]   Ibid.

[169]   Gray, *The U-boat War 1914–1918*, p.265.

[170]   Edwards, *War Under The Red Ensign*, p.178.

[171]   Hough, *The Great War at Sea 1914–1918*, p.175.

[172]   Thompson, *The War at Sea 1914–1918*, p.192.

There was however little enthusiasm on behalf of the British and Allied governments for retribution for the atrocities committed by the U-boats. Following the Armistice, sensitivities in Germany regarding the outcome of the war and the terms of Germany's surrender led the Allied powers to fears of civil unrest in Germany that could threaten the peace. Many in Germany felt that their nation had been unduly humiliated by the terms of the Treaty of Versailles in 1919, whereby Germany was to accept total liability and responsibility for the war. Article 231 of the Treaty had insisted that Germany should replace, ton for ton, and class for class, all merchant ships and fishing boats lost or damaged during the war. Following from this, every German merchant ship of 1,600 tons or greater, effectively all their ocean-going vessels, should be handed over, with large proportions of their smaller ships. Germany was also to use still operational shipyards to build ships for the Allies over a three-year period.

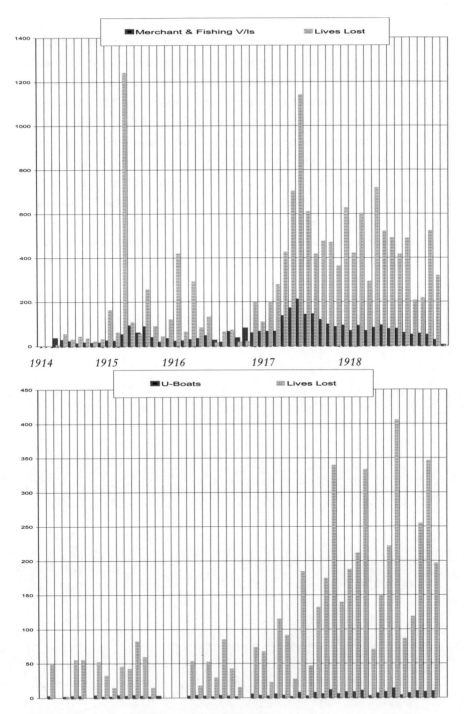

Figure 16.1 Comparisons of Lives Lost.

(Sources: Koerver, Gibson and Prendergast, www.uboatnet wwi)

Among the many accused of war crimes by the British government were 18 U-boat commanders, after much revision and dispute over which names were to be included. There was however considerable delay in progressing such matters and it was not until the Treaty of Versailles came into force on 10 January 1920 that any proceedings against the war criminals could be progressed. This was felt necessary to consider against the sensitivities of the widespread German view that they had been humiliated by the terms of the Treaty. Clearly there were many who were unhappy with this delay, with many of the protagonists dispersed all over the world and those, aware that they were named on the list of war criminals, having time to disappear.

Prosecution for war crimes is clearly a sensitive matter and what may be perceived as a crime by one party may be perceived as a necessary and legal, or possibly heroic, action by another. Indeed the German government argued that if they were to arrest many of those named it could bring the somewhat unstable German government down, as the list included names of men regarded as national heroes in Germany. Germany proposed that they would try the war criminals before the Supreme Court of Leipzig with the evidence submitted to the Supreme Court by British and Allied governments. This was accepted and, after further delay and discussion it was agreed that, by way of an experiment, British and Allied governments would put a list of 45 names before the Court for arrest and trial. Of this list of 45 names, six were put forward by Britain as representative of the war crimes, including the names of two U-boat commanders.[173]

The first of the U-boat commanders tried was *Kapitänleutnant* Karl Neumann, charged:

That he, being in command of the UC-67 on the 26th day of May, 1917, off the North Coast of Africa, attacked, torpedoed, and sank without warning, His Britannic Majesty's hospital ship Dover Castle, *well knowing her to be a hospital ship, in circumstances of extreme brutality, contrary to the laws and usages of war, thereby causing the deaths of six of her crew.*

The case was argued that the act of 'extreme brutality' was the torpedoing

---

[173] Mullins, *The Leipzig Trials, An Account of the War, Criminals Trials and a Study of German Mentality*, pp.7–10.

of the ship, and not any subsequent conduct on the part of Neumann, who stated that he was acting under the orders of the German Admiralty. He further stated that he and the German Admiralty believed that Britain abused the particular status of hospital ships by carrying troops and supplies, contrary to their non-belligerent status. Neumann was relaxed at his trial, convinced of the justice of his action and confident that although his action contravened the Hague Convention, he believed the Convention itself was being abused as the *DOVER CASTLE* was being used for military purposes. He also repudiated the charge of brutality by having allowed ample time for the survivors of the first torpedo strike to get clear of the ship before he fired the second to sink the ship and had at no time attempted to harm the survivors.

The Supreme Court made the finding that: '*The accused accordingly sank the* Dover Castle *in obedience to a service order of his highest superiors, an order which he considered to be binding. He cannot, therefore, be punished for his conduct.*'[174], [175]

The trial of the officers of U-86, Ludwig Dithmar and John Boldt, for the sinking of the hospital ship *LLANDOVERY CASTLE* and the subsequent murder of her survivors in lifeboats was regarded as the most important trial in some respects, as it was not held at the instigation of the British government but at the behest of the German authorities. The commander, *Kapitänleutnant* Helmut Patzig, aware that his name was on the list of war criminals, had fled, leaving his senior officers from U-86 to face trial instead. In this instance, the German Naval Command had given orders that hospital ships were only to be sunk within a given area – a considerable distance from the location of the actual sinking. In that event, it was clear that Patzig had been determined to eliminate as many of the survivors as possible, but one lifeboat with 24 men on board survived to give evidence of the atrocity, with 234 men and women dying.

The trial concluded that the two officers knowingly assisted Helmut Patzig in the mass killing, but that '*A direct act of killing, following a deliberate intention to kill, is not proved against the accused. They are, therefore, only liable to punishment as accessories.*' In assessing the sentence the Court found that,

---

[174] Ibid., p.107.

[175] The historian Martin Gilbert claims that Neumann was sentenced to imprisonment for four years (Gilbert, *First World War*, pp. 329, 330), but it is likely this sentence refers to a German Army soldier, Robert Neumann, who was a guard at a PoW camp.

A severe sentence must, however, be passed. The killing of defenceless shipwrecked people is an act in the highest degree contrary to ethical principles. It must also not be left out of consideration that the deed throws a dark shadow on the German fleet, and especially on the submarine weapon which did so much in the fight for the Fatherland. For this reason a sentence of four years imprisonment on both the accused men has been considered appropriate.[176]

Helmut Patzig, responsible for one of the worst atrocities of the war at sea, was never brought to justice. In fact, out of the 18 U-boat commanders listed as war criminals, not one was convicted or punished in any way. Only Patzig's subordinates, Dithmar and Boltd, were sentenced, and one was allowed to escape imprisonment and the other to serve only four months.[177]

Not only was there to be no sense of justice for the merchant seafarers from these trials of the U-boat crews who had acted with such brutality towards them, but there was little evidence of account having been taken of Admiral Jellicoe's request for some provision to be made by shipowners *'for the wives and children of those gallant fellows who have given their lives for their country.'*

Contrary to the fate of the crews of the merchant ships, however, shipowners fared well out of the war. As described earlier, the loss of a ship provided the scope for greater profit for the owner than if the ship made the port of destination safely. The only circumstances when profits were reduced were when the ship was delayed by waiting for, and sailing in, a convoy. Ship losses caused the values of the remaining vessels to rise and consequently many tramp ship owners sold out at great profit, escaping taxation on the grounds that they represented a return on capital.[178] Attention was drawn to the great increases in freight charges which helped to provide shipowners with soaring profits, while little of those profits were passed on to the seafarers whose wages were still stopped when a ship was sunk. The high profits of shipowners during the war was a topic which the then Chancellor

---

[176] Mullins, *The Leipzig Trials, An Account of the War, Criminals Trials and a Study of German Mentality*, p.132.

[177] Bridgland, *Outrage at Sea*, p.200.

[178] Woodman, *More Days More Dollars*, pp.207–208.

of the Exchequer, Bonar Law, as an investor in shipping himself, addressed in a speech to the House of Commons on 3 July 1917;

> *The sum of money I had invested in shipping, spread over 15 different shipping companies, was £8,100. Five per cent on that, which in ordinary times I should be glad to get, would be £405, but for 1915, instead of £405, I received £2,624, and for 1916 I received £3,847 after Excess Profits Duty had been paid.*
>
> *One of the steamers had either been sunk or sold. I do not know, either way she had been turned into money for me. In that ship I had £200, and after the very handsome dividend which I received on liquidation I received a cheque for over £1,000. There is another shipping company in which I invested £350. The other day I received a letter from the Managing Owner saying that because the cost of building ships was so high, they were going to make a division of the surplus capital. For that £350 of this division I received a cheque for £1,050.*

Apart from the profiteering, Bonar Law showed the callous disregard for the lives of the seafarers when he states that he did not know whether a ship had been sunk or sold and he also demonstrated a lack of understanding of the damage to shipping he and other investors like him caused.

Sir William Foxwood, a prominent Liverpool shipowner, businessman, banker and philanthropist was well aware that considerable damage had been done by the failure to properly coordinate merchant shipping as a national asset early in the war. He remarked on Bonar Law's statement:

> *The Chancellor of the Exchequer was undoubtedly carried away by his own amateur experience as a ship-owner, and thought there was no limit to the extent which might filch away the ship-owner's earnings, little recking that if the ship-owner is unable to put on one side a reserve to replace the tonnage he loses, he is forced to replace the tonnage he loses, he is forced to go out of the trade; and is also utterly disregarding the headway being made by neutral countries, who ... are profiting by high freights and using their profits to extend their mercantile fleets.*

Even after the war Foxwood, perhaps despairing of the loss 'beyond recovery' of the great national asset of shipping, stated '... *we shall rue the day when our Chancellor of the Exchequer became interested in four small steamers and drew conclusions from his experience which are not supported by the wider and more expert ... ship-owner.*'[179]

The outcome was of course that great capital and profits were made by shipowners and their investors, with little regard for those who crewed their ships. It is worth restating the words, already quoted, of Joseph Chamberlain as President of the Board of Trade in a speech in 1884 criticising a principle of marine insurance which appeared to be, '*buy your ship as cheaply as you can, equip her as poorly as you can, load her fully as you can and send her to sea. If she gets to the end of her voyage you will make a good thing of it; if she goes to the bottom you will have made a very much better thing of it*'. The words of Bonar Law showed that little had changed in the intervening years regarding the fate of those who crewed the ships.

It was only towards the end of the war that the seafarers of the Mercantile Marine, previously so poorly regarded by state, employer and general public, were regarded as a relatively valuable asset. The merchant seafarer became a comparative rarity, after that population had been so decimated by enemy action, sickness and enrolment in the Royal Navy and Army. Despite this, the U-boat crews responsible for perpetrating the greatest atrocities against the merchant seafarers remained unpunished. The true appreciation by the nation of their steadfastness however is surely shown in the words of the Prince of Wales at the end of the war, quoted in the Prologue of this book: '*It is the glory of our Merchant Navy, and will be so acclaimed by generations to come, that they faced without hesitation the tremendous odds and the frequent hazard of death, undaunted in spirit to the bitter end. Let us not forget, also, that had it been otherwise this country of ours must have perished.*'[180]

At the cessation of hostilities the merchant seafarers continued their livelihood without interruption as trade recovered, with supplies still being brought to a needy Britain and troops, armaments and civilians needing to be carried back home. There were few rewards for their actions, their living conditions and conditions of service were unchanged as was the stipulation that their wages would cease should their ship be lost, from whatever cause.

---

[179]   Ibid., p.208.

[180]   Hurd, *The Merchant Navy*, Vol. 3, Foreword.

EPILOGUE

The effectiveness of the U-boat activities in disrupting British trade was such that it could have brought about a different outcome to the war had it been more concentrated with a greater number of submarines, or if there had been a firmer commitment to unrestricted submarine attacks. In that sense, the U-boats may well have secured victory for Germany. In another sense, the unrestricted U-boat activities may be regarded as having been responsible in a large part for Germany losing the war, by bringing the United States into the Allied cause – the fear of which had made the Kaiser hesitate to give full reign to the proponents of submarine warfare.

As the post-war account of the conflict contained in the 28-volume British *History of the Great War Based on Official Documents* was nearing completion in 1923, the Admiralty declared that '... *their Lordships were not interested in overemphasising the role of German submarines*'. Several changes were made, particularly with regard to the material that dealt with the submarine activities in 1917, because:

1. *Those chapters provide gloomy reading from the British point of view and there is much to encourage potential enemies who may consider that it is in their competence to subjugate the Empire by a large submarine building programme.*
2. *The encouragement of these ideas by means of an official publication is very much to be deprecated, particularly at a time when we are advocating the abolition of the submarine.*[181]

In other words, the Admiralty did not wish the Achilles Heel of the Navy to be so prominently displayed, particularly after the Admiralty's focus on

---

[181]   Koerver, (ed.) *German Submarine Warfare 1914–1918 in the Eyes of British Intelligence*, pp.ix–x.

battleship strength in the years up to the war.

An earlier chapter reproduced the first verse of Kipling's poem 'Big Steamers'. The last verse of that poem is reproduced here:

> *For the bread that you eat and the biscuits you nibble,*
> *The sweets that you suck and the joints that you carve,*
> *They are brought to you daily by All Us Big Steamers*
> *And if anyone hinders our coming you'll starve!*

★ ★ ★

On a darkening evening of 3 September 1939, the Donaldson Atlantic passenger liner *ATHENIA* was heading out across the Atlantic bound from Liverpool, Glasgow and Belfast to Montreal with 1,102 passengers including over 300 Americans, plus 315 crew on board. A single torpedo was fired without warning by the German submarine U-30 sinking *ATHENIA* with the loss of 118 lives, including those of 16 children.[182]

The torpedo attack was just a matter of hours after the outbreak of the World War II.

The next generation of merchant seafarers was about to experience Balfour's earlier observation, *those who do not resist will be drowned, and those who do will be shot.*

---

[182] Woodman, *The Real Cruel Sea. The Merchant Navy in the Battle of the Atlantic,*
1939–1943, pp.11–19.

BIBLIOGRAPHY

Arthur, M., *The Faces of World War I*, London, Octopus Publishing Group, 2007.

Bone, D.W., *Merchantmen-at-arms: the British merchants' service in the war*, London, Chatto & Windus, Filiquarian Publishing, LLC/Qontro, 1919 and 2010.

Bridgland, Tony, *Outrage at Sea. Naval Atrocities in the First World War*, South Yorkshire, Pen & Sword Books, 2002.

Briggs, A., *A Social History of England*, London, Book Club Associates by arrangement with Weidenfield & Nicolson, 1983.

Cabinet Office/Admiralty War Staff. British Vessels Captured and Destroyed by the Enemy (Indus – 1914) and British Vessels Damaged or Molested by the Enemy but Not Sunk (Kingsmere – 1916).

Coles, A., *Slaughter at Sea. The Truth behind a Naval War Crime*, London, Robert Hale, 1986.

Course, A.G., *The Merchant Navy. A Social History*, London, Frederick Muller Ltd, 1963.

Edwards, B., *War Under the Red Ensign 1914–1918*, South Yorkshire, Pen & Sword Books, 2010.

Forstner, König, P. von und zu Peclelsheim, *U-Boat War 1914–1918*, Volume 2, Leonaur Books.

Gibson, R.H. and Prendergast, M., *The German Submarine War 1914–1918*, Uckfield, Naval and Military Press in Association with the Imperial War Museum,

Gilbert, M., *First World War*, London, Harper Collins, 1994.

Gray, E.A., *The U-Boat War 1914–1918*, London, Leo Cooper, South Yorkshire, Pen & Sword Books. 1994

Hall, J.A., *The Law of Naval Warfare*, London, Chapman & Hall, 1914.

Hoehling, A.A., *Lonely Command*, London: Cassell, 1957.

Holmes, J.W., *Voyaging*, Lymington, Nautical Publishing Co., 1970.

Hough, R., The Great War at Sea 1914–1918, Oxford, Oxford University Press, 1983.

Hohenzollern, Prince Franz Joseph von, *Emden. The Story of the Famous German Raider*, London, Herbert Jenkins, 1928.

Hope, R. *Poor Jack*, London, Chatham Publishing, 2001.

Hoyt, E.P. *The Last Cruise of the Emden*, London, Andre Deutsch Ltd, 1967.

Huberich, C.H and King, R., *The Prize Code of the German Empire as in force July 1 1915*. New York, Baker, Voorhis and Co., London, Stephens and Sons, 1915

Hurd, A. *The Battle of the Seas*, London, Hodder & Stoughton, 1941.

Hurd, A. *The Merchant Navy, History of the Great War Based on Official Documents*, Vols. 1–3. Uckfield By direction of the Historical Section of the Committee of Imperial Defence, Naval and Military Press in Association with the Imperial War Museum.

Jarvis, S.D and Jarvis, D.B., *The Cross of Sacrifice. The Officers, Men and Women of the Merchant Navy and Mercantile Fleet Auxiliary 1914–1919*, Uckfield, The Naval and Military Press Ltd, 2000,.

Koerver, H.J. (ed.) *German Submarine Warfare 1914–1918 in the Eyes of British Intelligence*, LIS Reinisch, A-7441, Steinbach 2012.

Mullins, C., *The Leipzig Trials*, London, H.F and G. Witherby, 1921.

Poolman, K., *Armed Merchant Cruisers*, London, Leo Cooper in association with Secker & Warburg, 1985.

Putnam, W.L., *The Kaiser's Merchant Ships in World War I*, North Carolina, McFarland & Co. Inc., 2001.

Tennent, A.J., *British Merchant Ships Sunk by U-Boats. World War I*, Penzance, Periscope Publishing Ltd, 2006.

Thompson, J., *The War at Sea 1914–1918*, London, Sedgwick & Jackson in association with the Imperial War Museum, 2005.

Trevelyan, G.M., *English Social History*, London, Book Club Associates, 1973.

Wheeler, H.F.B., *Daring Deeds of Merchant Seamen in the Great War*, London: Harrap & Co. Ltd, 1918 (republished by BiblioLife).

Woodman, R., *A History of the British Merchant Navy*, Vol. 3, *Masters Under God. Makers of Empire: 1816–1884*, Gloucestershire, The History Press, 2009.

Woodman, R., *A History of the British Merchant Navy*, Vol. 4, *More Days, More Dollars. The Universal Bucket Chain: 1885–1920*, Gloucestershire, The History Press, 2010.

Woodman, R. *The Real Cruel Sea. The Merchant Navy in the Battle of the Atlantic, 1939–1943*, London, John Murray, 2004.

ARCHIVES

Central Library, Liverpool
Central Library (The Bowen Collection), Southampton
Cobh Museum, Cobh, Ireland
Imperial War Museum, London
Little Museum of Dublin
London Metropolitan Archives, London
Maritime History Archives, Newfoundland
Merseyside Maritime Museum, Liverpool
Mitchell Library, Glasgow
National Maritime Museum, Greenwich
Ships of the Sea Museum, Savannah, Georgia
The Great War Documents Archive, Arizona
The National Archives, Kew
www.uboatnet ww1
www.wrecksite.eu/wreck

INDEX